VOLUME EDITOR

SHEILA LINTOTT is an Assistant Professor of Philosophy at Bucknell University, and the mother of two children. She is co-editor (with Allen Carlson) of *Nature, Aesthetics, and Environmentalism: From Beauty to Duty* (2008) and was co-editor of the *American Society for Aesthetics Newsletter* (2005–2008).

SERIES EDITOR

FRITZ ALLHOFF is an Assistant Professor in the Philosophy Department at Western Michigan University, as well as a Senior Research Fellow at the Australian National University's Centre for Applied Philosophy and Public Ethics. In addition to editing the *Philosophy for Everyone* series, Allhoff is the volume editor or co-editor for several titles, including *Wine & Philosophy* (Wiley-Blackwell, 2007), *Whiskey & Philosophy* (with Marcus P. Adams, Wiley, 2009), and *Food & Philosophy* (with Dave Monroe, Wiley-Blackwell, 2007).

PHILOSOPHY FOR EVERYONE

Series editor: Fritz Allhoff

Not so much a subject matter, philosophy is a way of thinking. Thinking not just about the Big Questions, but about little ones too. This series invites everyone to ponder things they care about, big or small, significant, serious ... or just curious.

Edited by Sheila Lintott

MOTHERHOOD

PHILOSOPHY FOR EVERYONE

The Birth of Wisdom

Foreword by Judith Warner

WILEY-BLACKWELL

A John Wiley & Sons, Ltd., Publication

This edition first published 2010

© 2010 Blackwell Publishing Ltd except for editorial material and organization © 2010 Sheila Lintott

Blackwell Publishing was acquired by John Wiley & Sons in February 2007. Blackwell's publishing program has been merged with Wiley's global Scientific, Technical, and Medical business to form Wiley-Blackwell.

Registered Office
John Wiley & Sons Ltd, The Atrium, Southern Gate, Chichester, West Sussex, PO19 8SQ, United Kingdom

Editorial Offices
350 Main Street, Malden, MA 02148-5020, USA
9600 Garsington Road, Oxford, OX4 2DQ, UK
The Atrium, Southern Gate, Chichester, West Sussex, PO19 8SQ, UK

For details of our global editorial offices, for customer services, and for information about how to apply for permission to reuse the copyright material in this book please see our website at www.wiley.com/wiley-blackwell.

The right of Sheila Lintott to be identified as the author of the editorial material in this work has been asserted in accordance with the UK Copyright, Designs and Patents Act 1988.

Library of Congress Cataloging-in-Publication Data

Motherhood – Philosophy for Everyone : the birth of wisdom / edited by Sheila Lintott; foreword by Judith Warner.
    p.   cm. — (Philosophy for everyone)
    Includes bibliographical references.
    ISBN 978-1-4443-3028-1 (pbk. : alk. paper) 1. Motherhood—Philosophy. 2. Mother and child.   I. Lintott, Sheila. II. Title: Motherhood – Philosophy for Everyone
    HQ759.M873819 2010
    173—dc22

                                                2010010365

A catalogue record for this book is available from the British Library.

Set in 10/12.5pt Plantin by SPi Publisher Services, Pondicherry, India
Printed in Singapore

1   2010

To my mother,
Dorothy June Lintott

CONTENTS

JUDITH WARNER

FOREWORD

How fitting it is to have a book of essays dedicated to the subject of motherhood and philosophy. For ours is an age where philosophies of motherhood abound. They clash. They compete. They battle for preeminence. They are not, for many of their adherents, mere matters of personal preference or individual parenting style. Breast or bottle, co-sleep or cry it out, home school or preschool, 2 percent or skim, opt-in (to our competitive, per-formance driven society) or opt out – all of these things are discussed and debated, argued over, made obsessions, with a sense of urgency that is all but universal among mothers in our time. They provide fodder for endless moralizing – a not-too-moral activity very different from the serious considerations of the moral issues surrounding motherhood you'll find here in the sec-tion devoted to "Mom's Morality." They are the material of elaborate self-justifications, the basis of too-easy judgments. They are, for many women now it seems, the building blocks of identity.

One would think that motherhood, of all categories of activity or states of being, could, in the abstract, at least, be something that one could just do. That a mother might be someone you could just be. That's an impossible dream in our culture, of course; in any culture, most likely. But still: Does motherhood really have to be as complicated as we – the current generation – have made it seem? Does every gesture, every decision, every plan of action, every choice, really have to be so freighted with meaning?

We have seen, over the past ten years or so in America, a number of trends regarding the emotional experience of motherhood. There was, first, the unquestioning embrace of a kind of child-centeredness that led mothers to sell their souls for a shot at maternal saintedness – the trend I've long come to think of as Total Reality Motherhood or called the motherhood religion. And then there was a backlash: the I'm-too-cool-for-that, slacker mom, three-martini-playdate moment of correction. These days, I often hear mothers, and a new wave of younger mothers in particular, striving to achieve a kind of balance in their emotional approach to motherhood. They want to bond without fusing, to be present for their children without disconnecting from themselves. They love their children and care deeply about mothering them, of course. But they don't necessarily want to make a fetish of motherhood. They have looked hard at those of us who have been defining motherhood for the past decade or two. And they don't want to be like us at all. They raise the possibility that there is perhaps room for thinking seriously and carefully about motherhood without making it into a religion or an all-consuming obsession; that perhaps a "Mommy Brain" can think *and* be, as the authors in the first section of this collection aim to do.

Despite all this, in the media, and in particular, in the blogosphere and the hellish domain of mommy chat rooms like UrbanBaby, Mommy War battles continue. They're not really about that old saw, working vs. non-working motherhood. (In this recession, or jobless recovery, just about everyone is working or wants to be.) But they're about everything and anything else and generally boil down, as Ayelet Waldman made so clear in her book *Bad Mother: A Chronicle of Maternal Crimes, Minor Calamities, and Occasional Moments of Grace*,[1] to turn around the theme of who's in and who's out, who's good and, in particular, most deliciously, who's bad. (For a discussion of some purportedly good/bad celebrity examples, see chapter 15 in this collection.)

Of those mothers deemed bad, Waldman writes, "By defining for us the kinds of mothers we're not, they make it easier for us to stomach what we are." She asks: "Is there really no other way to be a mother in contemporary American society than to be locked into the cultural zero-sum game of 'I'm okay, you suck'?"

There could be another way.

"Pain is inevitable: Suffering is optional," contributor Sheryl Tuttle Ross reminds us at the beginning of her splendid essay, "Mindful Mothering." Confusion, exhaustion, frustration, sadness, but also joy, pleasure, inspiration, and hope are all inevitable parts of motherhood. So much more – the anguish over breastfeeding, over sleeping arrangements, over how to live, how to teach, how to be a role model; in short, how to *perform* motherhood are optional. The degree to which we turn ourselves inside-out about motherhood, the degree to which we torture ourselves in striving to master it, the investment we make in our decisions, the degree to which we confound our identities with our mothering decisions – all these things can be taken or left. The practice of motherhood does not have to be elaborated into an identity-decreeing philosophy. The practice should be able to be enjoyed and fully, deeply experienced, as the authors in the section here called "Labor Pains" explore.

Yet, how we talk about motherhood influences what we think of mothers and what mothers think of themselves. So, the ideology of motherhood is not just of theoretical importance, it has an impact on how mothers live and how mothers feel. The divide between the fantasy world of contemporary motherhood and the real life experience is canvassed from various perspectives in the final section of this volume, "Is It Everything You Thought It Would Be? Fantasy Meets Reality."

Certain dilemmas of motherhood – or, more accurately put, of motherhood in our society – are inevitable. It is inevitable that mothers living in a society that has refused to march forward into modernity with them will experience great difficulties. I believe it's the material conditions of mothers' lives in America that has led to the base levels of unhappiness, overwhelmedness, self-doubt, anxiety, and guilt (feeling "crappy," as Waldman once put it to me) that plague so many mothers and cause them – as crappy-feeling people will – to lash out at other mothers who differ from them. It's the outer-directed symptom of what Elizabeth Butterfield so convincingly describes here, in her essay "Days and Nights of a New Mother." Mothers' anxiety about their lives causes them to cloak themselves in the inauthentic identities she describes, the false selves which serve as a form of self-protection. Buttressing these false selves are the reified philosophies that set mothers apart, lock them into attack mode, and, maybe most tragically, guarantee that they won't face squarely the objective contradictions of their lives.

One might argue that perhaps it's the choices that mothers have in this generation – the greater spectrum of possibilities for self-definition, with the greater anxiety such freedom necessarily entails – that lead them now to so insistently and assiduously take refuge in such highly elaborated forms of self-armor as the "serious mother" stance that Butterfield explores. But I don't think that's truly the case.

I think it's the limits that are placed on mothers' freedoms, the impediments that stand in the way of their making truly free choices that, in fact, cause them so much pain. Mothers today have been led to believe that they are free to choose. They've been told that – if they are at all well-off or well-educated – they have no right to yearn for more. It's been made clear to them that demanding more – like structures to promote work-family balance – is just a sign of being spoiled; mere "whining." And they've been sold a bill of goods that teaches that their problems are theirs alone, and if they can't work their lives out, in ways that are satisfying and on a most basic level just make sense, it is their fault alone.

Yet, the truth is, most of the time, mothers who want to balance work and family simply face a wall of impossibility. Full-time work in most professions demands extremely long hours and around the clock availability. Part-time work – which poll after poll shows mothers would prefer – is only in the rarest cases economically feasible and virtually never comes with benefits. Childcare is so expensive that it often forces lower-paid mothers out of the workplace. Afterschool programs are too few and often too mediocre to give most families meaningful and guilt-free coverage in the afternoons.

The list of lacks facing mothers, and families, in all demographics, goes on and on. But the bottom line is: in response to an unchanging landscape of roadblocks and impossibilities, mothers, feeling powerless, resort to magical thinking. They spin stories that will protect themselves and their children from the callous indifference of the outside world. As self-justifying philosophers of motherhood, they find ways for the ambiguities of existence to resolve themselves into solid certainties. And reality just gets blurrier and blurrier. We need books like this one to deconstruct such magical thinking and ground us in solid thought.

Does long-term breastfeeding inoculate children against stress and strain, rejection and failure, cruelty and despair? Probably not. But it does offer mothers and babies an oasis of calm and connection in an otherwise dislocated and harshly demanding world. Does co-sleeping produce children who will venture forth in life forever swaddled in warmth and surrounded by love? Probably not. But it does compensate parents and children cozily for the stressful lives they must live out in the world. These are valuable things. But the truth is: except for behavior that flies to extremes, most of what we do as mothers is pretty much good enough. Mostly not perfect and mostly not so bad.

Does attacking mothers' choices produce anything of value for children? Surely not – but perhaps in a world in which most mothers feel they don't have the power to really change things for their families, the attacks feel like social activism.

It would be so much more constructive to be honest with ourselves. To "stay with" the anxiety and anger and frustration and despair that result from mothering in a political culture that refuses to join the rest of the developed world in making family life livable and workable and, even, pleasurable.

Being fully present for our children – the goal, I believe, we all aspire to – also means being willing to be fully aware of all the unacceptable contradictions in our lives. And it means trying to do something about them. This multifaceted, inclusive, inviting essay collection provides a space in which we can start to think critically and honestly.

NOTE

1   Ayelet Waldman (2009) *Bad Mother: A Chronicle of Maternal Crimes, Minor Calamities, and Occasional Moments of Grace* (New York: Doubleday).

ACKNOWLEDGMENTS

This project has been a labor of love for me, pun intended, and at this point in my life it has seemed equally impossible (I am, after all, a philosopher with two little kids) and inevitable (I am after all, a philosopher with two little kids). My reflections on motherhood are rooted in the ancient history of my childhood, in the time I spent with my mom – most memorably, our many long days together at the beach – and in my thinking about my mom – something I have done and will in all likelihood do every day of my life. So, my largest debt of gratitude for helping to make this book, and much else, possible is owed to my mother, Dorothy June Lintott. I thank too the mothers and allomothers who have helped me understand, through their lived examples, the philosophical significance of motherhood and mothering. Through their modeling and talking with me about mothering, I have learned much of practical and theoretical value. These people include, although not exclusively, my husband Eric Johnson, sisters Kathy Bice and Monica Lintott, sisters-in-law Christine and Greta Lintott, aunts, cousins, nieces, grandmothers, in-laws, and, lucky for me, many friends, notably Martha McCaughey and Maureen Sander-Staudt, who provided prompt and critical review when I most needed it, and all of the "Bucknell Mamas," who provide support, laughter, and wine when I most need them. My children, Sonja and Jack, teach me more about mothering and about myself than anyone or anything, sometimes, in fact, more than I care to know. Singly and jointly they have helped me become a mother and have opened my world to emotional and intellectual expanses I never dreamed possible before them. Eric has my deep gratitude for being a real partner with me and a patient editor for me during this project and every other one I've been involved with since we met, including our favorite "projects," those we lovingly call "Sonja" and "Jack."

Amy Ramírez was my research assistant at Bucknell University during the final stages of this project and she was a tremendous help in stylistic, technical, and substantive matters. She has been not only a thoroughly competent and intelligent assistant, but great fun to work with besides. Darren Hick assisted me in thinking through various organizational patterns I might impose on the book and cheerfully helped me format the pictures that help make this volume in part a family album.

I am grateful for Judith Warner's interest in this project and willingness to contribute a foreword to it. In her weekly *New York Times* column, "Domestic Disturbances," Warner confronts a broad range of issues, from the (mis)representation of mothers in media and popular culture to children's mental health issues and treatment, mother's mortality, competition between mothers, breastfeeding rights and controversies, and domestic violence – always speaking with brave honesty and humble self-reflection. Warner is also the author of the best-selling *Perfect Madness: Motherhood in the Age of Anxiety* (2005), a motherhood book among motherhood books! Although she declares clearly on the first page of *Perfect Anxiety* that it is not a self-help book, her analysis of the anxiety surrounding motherhood today and its root causes helped me, for one, to put my own motherhood anxiety in perspective. Warner writes to and for mothers as friends; indeed, when I read her work, I am reminded of David Hume's observation that one chooses a favorite author as one chooses a friend. Warner is definitely one of my favorite authors and I believe she is a friend to all mothers. Hers is an important voice of our time and I am delighted to have it as part of our maternal chorus.

An impressive number of scholars submitted their work for consideration for publication in this volume. Those selected worked very hard, many taking time away from their own families to do so, and I am extremely appreciative for the time and energy they devoted to this project. Much credit is due to Agnus, Aeden, Aiden, Alice, Arden, Ariadne, Benjamin, Eleanor, Ella, Emilie, Gary, Gavin, Graham, Jack, Jacob, Jayden, Jayden, Joie, Joseph, Julia, Kevin, Leah, Liam, Maddy, Matilda, Michelle, Molly, Ruby, Sam, Sonja, Stephen, Toby, Tula, William, Wilkes, Zack, and Zoe for letting their mommies and/or daddies do a little work from time to time.

I thank Wiley-Blackwell Publishing for taking this project on and for seeing the philosophical significance and wide appeal this inquiry has. In

SHEILA LINTOTT

particular, I acknowledge Fritz Allhoff, Jeff Dean, and Tiffany Mok. I am sure each of these individuals will be happy to put this project to bed (although not without dinner) and to thereby regain some space in their email inboxes.

This book was originally conceived during a research leave funded by Bucknell University and I am grateful to the university and my department, the Department of Philosophy, for their support.

I also thank you, the reader, for your curiosity and open minded interest in motherhood. I hope you enjoy the volume, that it encourages you to think more about mothers, mothering, and motherhood, and that it reminds you of the many relationships that mothering fosters – including the unique mother-child relationship, but also bonds between women, between women and men, between generations, and more. May reading this volume also prompt you to call your mother if you are lucky enough to be able to do so. Finally, I extend a sincere "thank you" to moms everywhere. This is as much a celebration of you as it is an inquiry into your realities.

Sheila Lintott
Lewisburg, Pennsylvania

SHEILA LINTOTT

NAVEL-GAZING AT ITS FINEST

An Introduction to *Motherhood – Philosophy for Everyone*

navel (nā-vəl) n. 1. the depression in the center of the surface of the abdomen indicating the point of attachment of the umbilical cord to the embryo. 2. The central point or middle of any thing or place. Navel-gaz·ing (nā-vəl-gā-ziŋ) n. 1. useless or excessive self-contemplation.

In the pages of *Motherhood – Philosophy for Everyone* readers will find some serious navel-gazing, navel-gazing at its finest, navel-gazing that is not in the least useless or excessively self-contemplative. The association of philosophy with navel-gazing at its worst, with philosophy as a nitpicky academic enterprise, completely uninteresting and unnecessary, is, of course, familiar. But this negative association is a mistake. A more accurate way to think of philosophy is articulated by C. S. Lewis, who admits that philosophy isn't strictly speaking necessary, but without it, like without friendship or without art, life wouldn't be worth living: "Friendship is unnecessary, like philosophy, like art. . . . It has no survival value; rather it is one of those things that give value to survival."[1] One *need* not think about one's situation in life, one's duties, the nature of the beauty that surrounds her, and the spirit of the relationships she enjoys. However, such contemplation is a joy in itself and can yield insight that allows one to further appreciate the complexities of the life she lives. This is the sort of contemplation – honest, fresh, insightful, and even fun – that the reader will find in the pages that follow.

Navel-gazing is also associated with pregnancy, motherhood, and mothering, as it makes direct reference to contemplation of the "point of attachment from the umbilical cord to the embryo." It is actually more than a bit alarming that we live in times when contemplating the connection of mother and child, the center of all of our lives for a time at least, is likened to anything that might be considered a useless or excessive activity. Really, what's notable isn't so much what Adrienne Rich says as *that* she has to say it, when she states, "All human life on the planet is born of woman. The one unifying, incontrovertible experience shared by all women and men is that months-long period we spend unfolding inside a woman's body."[2] Navel-gazing in the form of thinking about mothers, mothering, and motherhood should be encouraged, even required! And in putting this collection together, I did both. For many years feminist philosophers have examined motherhood as a site of rich philosophical significance, and many of the essays in this anthology draw on this work. My hope for this present collection is that it might introduce the non-radical idea that motherhood is philosophically significant to a broader audience, maybe even showing some mothers along the way the philosophical significance of their experiences and reflections, as for too long mothers have assumed that their mothering work is mindless and monotonous.

The essays here inquire into motherhood and its intersections with serious philosophical *and* practical matters such as the relationship between a mother's knowledge and the guidance she seeks from the so-called experts, the meaning and beauty a mother can find in her mothering work, what moral virtues help a mother succeed, and whether and to what extent we should seek to control our children. One aim of the Wiley-Blackwell series in which this book appears, *Philosophy for Everyone*, is to incorporate more than just academic philosophers. *Motherhood – Philosophy for Everyone* includes perspectives from outside the academy, those of a stay-at-home mom and a nurse/lactation consultant, and work from diverse academic perspectives, including – in addition to philosophy – art, psychology, education, and theological studies. This collection is unique in a related manner, as the vast majority of the contributors are practiced in the field. That is, the vast majority of contributors are mothers. Thus, this is a book written largely by and mostly for mothers; yet, it is truly a book for anyone who cares about any mother or about the philosophical lessons that can be learned from mothering. Let's hope that's all of us.

For me, this is a very personal project. So, let me tell you a personal story. During a recent visit to bring the kids to see grandma, as I busied myself with potty negotiations with my toddler, nursing my infant, and a host of other activities that come with the responsibility of having children, my mother said something that shook me to my core. Watching me hurry around, she remarked, with a hint of surprise in her tone, "You're not a philosopher, you're a mother." I am sure she meant nothing negative by it; in fact, I'm sure it was intended as a compliment. After all, as the mother of five children and grandmother to nine, she understands the value and work of being a mother. Nonetheless, I was stymied by my mother's comment and after the initial shock wore off, I said, "I'm both." That was a while ago and my thoughts have returned to that moment over and over, obviously because I want to better understand the comment and my feelings about it. As a feminist, as a woman, as a mother, as a philosopher, I know that being a mother doesn't preclude my being a philosopher, or vice versa. Yuriko Saito, a philosopher I greatly admire, and a mother as well, advised me during my first pregnancy that being a mother would make me a better philosopher. I have returned to that sentiment for comfort more times than I can count, and I do believe that being a mother has made me a better philosopher; sometimes I am also confident that philosophy makes me a better mother. I *am* a philosopher and a mother: a mother-philosopher/a philosopher-mother (and more, of course). In the pages of this anthology the reader will find various perspectives on mothers' multiple identities and reflections on the extent to which all mothers are philosophers.

The Enlightenment philosopher Immanuel Kant posed three great philosophical questions, explaining that "all the interests of [his] reason, speculative as well as practical, combine in the three following questions:

1 What can I know?
2 What ought I to do?
3 What may I hope?"[3]

What mother doesn't ask these questions on a regular, even daily, basis? The authors here investigate issues that present versions of these questions in the lives of contemporary mothers. Some of the authors focus on issues raised by Kant's question of *what can I know?* in attempting to articulate the role that knowledge and truth play in motherhood; such issues include how becoming a mother might alter one's beliefs about gender, abortion, what it means to be a "good" mother, and, of course, sleep. Other authors confront *what should I do?* – questions in discussing some of the many ethical challenges that arise in mothering, for example, the morality of public breastfeeding, letting a child cry herself to sleep, lying to children, or wishing you could turn your child *off*. Finally, some confront topics more related to matters of *what can I hope?* as they dwell on the spiritual, existential, and aesthetic meaning that motherhood can help unearth.

In the remainder of this introduction, allow me to give you a better sense of what this anthology contains. The volume is framed by a foreword by Judith Warner and an extensive bibliography of feminist theoretical work on mothering compiled by philosopher Amy Mullin. Warner, a *New York Times* columnist, is a well-known voice for mothers and about motherhood in the United States. Warner's is the perfect voice to begin this collection of essays on motherhood, not because she a high-profile mother (which she is), but more importantly, because she is a thoughtful and probing critic of the cult and culture of motherhood in the United States, while simultaneously being a hardcore advocate for real mothers. The bibliography that ends the volume is intended to offer a list of suggested readings for readers whose appetite is whetted by the selections contained here.

The essays that make up this volume are dived into four sections: "Mommy Brain," "Labor Pains," "Mom's Morality," and "Is Motherhood Everything You Thought It Would Be?" I decided to begin with a section examining mothers' knowledge and their obligations and choices in light of that knowledge because I think, with philosopher Sara Ruddick, that it is appropriate to start a philosophical inquiry into motherhood with some serious "thinking about mothers thinking."[4] Yes, as Ruddick declares, whatever else mothers are, they are decidedly thinking beings:

> Daily, mothers think out strategies of protection, nurturance, and training. Frequently, conflicts between strategies or between fundamental demands provoke mothers to think about the meaning and relative weight of preservation, growth, and acceptability. In quieter moments, mothers reflect on their practice as a whole. As in any group of thinkers, some mothers are more ambitiously self-reflective than others, either out of temperamental thoughtfulness, moral and political concerns, or, most often, because they have serious problems with their children. However, maternal thinking is no rarity. Maternal work itself demands that mothers think.[5]

The authors of the essays in the first section are prime examples of thinking mothers.

In the first essay of "Mommy Brain: Truth, Knowledge, and Belief in Mothering," Sue Ellen Henry, a professor of education at Bucknell University, exerts her mental energy to explore and explain the relationship between mothers and "the experts" whose advice moms frequently seek as we try to navigate the seemingly dangerous and high-stakes terrain of motherhood. In her essay, "How Many Experts Does It Take to Raise a Child? Mothering and the *Quest for Certainty*," Henry argues that the certainty parenting experts promise is a myth, and our quest for it alienates mothers in a variety of ways, including from their own instincts and intuition and from other mothers – friends and family, near and far. Feminist philosophers such as Adrienne Rich and Alison Jagger[6] discuss motherhood in terms of alienation as well, but do so from different perspectives and with a different focus than does Henry. Henry takes a pragmatic approach, focusing on the Deweyan ideal of integrated knowledge. She advocates a thoughtful approach to one's mothering activities, a process that is open to insight and information from experts while being distinctively unique for and guided by each mother in each situation, a process that is, importantly, always open to edification.

In the second essay, Amy Kind confronts those of us – well, those like me – who sometimes lie to our children. After I confessed to her the complicated nighttime doozey I fabricated to get my 4-year-old to go to sleep, Kind replied via email, "Wow! You're much more elaborate in your lying than I am!" Nonetheless, in her "Creative Mothering: Lies and the Lying Mothers Who Tell Them," she admits that it's actually quite difficult to be wholly and completely honest with children. We're normally not too worried about lying to children, as we feel the lies we tell them, although perhaps not in every case, are usually justified. As any good philosopher would, Kind challenges our intuition that it's generally okay to lie to kids, considering a series of possible reasons one might use to justify these transgressions. She considers whether parental lying doesn't really count as lying (a defense that might employ some of Bill Clinton's linguistic finesse along the lines of "It depends what the meaning of 'is' is"), if parents' lies only protect children from the ugly facts of life with which they can't yet deal (*à la* Jack Nicholson's character in *A Few Good Men*: "you can't handle the truth"), or maybe we just don't owe children the truth (Kind admits to feeling a bit squeamish about this justification). After careful and engaging analysis of the reasoning *and* rationalizations parents offer to justify lying to their children, Kind concludes that honesty is frequently the best, but also the most difficult, policy. Alas, doesn't this conjunction obtain for virtually all parenting decisions?

"Pro-Choice Philosopher Has Baby: Reflections on Fetal Life" is a consideration of how pregnancy can change one's views. Bertha Alvarez Manninen discusses how her thinking about abortion changed the moment she saw the image of her daughter during her first ultrasound, an experience that she and her husband Tuomas both found truly awe inspiring. The challenge, as she sees it, is to reconcile her newfound respect for fetal life with her unshaken conviction that a woman has the right to choose whether to continue a pregnancy. This is indeed a challenge, for advocates of a woman's right to choose tend to base their case on the claim that fetal life is not the sort of life that demands respect. Rejecting the notion that abortion rights hinge on the issue of whether the fetus is a person, refuting the equivocation that calls "pro-choice" supporters "pro-abortion," and questioning claims that liken the moral status of abortion to morally neutral acts like getting a haircut, Alvarez argues that a profound respect for fetal life is compatible with supporting women's legal right to refuse to save another life via sustained intrusion into their own bodies. Manninen also problematizes the rhetorical position that paints women who have abortions as typically taking it lightly, exposing it as uninformed and terribly unsympathetic. Alvarez suggests we have much to learn from other cultures and that Americans would benefit from social grieving rituals that would offer the chance to mourn the loss of fetal life without demonizing or criminalizing women who procure abortions.

In the final essay of the "Mommy Brain" section, Kim Anno, professor of art at California College of the Arts, reflects on how mothering her son has rocked her previous understanding of the social construction of gender. Anno tells how she and her partner adopted Zack at birth and aimed to afford him ample space for expressing himself in a variety of gendered and gender-free ways. Zack, it seems, had some other plans. The shock and even the delight that register as Anno and her partner raise this masculine little boy is captured in the essay's title: "Kim, Ellen, and Zack's Big Adventure: Lesbian Mothers Raising a Boy Steeped in His Masculinity." Anno draws on the work of bell hooks and Judith Butler in her discussion of the difficulty of facing other people's, even other children's preconceptions and prejudices about her masculine, African-American son. For example, she tells of the sting of noticing "parents gathering up their children and moving them away from him at the park or the pool" and how these experiences rouse the "mother tiger" in her. Her reflections tell us as much about our culture's failures as about her own successes as a mother.

The second section is "Labor Pains: The Work and Wonder of Being a Mom." Everyone knows, especially moms, that being a mom is hard, hard work; true enough, but it is also sometimes amazingly wonderful – sometimes it is both at the same time. The authors in this section reflect on the toil involved with mothering, while revealing some of the wondrous moments that remind us of why so many women love being mothers. Elizabeth Butterfield sets the stage with some existential reflections on early motherhood in "Days and Nights of a New Mother: Existentialism in the Nursery." Butterfield, a professor of philosophy at Georgia Southern University, speaks honestly and from personal experience of the exhaustion, desperation, depression, and pain that a new mother can feel in response to the physical and psychological demands a new baby makes. Butterfield recalls feeling "a devastating loss of self" and a realization that "for better or for worse, [she] would never be alone in her cares again." Oh, I know that realization! And I rehearse it frequently. But there is more to motherhood than a loss of self. Butterfield speaks as well of the beauty of a deep commitment to another she feels as a mother, and she finds in existential philosophy, primarily in the work of Simone de Beauvoir, insights that help make sense of the profound and beautiful aspects that come with the loss of her former, relatively carefree self. Butterfield investigates motherhood as a site which challenges and encourages us to face our freedom, our responsibility, and the ambiguity of life, and as such, motherhood offers the opportunity to come face to face with the human condition and to face it authentically.

The theme of the experience of beauty is considered from a Buddhist perspective in Sheryl Tuttle Ross's "Mindful Mothering: How Feminist Buddhist Practices Enhance Experiences of Beauty." Ross, a philosopher and practicing student of Vipassana meditation, examines three of the noble truths of Buddhism with a focus on their application to contemporary mothering. The three noble truths she discusses are (1) pain is inevitable; (2) pain arises from attachment; and (3) the end of suffering is possible. In considering these truths as they apply to the lives of mothers, Ross first discusses the difficulties, disappointment, and pain that can be involved in trying to get pregnant, and telling of how, as many hoping-to-be-mothers learn, it isn't always as easy to get pregnant as we were led to believe in health class. The attachment in mothering seems almost inescapable and to most it seems desirable. Ross admits as much, while pointing out that being overly attached to anything – a person, an idea, a hope – can be a source of suffering; motherhood can teach us how little control we have. The second noble truth urges us to accept the difference between the way things are and they way we believe they should be, which can be a constant challenge for most mothers. Ross offers not only a theoretical discussion of Buddhist mothering, but also some practical advice and "mommy meditations" for mothers: breathe, become aware, recognize it is a socially defined role we are playing, and aim for a wise and kind response. Ross's essay is an inspiration for being present.

Another perspective on beauty is offered by philosopher of art Glenn Parsons in "A Face Only a Mother Could Love? On Maternal Assessments of Infant Beauty." Parsons is intrigued by the common idea that mothers find their infants beautiful – and likely *more* beautiful than others find them. Wondering first whether this common perception of mothers as in a sort of aesthetic overdrive is correct, he turns his attention to what such overdrive might tell us about mothers' aesthetic abilities. Are mothers, perhaps, better judges of their babies' beauty than are others, possessing what Hume calls "a delicacy of taste"? Are they literally able to see more of the beauty that is actually there than the rest of us? Or is it more plausible to think that they are simply biased, so in-baby-love that they would find their babies beautiful if they resembled Gollum. (In fact, my own beautiful baby boy looked very much like Gollum at birth and during early infancy; I knew it, but I also *knew* he was – and is – absolutely beautiful.) Parsons finds mothers' aesthetic appraisals of their babies to be evidence that the complex matters involving differences in artistic taste are increasingly complicated in the aesthetic matters transpiring outside the artworld. He maintains that there may be a sense in which some mothers' assessments are distorted. However, there is another, more important sense in which a mother's ability to bask in the beauty of what might appear to others to be an aesthetically challenged infant is just right. A mother's good taste encourages her to love, bond, and bask. Why would anyone want to get in the way of that?

Laura Newhart relives the process of adopting her son. "Kevin, Coming Into Focus: On Getting to Know My Son" is a poignant textual and photographic essay. The wonder of motherhood is captured in precious detail here as she remembers coming to know her son, whom she adopted from Guatemala in 2007, through photographs and emails sent to her prior to the adoption. The process of coming into focus continues as Laura and her partner travel to Guatemala to meet Kevin's foster mother and bring Kevin to his new home in the United States to begin their life together as a family. She confesses that she still looks at him in wonder, realizing that she still doesn't fully know him. Of course, one of the most delightful things about children is that they are always a source of surprise; we are

🐝 SHEILA LINTOTT

always getting to know them. Further, Laura imagines, or tries to imagine, how Kevin will continue to come into focus as he matures and grows. Beneath the surface of this touching narrative are multiple other narratives – of Laura coming to be a mother, of Kevin and Laura coming to be mother and son, of the family coming to be a family. Newhart's account reminds us that we are all, in so many ways, coming into focus.

The third section, "Mom's Morality: Ethical Issues in Mothering," comprises four reflections on breastfeeding, breastfeeding in public, co-sleeping, and natural birth. No mother I know is ignorant of these debates; however, the authors in this section have new perspectives and increased clarity to offer. In the first essay, Chris Mulford, a nurse and lactation consultant, peruses the range of interests, rights, and responsibilities involved in the choice to breastfeed. Mulford blends philosophical reflection with knowledge gained from years of working with nursing women and researching the history and practice of breastfeeding. Clearly an advocate for breastfeeding, Mulford does note that breastfeeding involves effort, planning, work, and sometimes notable discomfort and pain on the nursing woman's part. She is also eager to point out that

if anyone has a duty toward breastfeeding, it is not exclusively or even primarily mothers. It is all of us collectively. An individual woman has to make the choices that seem right for her. However, she chooses within an environment that limits or expands her options, both by influencing what she thinks and by putting assistance or obstacles her way. Just as artificial feeding requires an infrastructure of public sanitation and food distribution, so too breastfeeding requires an infrastructure of support for women and families, gender equity, and public information, if it is to survive in the modern world.

In "Lactational Burkas and Milkmen: On Public Breastfeeding and Male Lactation," Maureen Sander-Staudt picks up on just this issue of the required infrastructure needed for breastfeeding to be a supported and feasible norm in American culture rather than a burden placed on individual women. Sander-Staudt begins with a brief thought experiment: what would be different if men could breastfeed? She speculates that, among other things, sports clubs might be designed with booths comfortable for nursing and television watching and gyms might include equipment designed for simultaneous milk and iron pumping; most to the point, she is confident that breastfeeding would be better accommodated than it is today. She takes a feminist ethics of care approach to discussing the type of reciprocity a nursing woman should be able to expect in terms of the accommodation of her public nursing, while attending to the intimacy of the act and its alleged obscenity. Using the metaphor of a lactactional burka, Sander-Staudt maintains that nursing in public should be something that, to a large extent, individual women should be free to choose whether, when, and how to do. Moreover, she tells us of something quite surprising. Her opening thought experiment is not mere fantasy: "men have full mammary glands, and their capacity to breastfeed can be developed to the same extent as women's by using a breast pump for around twenty minutes daily for several months, and by increasing the levels of the hormone prolactin." Well, who knew? That changes things a bit now, doesn't it?

The third essay of the section deals with a very contentious matter indeed: how to get baby to sleep. The topic of sleep is perhaps the most pressing one for new parents. After the birth of my first child, I recall *everyone* asking me, "Getting any sleep?" (No.) "How's the baby sleeping?" (She's not.) "Is she a good sleeper?" (She's good at not sleeping.) "Sleeping through the night yet?" (Is that supposed to be funny?) And I recall asking *everyone* in desperation, "How can I make her sleep? I need sleep!," even sending late-night, sleep-deprived, and wildly desperate emails to anyone and everyone I thought might have an answer. Nobody did, but I got lots of interesting "advice." In their essay, the Elliotts – Kevin, a philosopher, and Janet, a former teacher and present stay-at-home mom – maintain that there are good reasons to prefer co-sleeping to the "crying-it-out" method of getting a baby to sleep. "Crying-it-out" is a method usually associated with pediatrician and author of books on infant sleep Dr. Richard Ferber, and made infamous by the Robert De Niro character Jack Byrnes' adherence to the method in *Meet the Fockers* (2004). The Elliotts argue on utilitarian grounds that the suffering "crying-it-out" involves for the baby must be counted against any other interests that might be served. It's worth noting, as the Elliotts do, that the "crying-it-out" method is not easy on parents either; they even report knowing parents who resorted to the use of earplugs to get some sleep amid the crying. (Um, yours truly is guilty as charged.) In the end, although the Elliotts believe that co-sleeping is a viable alternative to other methods, they do not recommend a single solution to all parents, aiming instead to illustrate how philosophy raises issues for parents to consider and can help parents make the choices that are right for them and for the members of their family.

SHEILA LINTOTT

In the final essay in this section Jen Baker maintains, well, just what her title suggests, that "Natural Childbirth is for the Birds." However, although the title might make readers anticipate a series of arguments against natural childbirth, Baker takes a different tack, carefully examining whether there are any convincing reasons to judge natural births to be better than non-natural births. Her essay takes on some very difficult issues, as she asks questions such as *what does it mean to say that a birth is natural?* and *why think natural is good?* In the end, she maintains that natural childbirth is akin to a sort of thrill-seeking endeavor, like climbing a mountain or parasailing. Moreover, as such, although it might be worth doing for a variety of reasons, it is not in any way morally superior to a happy birth in which the welcome assistance of an epidural helps manage the pain. (And here I draw on personal experience when I call an epidural "welcome"!)

The final section of *Motherhood – Philosophy for Everyone* collects four essays dealing with the differences between the way we *think* about motherhood, mothering, and mothers and the *realities* of motherhood, mothering, and mothers. This section is entitled "Is Motherhood Everything You Thought It Would Be? Fantasy Meets Reality" and the authors discuss, in turn, fantasies of child control (as in "where's the off button on this thing?!"), the virtues required for and fostered in mothering, the representations and evaluations of celebrity mothers in the mass media, and the implications and challenges to thinking of God as Mother.

Sara Goering's "The Off Button: Thought Experiments and Child Control" is a study in parental wishes and the old saw, *be careful what you wish for.* Goering observes that her fantasy of being able to turn her children off, for a time, is not idiosyncratic. Most caregivers, she notes, likely entertain this particular fantasy on occasion. She wonders what this fantasy says about us and whether we should indulge it, even if we could. Thought experiments are used by philosophers to examine our intuitions and the consequences that might follow from a certain scenario. From Plato's "Ring of Gyges"[7] (a ring that makes it's wearer invisible) to Descartes' "evil genius"[8] (a demon who may be deceiving you about even the most seemingly basic truths) to Philippa Foot's "trolley problem"[9] (you're faced with the choice of saving five people in the path of a trolley but, in so doing, you'll kill another person) philosophers love to imagine "what if?" in order to think about what follows. While registering some thoughtful skepticism about what thought experiments can tell us about the world as we know it, Goering argues that access to off buttons for children would lead to undesirable consequences, including both parents and children missing out on valuable learning experiences.

In "The Virtues of Motherhood" Nin Kirkham explores the great divide between reality and the way one might imagine herself as a mother who will feed only nutritiously dense meals and never yell and whose children will never throw tantrums and will always go peacefully to bed. But becoming a mother can bring such illusions to a crashing halt, leading to a more realistic conception and appreciation of what it means to be a good mother. Her conception of a good mother is rich, making room not only for a mother's ability to do right by her child(ren), but equally for her own flourishing and happiness, what virtue ethicists following Aristotle call *eudaimonia*. A good mother will live a life characterized by *eudaimonia* not *despite* being a mother, but in part *because* she is a mother. Kirkham mines virtue ethics for insight into the virtues of motherhood, focusing on the virtuous practice of endurance, liberality, and moral exemplarity in mothering. While Kirkham explores the virtues of motherhood, she is opposed to the common, all-too-common tendency to judge mothers. Wherever this tendency comes from, and there are surely multiple sources, Kirkham believes that becoming a mother increases one's awareness of the mother-blame game, about how automatic, harsh, and unfair many of our judgments of mothers are. Refusing to engage in this favorite pastime is yet another virtue mothers and nonmothers can practice.

In the penultimate essay, psychologists Clemence Due and Damien Riggs expand on this phenomenon of judging moms as "good" or "bad" through a discussion of the "recent explosion" of mass media representations of celebrity mothers. Interested in how the public engages with such images, they reflect on a class exercise conducted in psychology classes at the University of Adelaide in Australia. Students in these classes read and responded to a series of articles about such celebrity moms as Brittany Spears, Angelina Jolie, Jodie Foster, and Nicole Richie. Due and Riggs found that students would go beyond the stories as presented by the media in order to judge the women as mothers, favorably or unfavorably. Their judgments, therefore, depended on their preconceived notions about what a "good" or "normal" mother does and what sort of life a mother is expected to lead. One of their most disheartening, although not surprising (which is even more disheartening), findings is that motherhood and the work it involves are as undervalued today as they ever were. Moreover, the more a woman appeared to mother intensively (mothering to the exclusion of every other interest or desire), the more "normal" or "good" she was judged, the more "boring" the article about her and thus her life seemed. Message? Motherhood, when done right, is boring. For the record, I have to say that I frequently *wish* for boring days amid the chaos of contemporary motherhood!

The final essay of this collection tackles the topic of motherhood in divine proportions. In "God, Mom! The Blessings of Breasts and Womb," George Dunn considers resistance to and ramifications of the idea of God as a mother. Dunn explains that the idea of a maternal God is not new, having not only biblical roots, evidenced perhaps in the Book of Job, but also prehistoric roots, evidenced perhaps by fertility goddess statues. His discussion of divine motherhood introduces us to classical ideas in philosophical theism – to the thought of Anselm and Aquinas – and to the sexism of Aristotle, the ancient Greek philosopher whose claims that women were "defective and misbegotten" we are still trying to dislodge from our culture. Explaining that all language about God must be metaphorical or analogical, since God is, by definition, beyond our experience and understanding, Dunn argues that a comparison between God and Mother might be more apt than one between God and Father. In any case, he maintains that the image of God as Mother tempers the perceived harshness of God's wrath without doing away with responsibility or morality. Moreover, given that how we think of God affects how we think of ourselves, Dunn postulates that thinking of God as the epitome of maternal care might make salient new reasons to honor our own mothers.

Now there's a thought experiment for all mothers: What *if* God were one of us …?

NOTES

1 C. S. Lewis, *The Four Loves* (New York: Harper Collins, 2002), ch. 4.
2 Adrienne Rich, *Of Woman Born: Motherhood as Experience and Institution* (New York: W. W. Norton, 1976), p. 11.
3 Immanuel Kant, *Critique of Pure Reason*, trans. Normal Kemp Smith (New York: St. Martin's Press, 1965), p. 635 (A805/B833).
4 Sara Ruddick, "Thinking About Mothers Thinking," part one of *Maternal Thinking: Toward a Politics of Peace* (Boston: Beacon Press, 1989).
5 Ibid., p. 24.
6 Rich, *Of Woman Born*; Alison Jagger, *Feminist Politics and Human Nature* (Tottowa: Rowman and Allanheld, 1983).

7 Plato, Book II, *Republic* in *The Collected Dialogues of Plato* (Princeton: Princeton University Press, 1961), pp. 606–8 (359a–360d).

8 René Descartes, "Meditations on First Philosophy," "Meditation I: Of the Things Which May Be Brought Within the Sphere of the Doubtful," in *The Philosophical Works of Descartes*, Vol. 1, trans. E. Haldane and G. Ross (New York: Cambridge University Press, 1979), pp. 147–9.

9 Philippa Foot, "The Problem of Abortion and the Doctrine of Double Effect," *Oxford Review* (1967): 5, 5–15.

PART I

MOMMY BRAIN

Truth, Knowledge, and Belief in Mothering

SUE ELLEN HENRY

CHAPTER I

HOW MANY EXPERTS DOES IT TAKE TO RAISE A CHILD?

Mothering and the *Quest for Certainty*

Jacob, my first son, was born on a hot day late in July 2000. He had a rough birth; only after a few days in the NICU were we able to bring him home. Perhaps it was the difficulties he endured during his entry into the world outside my womb that made him seem especially fragile and I so incompetent to care for him. But I don't think this is the whole story. Another part of the story must be told, for, as a new mother, I felt, as I suspect most new mothers feel, completely inadequate to take care of a baby. The data to suggest that I didn't know what I was doing were all around me; I couldn't help Jacob stop crying and I was having trouble successfully nursing him. Beyond these routine difficulties, for several days I admired the lovely olive-toned skin I thought Jacob inherited from his father; soon the doctor announced that Jacob was jaundiced and needed light therapy. Who knew? Not me.

While I came to my mothering gig without so much as ten hours babysitting in my entire life, what I did have was a solid doctoral-level education in philosophical and sociological pragmatism *à la* John Dewey. As someone who had spent a lot of time in school, I had developed a way of approaching new problems that worked exceptionally well in an academic setting: read everything. Knowing that I was approaching motherhood with very few practical skills and even less actual experience, I did what I knew best. I read everything. So it's not surprising that just a few days after getting Jacob home I exclaimed, "I need a theory!" when confronted with the problem of whether to pick Jacob up when he started crying (my instinct) or whether to let him "cry it out" (as some of the books I had read suggested).

Thus began my "quest for certainty" in motherhood and mothering. In seeing these choices (between cuddling him and allowing him to cry it out) as separate and distinct, I had already fallen victim to the faulty thinking that Dewey maintained was predicated on the illusion of a separation between knowledge and belief. Informed by his lifelong attempt to heal Cartesian dichotomies (between, for example, mind and body, emotion and reason, and subject and object) that he believed ran thinking off into a ditch, Dewey critiqued such a "quest" as centered on a false dichotomy between knowledge and belief. In separating knowledge (in this case, the "expert" advice found in some parenting/mothering books) from my extant, albeit budding beliefs about mothering (in this case, babies should be comforted), I had conceived of mothering in a bifurcated way. There was, on the one hand, "right mothering," confirmed by book advice; on the other, there was "possibly wrong mothering," ruled by instinct. Such a segregation of knowledge from belief, Dewey wrote, led to the idea that knowledge was more certain, universal, and thus better than belief, which was cast as uncertain and provisional. Instead, Dewey saw both knowledge and belief as forms of partial truths, that when put together could productively inform knowledge in action.

As an acolyte of Dewey's, I was and still am drawn to such thinking: let's use all the tools we have – knowledge, beliefs, experience, intuition – to figure out the most fitting, appropriate, and thoughtful solutions to the problems we face. After all, if they are worth our effort to try to solve, we might as well hit them with everything we've got. In my work as an academic I applied this type of thinking to theoretical and real problems found in schools. I felt confident using this approach in my professional life. But, for reasons that escaped me at the time, the situation was different in my mothering life. In the face of mothering, I developed a new response: "I know, I know – but I need answers because the stakes are so high!" I thought to myself over and over. As Dewey maintains in the first sentence of *The Quest for Certainty*, "man [sic] who lives in a world of hazards is compelled to seek for security."[1] Nothing exemplifies my

SUE ELLEN HENRY

notion of hazards better than my first few months as a new mother. The stakes as I saw them were enormous; if I mothered him badly, Jacob might be hurt psychologically, physically, mentally, cognitively, emotionally, and any number of other ways. Even in my sleep-deprived ride on the emotional rollercoaster of new motherhood, I could clearly see, maybe *too* clearly, the risks omnipresent in my world. I needed security, I needed it fast, and I attempted to find it in strictly following the step-wise advice offered in the books I had gathered.

While my move toward "expert" texts was lodged in a need for security, few of them discussed my need for an integrated response to mothering. More often, these texts broke my holistic question of "how do I care for this baby?" into smaller, discrete topics, characterized as "problems": sleep problems, eating problems, issues of cognitive development, and the like. My need for security was confounded by a growing sense that *my* actions, as Jacob's mother, were most essential to his health and happiness. Through a detailed analysis of the language and rhetoric found in popular parenting texts of the 1980s, Harriett Marshall found that such emphasis on the actions of mothers (as opposed to other important caregivers to young children) is very common.[2] Marshall asserts that in focusing almost exclusively on the actions of mothers, often omitting the work of others, these texts cement in mothers the crucial and, more importantly, sole responsibility for a child's "normal development" toward being a "well-adjusted individual."[3] In my own case, two outcomes emerged from this situation: (1) in many cases I elevated these texts as sources of authority over my own judgment and (2) I got the message that it was all on me. Taking these outcomes in tandem, it is no surprise that I came to believe that to manage the stress of this situation, I'd better continue consulting these texts because the stakes were so high, which, of course, led to more stress about following the books' prescriptions accurately.

Dewey suggested that many problems grow out of thinking that segregates knowledge from belief, particularly in the context of social problems. Confronted by the vast uncertainty of new mothering, mothers may be more likely to turn to "expert" texts for guidance, guides which are ubiquitous in American culture.[4] In relying on "expert" knowledge and seeing it as validated and more influential than her own experience and beliefs, a new mother can sense enormous alienation from her own actions and her developing identity as a mother. This outcome is especially likely given that, as we will see, being a "modern mother" is framed in such texts as seeking out and adhering to the advice of physicians, psychologists, and other "experts." Confounding the new mother's need for support is the fact that in reinforcing their authority, some of these texts fail to mention that other women, family members, neighbors, or other mothers, can be sources of local expert knowledge. Thus, for the modern mother, nearly exclusive adherence to the texts and the "expert" advice is not only required, but turning to this advice and away from other possible sources of information is advocated. In following such a path, a peculiar, although predictable form of isolation results, segregating the new mother's instincts and what she believes, intuits, or feels to be good care for her child (her beliefs) from that which she "knows" from the mothering books (her knowledge). The argument here is this: singular reliance on texts for developing a personal and integrated theory of mothering leaves one vulnerable to its ontological opposite: alienation. Action which is "right" but unattached to a more coherent and evolving theory of mothering – a system of mothering – will likely leave the mother feeling like someone employing the techniques of mothering without being a mother.

Finding Answers to Mothering Questions

I'm walking through a parking lot with Jacob at 5 months old, in a front pack on my chest. For once, he is quiet; normally he is crying or fussing in some way. As I'm walking past the building that houses my university office, I feel a sense of lost competence that I remembered in my professional role. Another competing feeling immediately enters my head: there's nothing in my past that has prepared me for the decisions I may have to make about how to care for Jacob in the next five minutes. He might need a diaper change (I'm nowhere near a restroom with a changing table – is there even a changing table anywhere on campus?); he might need to be fed (I'm nowhere near a quiet place where I can nurse and not offend the easily offended); he might start crying without known cause, as he is wont to do (I'm standing where we will be easily heard, as we're surrounded by office windows). While I felt incredibly insecure as a new mother, what I didn't know at the time was that my security would hardly be found in the use of expert parenting texts. Indeed, the use of these texts exacerbated and intensified my insecurities. Even my reliance on such texts felt, in many ways, like a personal failure. What kind of mother has to rely on a textbook to teach her how to get her baby to sleep, much less, eat?

Little did I know that the idea of following "expert" advice in mothering, the age of "scientific motherhood,"[5] began in the mid-nineteenth century, predicated on the idea of "add science to love and be 'a perfect mother.'"[6] Childcare was "medicalized" by (mostly male) physicians whose advice, aided by the printing press and growing literacy rates, ushered in the notion that women needed professional medical and scientific instruction in mothering.[7] These texts offered extensive explanation and detailed instructions on the most routine of mothering duties, including bathing, feeding, and clothing newborns and infants, as well as information on more scientific topics such as disease prevention. On the heels of significant medical advances such as a vaccine for diphtheria and the discovery of bacteria, doctors asserted that improving infant mortality rates required that mothers mother according to their advice. As one physician wrote in 1887: "How many mothers undertake the responsible management of children without previous instruction, or without forethought; they undertake it as though it may be learned either by intuition, by instinct, or by affection."[8] Unlike earlier mothering texts, such as those by women's education advocate Catherine Beecher, which supported the centrality of mothers and their local family's knowledge in childcare coupled with advancing gains in science and the medical establishment, texts written by doctors urged women to follow their lead and to deny or ignore their own judgment gained from personal experience and local practices. Abraham Jacobi, largely credited as the father of modern pediatrics, popularized his version of childcare with a pamphlet distributed to mothers in the poorer sections of New York City in the 1860s. According to Rima Apple, Jacobi "extolled the role of the medical practitioner" by reminding women that their doctors, not their neighbors, should be their guides.[9] Apple asserts that contemporary women have found unique ways to draw important information from science, medicine, and other "experts," together with their developing personal sense of mothering, and are generally resistant to the heavy-handed advice of "experts." She argues that cooperation between mothers and experts should be our goal today, and that while the balance of power between mothers and physicians is not yet equal, both parties should work toward making it so. In so doing, Apple advances a pragmatic approach to motherhood reminiscent of Dewey's call for intelligent inquiry, an approach that considers beliefs, knowledge, and experience to have important bearing on the understanding of and possible responses to social issues such as those found in parenting. And yet, while well schooled in Dewey's approach, in these early months of mothering it seemed inconceivable to me that better solutions to the issues I had in caring for Jacob could be found in the intermingling of "expert" advice and my own inclinations. In retrospect, it wasn't science or the actual message of these "expert" texts, *per se*, that was so disconcerting to me as a new mother: it was more the delivery of the message. These texts, much like ads promising quick weight loss, sent the message that properly following this plan would result in a blissful state of infant and maternal happiness in the form of a good sleeper, a voracious eater, and an overall contented and cheerful baby. Failure to apply the technique wholly and correctly would, it was implied, result in inadequate outcomes. Moreover, and most damning to my confidence as a mother, inadequate outcomes were evidence of a failure to apply the technique wholly, consistently, and correctly. That's how I knew *I* was failing at getting Jacob to sleep, eat, be calm, etc. In fact, Marshall's review of contemporary parenting texts finds that while these guides often include the rhetoric of "flexibility," they also reinforce certain "rules" that a good, modern mother should follow: "the first rule made explicit in some manuals is that mothers should look to the experts for guidelines and that the experience passed on by other mothers is not sufficient."[10] I recall being drawn to a biomedical model during pregnancy, when my body felt like a human petri dish. I was extremely curious about what was happening to me physiologically, and relied on several texts that described in great detail the growth of the baby, as well as the hormonal and physical changes my body was undergoing. I also wanted the "certainty" that the biomedical model offered when Jacob was in the NICU following his difficult birth. It became hard to give up that "certainty" when he was ready for home care because I'd grown accustomed to the dichotomy of the "right" care vs. "good" care. Indeed, in the biomedical model, they are one and the same. Problematic, too, was that very rarely did these "expert" texts emphasize that *this is a human being we're dealing with here*, perhaps the least predictable and most idiosyncratic entity on the planet. Thus, when Jacob slept as the book technique suggested he would after following the step-wise procedure, I took it to mean two things: (1) I was applying the technique correctly, wholly, and consistently, and (2) Jacob was a good boy and no longer had a sleep "problem." When Jacob didn't sleep, I read just the opposite message. I had failed him and in the process, he failed me. There were times we were just miserable together.

This cycle of "technique–response–infrequent success/failure" continued in nearly every realm of our lives together. In particular, I had a lot of difficulty nursing Jacob in those early months, but remained committed to doing so. One morning in an act of support, my husband suggested that I call a friend of mine. She had a year-old baby and had also experienced similar difficulty in nursing. Through my tears I told him

"I can't call her, I just can't." I was embarrassed to call. I really believed that by following the expert advice I was doing the best that I could and that lay people probably would have little to add. I continued to consult my "expert" guides on nursing, holding tight to the notion that if I just did it right and followed the plan, then I'd be able to get the nursing to work. I continued to work in isolation until my doctor became worried that Jacob was developing acid reflux and would have to start on a course of medication. At this point, I knew I had to get more help and I warmed to the idea that there might be other wisdom out there to help me with my nursing challenges *and* that I needed human support in making this work, support beyond that which a text could provide.

Finally, I met with my local La Leche League gals. Mothers themselves, with a combined total of hundreds of years experience in parenting not only infants but older children too, these women were a godsend. Exemplary of the Catherine Beecher-style of mothering advice, these women brought together scientific knowledge on child development and nutrition with experiential advice gained from raising hundreds of babies by a multitude of mothers. They had techniques, too, just as the "expert" texts did, but they also sent this message: "If this technique doesn't work, you just haven't found what works for you and your baby. Keep trying."

This message is key to a Deweyan approach to intelligent inquiry. Dewey believed that the best solutions to social problems included all people implicated in the problem. Working with a 5-month-old is probably a bit different from what Dewey had in mind, but nonetheless, the approach to problem-solving still works, in part because it requires continual feedback to monitor the unanticipated side effects of selected solutions and requires that everyone invested in the work of the solution be part of the planning. This system was built on the notion of reframing the dichotomy between knowledge and belief that is so frequently found in scientific "expert" knowledge and exemplified by the early pediatric texts on mothering toward the notion of knowledge in action.

Both/And Not Either/Or

There are good reasons for science (particularly medical science) to focus on the production of valid claims about the relationships between variables, and not attend to the relative importance of beliefs. Experimental science works on principles of isolation; the most certain way of saying that something is correlated with a particular outcome is to isolate the other potential variables that might interfere. Because science is predicated on the notion of testing relationships among variables, isolation is a key component of such important work. The capacity for experimental science to demonstrate such correlations between variables (for example, smoking cigarettes is highly correlated with lung cancer) makes it powerful and important. Yet in the context of good mothering, there are few correlations between actions and outcomes that are really this concrete (one example is the relationship between shaking a newborn baby and brain injury). An apt example of a scientific "rule" that really is more of a set of preferences can be found in the advice on toilet training. According to Apple, early in the twentieth century doctors advised mothers to train their children at a few months of age. By the time of Dr. Spock in the mid-twentieth century, a much more permissive, "when the child is ready" approach to toilet training was taking hold and widely practiced by mothers. Indeed, the power of medical, scientific information coupled with strong rhetoric that modern mothers, *good modern mothers*, follow this advice and not the advice of lesser authorities, creates the likely elevation of this information to a potentially over-inflated status. Considering such information as a "rule" disregards the fact that the context in which this information will be put into action contains far more variables, many of which will be completely unknown and unaccounted for in the controlled nature of experimental science. The situation of the home, of the relationship between baby and parents, not to mention other family members, are all critical elements of the environment in which the scientific advice will be used. Dewey was sensitive to the situatedness of social problems, and thus advocated for an approach that tested responses to issues in the context in which they would be used in order to inform future action. The actions of the mother, father, child, and other family members, and their collective experiences, combine to form important information for future decision making. In fact, viewing mothering from a pragmatic point of view, one would see the home as the mother's laboratory, the place where she gains experience, and thus knowledge, about what works for her in the context of her family situation. Textbooks are a poor substitute for this experience; and experience, as Dewey maintains, is not separate from knowledge but another avenue for knowledge construction. In *Democracy and Education*, Dewey writes of a child who is learning to fly a kite as an example of how experience is a form of knowledge. Dewey asserts that working with the kite teaches the child, not because it relates directly to the principles of aerodynamics or other axioms of physics, but because it is a form of action. This action, when coupled with more conventional forms of knowledge, expands the person's capacity for intelligent inquiry by using all the forms of knowledge available: information, beliefs, experience, intuition. As Dewey explains, "senses are avenues of knowledge not because external facts are somehow 'conveyed' to the brain, but because they are *used* in doing something with a purpose. The qualities of seen and touched things have a bearing on what is done, and are alertly perceived; they have a meaning."[11] What I'm coming to realize now, as a mother of three (nine, seven, and four), and having successfully (which is not to say perfectly) mothered them in their infancy, is that I needed *both* "experts" and the support for the developing sense of myself as a mother that the La Leche League ladies offered me. I needed to know how the early substance from my breasts, which didn't look like milk at all, actually was so packed with nutrients that it made sense to pump and feed it to Jacob even though he was in the NICU and doing so was quite difficult. I needed to know that whole milk is best for my baby until age two because the fully-fatted variety supports brain development. I needed to know that honey is dangerous to the newborn baby because of the risk of botulism in a system that hasn't developed much immunity yet. Okay – some expert testimony is helpful. But in an age when individual mobility means that many, many new mothers live away from their families, from their sources of local knowledge and a network of people who can support their growing sense of identity as "mother and . . .," it is profoundly anti-pragmatic to rely primarily on external, "expert" texts that claim a position of singular authority without also considering the relationship between the advice, the theory of mothering, and the actions both underwrite.

Toward a Pragmatic Approach to Mothering

While I sadly came to mothering the first time with woefully little related experience, I did come to mothering with many beliefs about what good mothers do. Mothers nurse their babies and do not use formula. Mothers bathe their babies every day. Mothers knit blankets for their babies. Mothers are with their babies all the time. In my experiences mothering my daughter and second son as infants, every one of these "rules" was broken. My husband was also able to get me to reconsider the rigidity of these rules for Jacob, but only after revealing to me that these "rules" were an albatross and were preventing me and Jacob from being at peace with one another.

The "expert" texts I read didn't convey these rules; I brought this set of beliefs with me from somewhere. Thus, it's not the texts alone that are the problem. It's their authoritative tone and subtle assertion of exclusive authority, combined with the anxious reader's tendency to bring preconceived rules and standards to her assessment of herself as a mother. I now see that I, with my preconceived notions of what a good mother does and doesn't do, needed texts that would encourage me to reflect on the various "rules" about infant care that I brought to the situation; that canned the rhetoric of "this is the best information available"; that admitted their contribution to the experience (sometimes the ordeal) of mothering wouldn't be independently sufficient and thereby suggested that working with this information in the company of others might be helpful. In short, I needed the texts to promote a pragmatic approach to mothering that acknowledged my perceived need for certainty, remained supportive in managing the intense ambiguity of first-time mothering (indeed, perhaps every-time mothering), and didn't over-promise like a weight loss ad. The issue of nursing is particularly emblematic here. I had never ever seen anyone nurse a baby before I began nursing Jacob. My mother bottle-fed my brother and me on the "expert" advice of a physician who suggested that bottle-fed children were better sleepers, so my mother had no personal experience with nursing either. I imagine that other mothers are in this same boat. Of course, a breastfeeding class would probably have been useful; there were none offered in my area, and Jacob arrived three weeks early anyway, allowing us to attend only half of the infant care classes we signed up for. In the absence of all this experience, I substituted book knowledge and found myself floundering. I know now that I would have benefited from simply attending some La Leche League meetings, surrounded by mothers nursing their babies, in order to see what the range of "good care" looks like, to see the different positions, to see a successful latch on, to see, in other words, *what the experience of nursing looks like*. I might have had the same difficulties with nursing, to be sure, but what I would have had is some additional experiential information that could have helped to inform the "expert" texts I relied on.

The nursing example is especially apt in part because, before one has a baby to care for, one knows intellectually that it will be challenging and difficult at times. But it is hard to imagine and hard to conceive of just how much pressure one will feel in caring for this very delicate (yet hardy, too) newborn life completely reliant on others for everything. The commitment to nursing is particularly important because, in addition to clothing, cleaning, and nurturing, the mother is then also ultimately completely and solely responsible for the nourishment of the child. Oh, and there's no fluid meter indicating when the baby is full and when the baby is empty, nor is there similar equipment for the breasts! Sure, sure – watching the outputs (that is, dirty diapers) offers a window into the inputs. I know. But watching the outputs can be equally as baffling and stressful to a new mom. How much urine is sufficient? And, my word, how many colors can a bowel movement be?! When the pressure of knowing that even when it comes to feeding *it's all on you*, being instructed to count and evaluate dirty diapers isn't very reassuring.

A pragmatic view of mothering incorporates all forms of knowledge, experience, and beliefs together. It encourages the new mother to consider her unconscious beliefs about mothering, and to examine their usefulness to her, her baby, and the family, and the extent to which they are or are not conducive to the wellbeing of this set. This view seeks out experiences with others as important sources of knowledge that can both teach the new mother some techniques as well as offer the support necessary to develop an identity as a "mother and . . . ." A pragmatic view suggests to mothers that they are in an interaction with the texts they read, and that critical and open wondering about the authority of the text is important. Perhaps most of all, pragmatic mothering echoes a good friend's words to me during these early months: "Sue Ellen, there are probably a few really bad ways of parenting that most of us would agree on, but there are many, many good ways of parenting that just look different from one another."[12]

NOTES

1   John Dewey, *The Quest for Certainty: A Study of the Relation of Knowledge and Action* (New York: Balch, 1929).
2   Harriett Marshall, "The Social Construction of Motherhood" in Ann Phoenix, Anne Woollett, and Eva Lloyd (eds.) *Motherhood: Meanings, Practices and Ideologies* (London: Sage, 1991).
3   Ibid., p. 83. Interestingly, Marshall has also found that there is a regulatory function of pregnancy texts on shaping the person who is "fit to reproduce." (See Harriett Marshall and Anne Woollett, "Fit to Reproduce? The Regulative Role of Pregnancy Texts," *Feminism and Psychology* 10, 3 (2000): 351–66.) Additionally, fathers are often cast as sidekicks to mothers, according

to Jane Sunderland, "Baby Entertainer, Bumbling Assistant and Line Manager: Discourses of Fatherhood in Parentcraft Texts," *Discourse and Society* 11, 2 (2000): 249–74.

4 Type "parenting" into Google and 78 million hits result; "mothering" results in 3.3 million hits; "motherhood" renders 10.6 million hits.

5 Rima D. Apple, *Perfect Motherhood: Science and Childrearing in America* (New Brunswick: Rutgers University Press, 2006).

6 Ibid., p. 2.

7 Ibid.

8 Ibid., p. 17.

9 Ibid., p. 15.

10 Marshall, "The Social Construction of Motherhood," p. 73.

11 John Dewey, *Democracy and Education* (New York: Free Press, 1916), p. 142.

12 My enduring gratitude to Suzanne Wiltgen for this and many other important thoughts on parenting.

CHAPTER 2

CREATIVE MOTHERING

Lies and the Lying Mothers Who Tell Them

Bedtime Stories

Every night, as I am putting my 5-year-old son to bed, I tell him a lie.

About eighteen months ago, he started having nightmares almost every night. Confronted with the challenges of childrearing, our own mothers turned to Dr. Spock; we mothers of today turn to Dr. Google. A quick search taught me the four "Rs" of dealing with children's nightmares – reassurance, rescripting, rehearsal, and resolution – and provided some strategic suggestions for putting these into action. I was particularly taken with one bedtime "trick" recommended by BabyCenter: "Fill a spray bottle with water scented with a couple drops of vanilla extract . . . and let your child banish scary dreams by spritzing a little around his room before bed."[1] And thus, with the blessing of the self-proclaimed #1 global interactive parenting network, I lied to my son. I grabbed a bottle of air freshener and reported that "Bad Dream Spray" helps keep the bad dreams away and makes them less scary if they do come. His nightmares stopped the very first night I sprayed it. I now spray it every single night at bedtime, and though he still wakes up occasionally with a bad dream, he definitely finds comfort in the ritual of the spray and believes that it works. And more recently, when his younger brother began having the occasional nightmare, I started using the bad dream spray in his room as well.

In the grand scheme of things, deceiving my children to help them conquer their nightmares seems like a relatively harmless practice. Or at least I can fairly easily convince myself that it is. But the real problem is that my lie about bad dream spray is not an isolated one; in fact, I do a lot of lying to my children. And it turns out that I'm not the only one. According to one survey conducted in 2008 by The Baby Website, a British parenting site, 66 percent of parents routinely lie to their children to encourage good behavior, and the average child hears over 3,000 "white lies" from her parents as she's growing up. In a different poll conducted in July 2008, MSNBC found that over 70 percent of parents see no harm in telling an occasional white lie to one's children.

Once we start to recognize the pervasive role that lying plays in parenting – that deliberate deceit is embedded and interwoven throughout the practice of childrearing – it's not only much harder to convince oneself that it's okay, but it starts to seem downright frightening. Confronted with all the lies they hear, it's a wonder that more children don't end up like *South Park*'s Kyle who, having discovered that his parents have lied to him about Santa Claus, the Easter Bunny, and the Tooth Fairy, has an existential crisis. "I don't even know what's real anymore," he screams, before heading off to read the skeptical treatise of philosopher René Descartes.[2]

It's For Your Own Good; Or Is It?

In his influential and pioneering work on children's moral judgment, Jean Piaget proposed that most young children under the age of eight don't know the difference between lies and other forbidden words like swear words. When asked to explain what a lie was, the typical child in Piaget's study described it as "a naughty word," saying things like, "It's when you say naughty things you oughtn't to say."[3] Some children were able to give a more sophisticated answer, identifying lying as "when you say what isn't true," but even these children did not typically distinguish between mistakes, guesses, and exaggerations.[4]

As we become adults, we develop a more nuanced understanding of what lying is, but even so, there's a certain looseness to the notion. Think, for example, of Bill Clinton's infamous defense against lying about his relationship with intern Monica Lewinsky: "It depends on what the meaning of the word 'is' is." The statement to which he was referring – "there is no sex of any kind in any manner, shape, or form" – is undoubtedly misleading, and deliberately so, but if we define "is" as Clinton wants us to, it might technically be true.[5] Or perhaps the statement is not true even in some technical sense, but Clinton had deluded himself into thinking that it was. In that case, we might apply the reasoning used by George Costanza, master of deceit: "It's not a lie if you believe it."[6]

So should a false statement count as a lie, even if the speaker believes it to be true? Should a deliberately misleading statement count as a lie, even if it isn't false? In fact, philosophers have disagreed among themselves on precisely these issues. Some have claimed that a statement must be false in order for it to count as a lie, while others require only that the speaker believe the statement to be false.[7] But in thinking about the lies that we tell to children, we don't need to settle this disagreement. In virtually all (if not all) of the common sorts of parental fabrications, the statements that we're making are indisputably false, and we're under no delusions about this. We make false claims, and we know that the claims we're making are false. We're not going to get off the hook on a technicality.

But perhaps we can get off the hook in some other way. Though we can agree that most lying deserves our moral condemnation, perhaps parental lying constitutes an exception. In particular, in many cases when we lie to our children, *we do so for their own good.* Jack Nicholson's character in *A Few Good Men* gruffly tells Tom Cruise's character: "You can't handle the truth." We mothers seem to take a similar view of our children. So when a beloved pet dies, we make up stories about the farm in the country to protect our children from the cold, harsh reality of death. When nightmares intrude, we invent products like bad dream spray to protect them from whatever is making them afraid.

In her comprehensive analysis of the morality of lying, philosopher Sissela Bok notes that the special needs of children help explain why we think differently about lying to them in comparison with others:

> They, more than all others, need care, support, protection. To shield them, not only from brutal speech and frightening news, but from apprehension and pain – to soften and embellish and disguise – is as natural as to shelter them from harsh weather. Because they are more vulnerable and more impressionable than adults, they cannot always cope with what they hear. Their efforts, however rudimentary, need encouragement and concern,

rather than "objective" evaluation. Unvarnished facts, thoughtlessly or maliciously conveyed, can hurt them, even warp them, render them callous in self-defense.[8]

A mother who would never dream of lying to her partner, or her parents, or her friends, might thus lie to her children without blinking an eye – and we might think that she does best to do so.

But not all philosophers would agree with this analysis. Writing in the fifth century, the theologian St. Augustine famously argued that lying is always a sin. He even explicitly ruled out the possibility that we might be justified in lying to someone else in cases where we can bring about some positive results by doing so: "Nor should we suppose that there is any such thing as a lie that is not a sin, just because we suppose that we can sometimes help somebody by lying."[9] To defend his point, Augustine asks us to consider the parallel case of achieving some great benefit by stealing from someone with a vast fortune. Suppose that by embezzling $5,000 from Oprah Winfrey, one of her employees is able to secure some desperately needed medical treatment for himself. Given Oprah's estimated net worth of over $2.7 billion, the lost money is of essentially no consequence to her, but it dramatically improves the employee's life. Still, according to Augustine, the theft is a sin: stealing is wrong, no matter what our intentions in the matter, and no matter what benefits it can bring about – and likewise for lying.

German philosopher Immanuel Kant, writing in the eighteenth century, took a similar stance. For Kant, being truthful "is a sacred and absolutely commanding decree of reason, limited by no expediency."[10] Like Augustine, Kant explicitly rejects the possibility of a harmless lie; in his view, "a lie always harms another; if not some other particular man, still it harms mankind generally, for it vitiates the source of law itself."[11]

Of course, it's hard not to think that Kant and Augustine might have felt differently about the morality of lying had either of them had any kids. But even setting aside the case of parental lies, it's hard not to be troubled by the uncompromising nature of their view. One particularly forceful objection stems from situations in which a lie will save someone's life. Consider the case of Anne Frank and her family, who attempted to escape Nazi persecution by hiding in secret rooms on the third floor of an Amsterdam office building. Didn't those who kept them hidden do the right thing in lying to Nazi officials about their whereabouts? Telling the truth would have sent the Frank family to near-certain death. When we consider this kind of case, it's difficult to agree with Augustine and Kant that lying is always wrong.

In contrast to the hard line taken by Augustine and Kant, some philosophers have argued that there's nothing in principle wrong with lying. John Stuart Mill, a nineteenth-century British philosopher, advocated a moral theory called utilitarianism that judges the morality of actions based on their consequences; specifically, "actions are right in proportion as they tend to promote happiness; wrong as they tend to produce the reverse of happiness."[12] If lying to someone leads to more happiness overall than telling them the truth, as often seems to be the case when we parents lie to our children, then lying is the morally preferable course of action.

On first hearing, this view seems to go too far in the other direction; where Kant and Augustine viewed lying through too harsh a moral lens, the utilitarian view seems to treat it far too lightly, sacrificing principle for expediency. As Mill himself admits, "it would often be expedient, for the purpose of getting over some momentary embarrassment, or attaining some object immediately useful to ourselves or others, to tell a lie."[13] But Mill has an answer for his critics, since utilitarianism makes its moral calculation based on *all* of the consequences of the action. Lying to a child may make everyone happier in the short run, but if it has disastrous consequences down the road, then utilitarianism does not sanction it. A mother may lie to her son with the good intention of protecting him, but if he is so sheltered as a youngster that he grows up unable to cope with disappointment, or unable to enter into trusting relationships with others, it might be that he would have been happier overall having had to cope with the truth as a youngster.

(Then again, Mill himself serves as a sterling example of someone who might have had to cope with too much truth as a youngster. He was taught Greek at age 3, Latin at age 8, and by the age of 14 he'd read most of the classics in both of these languages and had mastered considerable amounts of history, mathematics, and economic theory. He then suffered a nervous breakdown at age 20, and as he recounts in his autobiography, he came to believe that his education had robbed him of all capacity to feel.)

Even if utilitarianism is not as forgiving about lying as it first seems, we may still find something uncomfortable in the thought that, on the utilitarian view, there is nothing in principle wrong with lying. Even once we take into account all of the consequences of a particular lie, it seems plausible that there will be plenty of situations in which the benefits of lying will outweigh the benefits of telling the truth, even if just slightly. In such a case, utilitarianism promotes lying as the morally preferred course of action – in fact, on the utilitarian view, lying in this sort of case would be morally required. And if there are any cases in which the consequences of lying turn out to be the same as the consequences of telling the truth, utilitarianism views the two actions as morally equivalent – there would be no reason to prefer the truth to a lie. So we might be able to call on utilitarianism to get ourselves off the hook for our parental lies, but we're hardly going to be able to use it to teach our children the value of honesty.

Truth, Lies, and Parental Whoppers

When I was a child, one way that I was taught the value of honesty was by the story of George Washington and the cherry tree. Ironically, this story itself is almost certainly a lie, one fabricated by his biographer Mason Weems. Now, as I reflect upon the story, what I find most unbelievable about it is not that young George would confess to having chopped down the cherry tree, but that the obvious rejoinder to his plaintive "I can't tell a lie" wasn't simply "Just wait until you're a parent yourself, George."

I say this partly as a joke – but only partly. It turns out that it's remarkably hard as a mother to be completely honest with your kids. And so it would be nice if there were some justification for it, at least sometimes. What we want is some kind of compromise position between the Scylla of Kant and Augustine and the Charybdis of Mill – one that allows us to recognize the intrinsic wrongness of lying without forcing us to denounce every lie as morally reprehensible. Bok's own position does just this. Although she doesn't endorse the hard line taken by Augustine and Kant, she rejects the claim that lies should be evaluated solely in terms of their consequences. In her view, irrespective of the consequences of lying, it should always be regarded as having an initial "negative weight," and she codifies this thinking in her *principle of veracity*: "truthful statements are preferable to lies in the absence of special considerations."[14] As she notes, the principle doesn't entail that lying should always be prohibited. But it does mean that we're obligated to look for truthful alternatives before opting to lie, and "only where a lie is a *last resort* can one even begin to consider whether or not it is morally justified."[15]

🐾 AMY KIND

Once we start to think carefully about the sorts of lies we ordinarily tell in our day-to-day lives, it becomes clear that most of them are not really the course of last resort. For example, many of us lie instinctively and without hesitation or question when we receive an unwanted present; I can't even begin to count the times I've smiled cheerfully and said, "It's lovely" or "It's just what I wanted," while internally debating whether it would be best to return it or regift it. Presumably in such cases, we lie simply because we want to be polite. But, as Bok points out, we can usually find something to say in those circumstances that would respect both truth and social convention. Opening a hideously ornate and overly cutesy sailor suit given to my son when he was a newborn, I unhesitatingly gushed over it while cringing inside, though it would have been just about as easy – and just about as nice – to say something else that was truthful: "What a gorgeous shade of blue – it matches his eyes perfectly."

In many of the cases where we lie, our lies are completely unnecessary. And unfortunately, many – I'd even be willing to say most – of our lies to our children fall into this category. Consider some of the lies that readers eagerly supplied to MSNBC's online survey of parental "whoppers":

> I told my daughter that I went to the doctor and had him fix my ears so I can't hear whining.
>
> My boys loved listening to Raffi. I liked it too . . . but I reached a point that I'd rather be poked in the eye with a hot stick than listen to one more Raffi song. So, I told my sons (ages 2 and 3) that Bruce Springsteen was Raffi's brother and that Raffi would really love for us to listen to the Boss.
>
> For years my nephews were under the impression that once batteries died, they couldn't be replaced. It saved a lot of headaches from noisy noisy toys.
>
> My husband and I would tell our daughter that if she didn't behave we would take her back to the kid store. One day she was acting up in the car and we pulled into a strip mall to "take her back."[16]

Children don't need to be protected from Raffi music or from noisy toys. And our desire (or even need) to stop them from misbehaving or whining has little to do with keeping them from harm or promoting their development. As Bok notes, "even apart from shielding and encouragement, strict accuracy is simply not very high on the list of essentials in speaking with children."[17] Rather, in these kinds of cases, our lies are motivated simply by convenience or expedience – or perhaps by sheer desperation.

When I've been chasing my younger son around all morning and his toy school bus starts to play "the horn on the bus goes beep beep beep" for the umpteenth time in a row, I may feel like I've reached the end of my rope, but even in this case, I can't deny that lying about batteries is far from my only option – even if I also discount the particularly appealing alternative of throwing the bus out the window.

Regrettably, when it comes to morality, there's no such thing as the Raffi excuse, and plenty of parents are able to achieve behavioral compliance in their children without resorting to lying (or other equally questionable practices). Nor can these parental lies simply be dismissed as harmless. The mom who threatened to return her daughter to the kid store readily admits the harm her lie caused; her daughter, now 31, "still needs therapy for that one." Even in cases where the particular lie itself causes no harm, children can be harmed simply through their exposure to the practice. According to the American Academy of Pediatrics, lying becomes increasingly common as children reach preschool age. Although this behavior can be explained in part by children's fear of punishment and in part by their overactive imaginations, it's no surprise to learn that one reason that children lie is that they are modeling behavior they see in adults.[18]

We might reasonably disagree with Kant and Augustine that lying always deserves our moral condemnation, but even so, we're not off the moral hook when it comes to parental lying. Desperation, and sleep deprivation, might explain why we do so much of it. But what explains why we think that it's okay?

Lies, Rights, and Rationality

Hugo Grotius, a seventeenth-century Dutch jurist whose work has been enormously important in philosophy, law, and political theory, famously argued that we're perfectly justified in lying to children; in his view, "it is permissible to say what is false before infants and insane persons." When we lie to competent adults, we infringe on what Grotius calls their "liberty of judgment," but since young children lack this liberty, we do nothing wrong if we lie to them. Perhaps then, following Grotius, we lie to children because we think they have no right to the truth.

Personally, I feel squeamish when encountering this line of reasoning. But there may well be something to it. If we think more about the wrongfulness of lying – and what, exactly, it is about lying that makes it

wrong – we can come to see why it might be reasonable to treat lies to children differently from lies to adults.

It's perhaps easiest to see this by returning to Kant's view, particularly the fundamental moral principle he calls the *categorical imperative*. Kant gives three formulations of the categorical imperative, but I'll focus on the one he calls the *formula of humanity*. Think of all the sorts of things that we rely on in our daily lives – our iPhones, our breast pumps, our double mocha lattes (or in my case, Diet Coke). All of these things are valuable to us, but they're valuable to us as means to some of our other ends – in these cases, to our needs as working mothers to multi-task and stay semiconscious throughout the day. In contrast, the value of a human being is different. Humans are not valuable as means to some other end; rather, our rational nature means that we have value in and of ourselves. In Kant's view, that means that we deserve special treatment, and his formula of humanity thus mandates that we treat our sister humans "always at the same time as an end, never merely as a means." Kant does not mean to deny that we can never ethically use other people as means towards our ends. The checkout clerk at Cosco serves as my weekly means to Kirkland baby wipes and multiple cases of Diet Coke, and in Kant's view, assuming that she's willingly undertaken the job, that's perfectly acceptable. But in my interactions with her, I shouldn't treat her *merely* as a means. I need to accord her the respect she deserves as a rational member of humanity.

The key role assigned to the notion of rationality also helps to explain why Kant judges lying to be so problematic. The formula of humanity requires us to respect each other as rational beings, and this in turns means that we have to respect one another's rights to make our own decisions. But lying to someone is inconsistent with this respect. Typically, when we lie to others, we're attempting to manipulate them for our own purposes. Even in those cases when we lie to others in an attempt to get them to do what we think is in their own interests, the deception prevents them from genuinely making the decision for themselves. The lie deprives the victim of the ability to reason accurately about the possible courses of action that are open to them.

Contemporary philosopher David Simpson, who offers an analysis of the immorality of lying in his paper "Lying, Liars, and Language," extends this Kantian point:

> When I lie to you I engage, at the core of the lie, the mutuality of our personhood. I do not just dismiss you as a person; I appeal to you as a person, and then use that against you.[19]

It's precisely for this reason, however, that we may be able to justify lying to children. Kant himself, while recognizing that children are not yet fully autonomous or rational, still believed that they should be treated in accordance with the formula of humanity.[20] But we might try to develop a slightly different position here. Children, especially young children, are not yet fully persons; they have not yet exercised the full potential of their rationality. Even when we're being entirely honest with them, parental conversations with children can never be the mutual engagements of personhood that take place in conversations between adults. Thus, we can't violate this mutuality by lying to them. Without going so far as Grotius – without saying that children have no right to the truth – it seems plausible to think that the fact that children have not yet fully developed their rational natures means that we have different obligations of truthfulness towards them.

Conclusion: It Isn't Easy Being Honest

The UN Convention on the Rights of the Child, ratified by the General Assembly in 1989, notes that "the child, for the full and harmonious development of his or her personality, should grow up in a family environment, in an atmosphere of happiness, love and understanding." Likewise, in his book *Parents and Children: The Ethics of the Family*, contemporary philosopher Jeffrey Blustein argues that our most important duty as parents is to provide children "with the kind of affectionate, appreciative, and supportive upbringing that gives them a sense of their own value and a confidence in their ability to fulfill their intentions."[21] In certain circumstances, it might be that we can best fulfill this duty by lying – and the fact that our children have not yet fully grown into themselves as persons might excuse us when we do so. But once we stop to think about it, it's easy to see that those circumstances are far, far fewer than we'd like to admit.

I'm not quite ready to confess to my children that Bad Dream Spray is really just ordinary air freshener. But I'm also trying, day by day, to do my best not to perpetuate any new lies. When my older son started worrying recently about how we get the chicken meat from the chicken (I think he'd vaguely thought that chicken meat comes from chicken the way milk comes from cows), it was very hard to tell him the truth. Even keeping the facts as simple and neutral as possible, I was sure they would devastate him. And in fact they did: since he learned the truth two weeks ago, he's become a vegetarian. (His younger brother will no doubt soon follow suit.) But here's a perfect example of a case in which only upon knowing the truth could he make a rational decision about his eating practices, or as rational a decision as one can make at the age of five. And, though the truth caused him considerable anguish, I'm glad that he knows it, because it empowered him to make his own choice in the matter.

On the other hand, whether the Tooth Fairy is going to leave him a present under his pillow when he loses his first tooth is something that I haven't yet decided.[22]

NOTES

1   See the discussion of nightmare prevention at www.babycenter.com.
2   "The Tooth Fairy Tats," *South Park* season 4.
3   Jean Piaget, *The Moral Judgment of the Child* (New York: Collier Books, 1962), p. 140.
4   In a recent study of children's attitudes toward lying, 38 percent of the 5-year-olds identified swearing with lying, as compared to 12 percent of 8-year-olds. The study also supports Piaget's claim that young children tend to identify all untrue statements as lying. See Candida C. Peterson, James L. Peterson, and Diane Seeto, "Developmental Changes in Ideas About Lying," *Child Development* 54, 6 (December 1982): 1529–35.
5   The initial claim was actually uttered by his spokesman, William Bennett. Clinton offered his lesson on semantics in his 1998 videotaped testimony to the grand jury empaneled by Independent Prosecutor Kenneth Starr.
6   George gives this advice to Jerry in the season 6 *Seinfeld* episode, "The Beard."
7   Thomas Carson, for example, claims that "In order to tell a lie, one must make a false statement." See Thomas Carson, "The Definition of Lying," *Nous* 40 (2006): 284–306. In contrast, Joseph Kupfer claims that "A person lies when he asserts something to another which he believes to be false with the intention of getting the other to believe it to be true." See Joseph Kupfer, "The Moral Presumption Against Lying," *Review of Metaphysics* 36 (1982): 104.
8   Sissela Bok, *Lying: Moral Choice in Public and Private Life* (New York: Vintage, 1999), p. 206. This essay is heavily indebted to Bok's work on lying.
9   St. Augustine, "The Problem of Lying," in *The Enchiridion: On Faith, Hope, and Love*, ed. Albert C. Outler (1955), available online at www.tertullian.org/fathers/augustine_enchiridion_02_trans.htm (accessed August 10, 2009).
10 Immanuel Kant, *Critique of Practical Reason and Other Writings in Moral Philosophy*, ed. Louis White Beck (Chicago: University of Chicago Press, 1949).

11 Bok, *Lying*, p. 269.
12 John Stuart Mill, *Utilitarianism*, 2nd edn., ed. George Sher (Indianapolis: Hackett, 2001), p. 7.
13 Ibid., p. 22.
14 Bok, *Lying*, p. 30.
15 Ibid., p. 31.
16 See the list online at www.msnbc.msn.com/id/25678284/.
17 Bok, *Lying*, p. 206.
18 Steven P. Shelov and Robert E. Hannemann (eds.) *Caring For Your Baby and Child: Birth to Age Five* (New York: Bantam Books, 1991), p. 373.
19 David Simpson, "Lying, Liars and Language," *Philosophy and Phenomenological Research* 52 (1992): 637.
20 See Jeffrey Blustein's discussion of related issues in *Parents and Children: The Ethics of the Family* (New York: Oxford University Press 1982).
21 Ibid., p. 129.
22 I owe a debt of thanks to my research assistant, Jackson Wyrick, for his invaluable assistance as I was writing this essay. Many thanks also to my partner in deception, Frank Menetrez. This essay is dedicated to my two wonderful boys, Stephen and Joseph. Being their mother is one of the greatest joys of my life. If they ever read this essay when they get older, I hope that they'll forgive the lies that I told them.

CHAPTER 3

PRO-CHOICE PHILOSOPHER HAS BABY

Reflections on Fetal Life

Pregnancy: Before and After

My husband Tuomas and I spent the first three years of our marriage doing everything in our power to avoid pregnancy. During this time, I firmly believed in a woman's right to choose whether to continue a pregnancy. If asked to defend my stance, I argued that a woman is very clearly a person, a being with moral and legal rights, whereas a fetus was clearly not a person, given its lack of rationality, moral agency, and self-consciousness.

Tuomas and I started trying to conceive after our first year as professors. After nine months of trying, we discovered our pregnancy on Saturday, May 10, 2008 – the day before Mother's Day. Twelve weeks later, we had our first ultrasound. The first image of our future daughter was, to use Rudolf Otto's term, awe-ful. The ultrasound technician pressed the wand against my belly and the little fetus somersaulted in response. While the technician continued to speak to us, my little tenant continued frolicking in my womb. Tuomas and I drove home in silence afterwards. While stopped at a red light he commented, out of the blue, that after seeing our fetus, he could never bring himself to abort it. My response seemed so foreign given my past beliefs: neither could I.

The months that followed reinforced my new respect for fetal life. The first time I felt my daughter kick overwhelmed me with tears. In the early hours one Wednesday morning, both still groggy from sleep, I placed Tuomas' hand on my belly and he felt her move for the first time. We constantly read and sang to her. I began what I hope will result in a life-long love affair with the Beatles by playing their songs against my belly for an hour a day (which seems to have worked – you should see her laugh when I sing "Yellow Submarine" to her). I realized that, regardless of philosophical debates about whether a fetus is a person, the fetus inside me was an independent entity in its own right. And it wasn't *just* a fetus – she was my daughter. In her book *Human Reproduction: Principles, Practices, and Policies*, Christine Overall writes:

> Paradoxically, the experience of carrying a fetus inside my body profoundly deepened my understanding of the abortion issue in two respects. First, the sensations of the active, unpredictable fetus with its turns and kicks, its hiccups, and its rare rest periods, convinced me that this entity within my body was definitely independent and alive, no mere appendage, and not a part of my body in the way that an arm or an eye or a heart is. At the same time, the experience of being "with child" was sufficiently engrossing, disturbing, even overpowering at times, to persuade me that no woman should ever have to go through this experience – an experience that philosopher Caroline Whitbeck has suggested is akin to literally being possessed or taken over by another being – against her will.[1]

Overall's experience accurately reflects my own. It was made apparent to me one day during the eighth month of pregnancy my little fetus already had her own personality. Tuomas and I rushed to the hospital one night at 9 p.m. after a full day of feeling no fetal movement. Of course, the minute the nurses strapped a fetal monitor on me, our baby started moving vigorously. Her stubbornness and desire to do things her way was already emerging. She was definitely, already, her own individual. And the utter feeling of terror that ran through me as I wondered what was

BERTHA ALVAREZ MANNINEN

going on inside my body, only inches away and yet almost inaccessible, reminded me of the extremely intimate state that pregnancy is.

I was troubled – how could I reconcile my pro-choice stance with my new respect for fetal life? My personal experiences would never hold up as evidence in a philosopher's court; they would most likely be dismissed as emotional or visceral reactions rather than considered to be from a privileged epistemological perspective. I did know I was no longer willing to say a human fetus lacked personhood, at least from mid-gestation onward. Indeed, even now, I have no idea whether a fetus is a person: Is it always a person? Never a person? Does it become a person sometime in gestation? If so, when? While some philosophers use mental criteria for defining personhood, non-philosophers might appeal to emotion, religion, biology, or other metaphysical beliefs in defense of their conception of personhood. The vastly diverging viewpoints about personhood held by so many people in our society render it unlikely that consensus will be reached on this issue.

Although much ink has been spilt in order to answer what now seems to be an intractable question, actually, it is unnecessary to determine whether the fetus is a person in order to decide if one is in favor of abortion rights. In what follows, I show how abortion rights still stand even if the fetus is considered a person with full moral status. Next, I discuss the possibility of being pro-choice and yet still displaying appropriate respect and reverence for intrauterine life. Seeing the possibility of being pro-choice *and* respectful of intrauterine life allows us to dispel the misconception, held by many, that being pro-choice means being pro-abortion.

McFall, Shimp, and Thomson's Ailing Violinist

In 1978 Robert McFall suffered from apalastic anemia, which required him to obtain a bone marrow transplant in order to survive. His cousin, David Shimp, had the only matching bone marrow physicians found, yet, although he willingly went through the testing, he refused to undergo the extraction procedure once the match was ascertained. McFall sued Shimp, hoping the Pennsylvania courts would force his cousin to submit to further testing and ultimately to the extraction. According to the court, the main ethical issue at stake was whether "in order to save the life of one of its members by the only means available, may society infringe upon one's absolute right to his 'bodily security?'"[2] The judges ruled that such an infringement could not be made. Forcing Shimp to donate bone marrow would violate our society's basic principles. The court maintained:

> Our society . . . has as its first principle, the respect for the individual, and that society and government exist to protect the individual from being invaded and hurt by another. . . . For our law to compel the defendant to submit to an intrusion of his body would change the very concept and principle upon which our society is founded. To do so would defeat the sanctity of the individual.[3]

Notice that the judges' conclusion was *not* that McFall lacked a right to life or moral status, or that his life was otherwise worthless or less valuable than Shimp's. Not by a long shot. The conclusion was that no person's right to life entailed that another person could be forced to submit to unwanted bodily intrusion in order to preserve that right. So, it wasn't that McFall's life wasn't valued by the judges; rather, the judges decided that no one's worth as a human being entailed that another human being's dignity or integrity could be compromised for the sake of it.

Every semester, medical professionals from local blood banks come to college campuses in the hopes of obtaining blood that will be used to help afflicted persons, and possibly save some lives. Sadly, they must offer incentives, from juice and cookies to monetary prizes, to entice individuals to donate. They often tell me, when I go to contribute, that the donations have been paltry. Having an ample supply of blood in blood banks is obviously important. One might wonder if it would be easier and more efficient if students, faculty, and staff were randomly selected and their blood forcibly extracted and stored for future life-saving purposes? Using the same logic, imagine how many people we could help if randomly selected healthy individuals were forced to "donate" one of their kidneys in order to save the lives of individuals with End Stage Renal Disease. After all, although some lifestyle changes need to be made to live with one kidney, they are not terribly onerous. A person with one kidney should consume nutritious foods, get regular exercise, and stay well hydrated. These are habits we should all adopt, so the cost to the forced "donor" is relatively low, but the benefit to the recipient is enormous: it is life-saving.

Such prospects should send chills down your spine because, as Donald H. Regan, professor of law and philosophy, puts it, "we are traditionally

BERTHA ALVAREZ MANNINEN

very dubious about the practices which involve direct invasions of the body or imposition of physical pain or extreme physical discomfort."[4] This is the thesis Judith Jarvis Thomson argues in favor of with her now (in)famous – at least among philosophers – violinist example in her article "A Defense of Abortion." Thomson asks us to imagine waking up and finding yourself hooked up to a famous violinist suffering from a deadly kidney ailment. The Society of Music Lovers has determined that only you have the ability to save him, and if you disconnect yourself from the violinist he will surely die. The attending physician reminds you that the violinist is an innocent person with a right to life, and that, although you also have a right to your bodily integrity, the violinist's right to life clearly supersedes that right. Nonetheless, according to Thomson, it is obvious that "you do not commit murder, you do not do what is impermissible, if you reach around to your back and unplug yourself from the violinist."[5] While it would be very nice of you to allow the violinist continued use of your body, you can't be *required* to do so. Thomson does not deny that the violinist is a person with moral worth and a right to life. She merely wants to show that "having a right to life does not guarantee having either a right to be given the use of or a right to be allowed continued use of another person's body."[6]

These examples help elucidate the argument in favor of abortion rights in a manner that does not deprive the fetus moral status or a right to life. McFall certainly had a right to life and moral worth; the same can be said about individuals afflicted with End Stage Renal Disease and Thomson's violinist. Yet their right to life and moral worth doesn't translate into forcing other people to surrender bodily autonomy or integrity in order to save their lives. Analogously, even if the fetus were considered a person with full moral status and moral rights, it doesn't follow from this alone that another person – the pregnant woman – can be forced to submit to unwanted bodily intrusions in order to sustain the fetus's life. As Regan writes: "it is a deeply rooted principle of American law that an individual is ordinarily not required to volunteer aid to another individual who is in danger or in need of assistance."[7]

We can find more support for Thomson's thesis by appealing to Immanuel Kant's moral philosophy. Kant maintains that all persons should "act in such a way that you treat humanity, whether in your own person or in the person of another, always at the same time as an end and never simply as a means."[8] That is, no person should be treated in a manner that is against her will and that she has not consented to; she cannot be treated as a mere instrument to obtain the ends of others. To force a woman to undergo pregnancy is to ignore all the emotional and physical hardships that may come with such a state, including, but certainly not limited to, debilitating nausea, hypertension, dizziness spells, migraines, gestational diabetes, exhaustion, and even sometimes extreme bleeding or possibly death. If a woman undergoes a caesarean section (as I did), she submits herself to major abdominal surgery with an exceptional amount of pain in its aftermath; pain that she is expected to overcome rather quickly in order to begin caring for a being that is completely dependent. It is hard to imagine *forcing* women to undergo such difficulties; difficulties that certainly surpass blood or bone marrow extraction, which we never force upon anyone. To ignore a woman's decision concerning such an extremely intimate and personal matter, to compel her to be possessed or taken over by another human being, even if that human being is a person, is an extreme intrusion of her body, mind, and emotional life. To endorse such treatment by outlawing abortion blatantly violates Kant's imperative. It is to treat the pregnant woman as a mere object; to ignore her physical and emotional interests and reduce her to nothing but an incubator for meeting the needs of the fetus.

Although Thomson's thesis has been subjected to many criticisms, I would like to briefly address the most common one: the responsibility objection. According to this objection, if a woman concedes to voluntary sexual intercourse, she has tacitly given the fetus permission to use her body for its sustenance. This is because fully aware of the possibility of pregnancy, she deliberately participated in an activity, sex, that caused the fetus's dependence on her. In this sense, she is responsible for the fetus's existence and its subsequent needs, so she has a moral obligation to sustain it until birth, an obligation that ought to be legally enforced by banning abortions.

Thomson responds to this objection by offering yet another interesting example. Suppose you know a burglar is on the prowl in your neighborhood, and yet it's hot and your air conditioning is on the fritz, so you leave your window wide open, allowing the burglar easy access to your house. Although you knew full well you may be robbed, you opened the window to enjoy the cool breeze nonetheless. You knowingly did something you would enjoy that also allowed the burglar entry to your house. Thomson denies that by doing so you forfeit the right to your property; the burglar does not have a right to rob you because you were careless in neglecting to fully secure your home against him. Similarly, Thomson argues, even if a woman voluntarily engages in sexual intercourse, even if she was careless in preventing pregnancy, the fetus does not thereby have a right to the use of her body.

What I take Thomson to be arguing is this: some rights remain with the right-bearer alone and are not automatically forfeited simply because the right-bearer was reckless in her behavior, knowingly putting herself in a position where her rights *could* be violated. It may be reckless for a woman, for example, to walk down a dark street alone in the middle of the night in a violent and crime-infested neighborhood. Her taking this walk does not amount to a forfeiture of her right to bodily and sexual integrity. In other words, another person does not thereby receive the right to rape her. More analogously to the typical case of pregnancy, have you ever heard of a situation where a drunk driver was forced to donate blood or a non-vital organ to help save the life of the innocent person he hit while driving drunk? Sound like a good idea? This may be more analogous to pregnancy because, like the victim of the drunk driver, the fetus may be considered an innocent person and its dependency on another for survival is due to the actions of that other. Yet even though the drunk driver was fully responsible for his behavior in the sense that we would say that he *shouldn't* have driven drunk, and even though he may be held accountable in other ways as well, he is never held so accountable that his bodily integrity is violated. He is never forced to submit to bodily intrusion to save the life of the innocent person he harmed. And he wouldn't be, even if he were the only person who could help the victim (as Shimp was the only person with matching bone marrow for McFall). Not forcing drunk drivers to do it for their victims leaves us hard pressed to find an argument that women should be forced to do it for their fetuses.

Women should retain the right to bodily integrity that was preserved for Shimp; the right to an abortion should be seen as a manner of protecting women against a potential type of bodily intrusion – pregnancy – that is unique to them alone. This is why I am pro-choice, even though I do have profound respect for fetal life. Indeed, I also have profound respect for the lives of individuals dying from kidney disease, aplastic anemia, or any other ailment, and I certainly feel sorrow for their deaths. Nevertheless, I cannot support a law that would force a subset of our population to submit to unwanted bodily intrusion to save the life of another subset of our population. Not even if the former were somehow responsible for the latter's state and no matter how tragic their death would be.

And I do believe that, more often than not, abortions are instances of tragic deaths, either because of the death of the fetus itself and/or due to the circumstances that resulted in the abortion.

Pro-Choice Does Not Mean Pro-Abortion

In her article "On the Moral and Legal Status of Abortion," Mary Anne Warren maintains that advocates of abortion rights do not regard abortion as "morally serious or extremely unfortunate" but rather as "closer to being a morally neutral act, like cutting one's hair.[9] Such a condescending attitude toward fetal life and a nonchalant perspective on the loss of fetal life turns many individuals away from the pro-choice position. Francis Kissling writes: "I am deeply struck by the number of thoughtful, progressive people who have been turned off to the pro-choice movement by the lack of adequate and clear expressions of respect for fetal life. . . . It almost seems as if there has been a 'hardening of the heart' resulting from the pro-choice position."[10]

In response to Warren's claims, philosopher Rosalind Hursthouse argues that the premature death of a human life that comes with an abortion "must make it a serious matter and hence . . . anyone who genuinely believes that an abortion is comparable to a haircut or an appendectomy is mistaken."[11] In Hursthouse's words, we can begin to find a way to respond to Kissling's concern that devaluing fetal life and approaching abortion as a morally innocuous action has led many to view the pro-choice movement as a pro-abortion movement; as a movement that callously celebrates or even encourages abortion (as when opponents of abortion refer to its defenders as "pro-abortion"). The challenge facing pro-choice advocates is to simultaneously defend the abortion right and to display adequate respect for fetal life, acknowledging in the process the serious and sad occasion that a procured abortion can be.

In Japan, abortion is acknowledged as an unfortunate social necessity, but there also exists grieving rituals, the *mizuko kuyo* memorial rites for instance, in the event that individuals who have procured an abortion wish to honor the fetus that died. Without such a grieving ritual, many Buddhists worry that the result would be "a kind of personal degradation . . . from repeated abortions to a flippant acceptance of the practice and from there to deterioration in a person's capacity for generalized sensitivity."[12] In American culture there are no socially sanctioned mourning rituals for fetal death after an abortion (not to mention miscarriages, which can be extremely painful for the families who experience them). I suspect this is the case because it is assumed that women have no need to mourn the death that they deliberately sought and caused. However, *contra*

Warren's contention, many women don't see abortion as a morally innocuous action or comparable to a haircut; many do suffer in the aftermath. (Men, it has been shown, also suffer as a result of their partner's abortion decisions and thus they too need some sort of socially sanctioned manner of expressing that suffering, not to mention access to post-abortion counseling.) One abortion nurse tells the story of a woman who, after having an abortion, "raised herself up on one elbow to see what had just come out, and she let out one of the most blood-curdling screams I have ever heard."[13] The same nurse tells a story of another woman who "reached out her beautifully delicate young hand, gently touched the cheek of her newly aborted fetus, and said, 'I'm sorry, baby.'"[14] Another woman who procured an abortion for a deformed fetus told her nurse that she didn't "'want to deny that this baby existed.' She gave it a name, had a funeral for it, and buried it in the family plot alongside her grandmother."[15]

Two things are clear from the above stories. First, the stereotype that all women who procure abortions are heartless baby-killers, or indulge in promiscuous practices only to then callously kill their infant, is inaccurate, incomplete, and insensitive. Second, there is a need to acknowledge that fetuses are entities deserving of respect; the abortion procedure is much graver than simply removing an appendage or getting a haircut and there is a need for a socially accepted manner of grieving fetal deaths that result from deliberate abortions. Americans need their own version of a *mizuko kuyo* ritual; acknowledging and encouraging grieving rituals for fetuses is one way that we can simultaneously recognize the right to an abortion and a call for respecting the value of intrauterine life.

Another way to emphasize that being pro-choice does not mean being pro-abortion is by supporting social programs that help women through the challenges of an unplanned pregnancy. There is evidence that some social programs significantly curb abortion rates by offering financial and medical support so that women do not automatically revert to abortion out of fear or being unable to support the ensuing child. (I find it sadly ironic that anti-abortion and anti-welfare rhetoric seem to find a common home in political debates and ideology, seeing evidence in this that we care more about children before they are born than we do after. If the pro-life philosophy extended to extrauterine life with the same vigor, perhaps that can do more for curbing abortions than simply outlawing it.) For example, a recent report released by the Catholics in Alliance for the Common Good finds that the abortion rate among women living below the poverty level is more than four times that of women above 300 percent of the poverty level. This study of all US states from 1982–2000 finds that social and economic supports such as benefits for pregnant women and mothers and economic assistance to low-income families have contributed significantly to reducing the number of abortions in the United States over the past twenty years.[16]

By supporting social programs that help pregnant women in need, we illustrate respect for fetal life by doing what President Barack Obama has implored both sides of the abortion debate to do: look for ways to decrease the demand for, and consequently the incidence of, abortion.

Women (and men) should be given the opportunity to openly talk about past and present abortions they may have obtained, and they should be encouraged to express their feelings honestly, from relief to regret, without criticism or condemnation. In addition, acknowledging that pregnant women can suffer from the loss of fetal life when procuring abortions, and giving validity to that suffering by making grieving rituals available to them if they so wish to publicly mourn, does not undermine the contention that women have the right to an abortion. These rituals *would*, however, undermine Warren's contention that fetal life is no more valuable than the life of a fish and that abortion is a morally innocuous, insignificant action. But undermining *this* perspective only serves to advance the pro-choice movement in the eyes of the general public. There need not be a "hardening of the heart" as a result of being pro-choice.

NOTES

1   Christine Overall, *Human Reproduction: Principles, Practices, and Policies* (Toronto: Oxford University Press, 1993), pp. 1–2.
2   10th Pennsylvania District Court, *McFall v. Shimp* (1978). Available online at www.ucs.louisiana.edu/~ras2777/judpol/mcfall.html (accessed June 18, 2009).
3   Ibid.
4   Donald H. Regan. "Rewriting Roe v. Wade," *Michigan Law Review* 77, 7 (1979): 1583–4.
5   Judith Jarvis Thomson, "A Defense of Abortion," *Philosophy and Public Affairs* 1, 1 (1971): 52.
6   Thomson, "A Defense of Abortion," p. 56.
7   Regan, "Rewriting Roe v. Wade," p. 1569.

8   Immanuel Kant, *Grounding for the Metaphysics of Morals* (Indianapolis: Hackett, 1785), p. 36.

9   Mary Anne Warren, "On the Moral and Legal Status of Abortion," *The Monist* 57 (1973): 43–61.

10 Francis Kissling, "Is There Life After *Roe*? How to Think About the Fetus," *Conscience: The News Journal of Catholic Opinion* (2004). Available online at www.catholicsforchoice.org/conscience/archives/c2004win_lifeafterroe.asp (accessed June 18, 2009).

11 Rosalind Hursthouse, "Virtue Theory and Abortion," *Philosophy and Public Affairs* 20, 3 (1991): 237.

12 William R. LaFleur, "Contestation and Consensus: The Morality of Abortion in Japan," *Philosphy East and West* 40, 4 (1990): 534–7.

13 Bobbie Jean Kennedy, "Dilemmas in Practice: I'm Sorry, Baby," *American Journal of Nursing* 88, 8 (1988): 1068.

14 Ibid., p. 1067.

15 Ibid., p. 1068.

16 Catholics in Alliance for the Common Good, "Reducing Abortion in America: The Effect of Economic and Social Supports" (2008). Available online at www.catholicsinalliance.org (accessed June 18, 2009).

CHAPTER 4

KIM, ELLEN, AND ZACK'S BIG ADVENTURE

Lesbian Mothers Raising a Boy Steeped in His Masculinity

We adopted Zack at birth; in fact, we were present at his birth. He was three years old when we found him early one morning, nose pressed to the window, eagerly waiting to catch a glimpse of the garbage truck making its rounds through our neighborhood. That's when we first knew something was up with biology and that the social construction of gender was a bit more complicated than we had thought. As lesbian mothers, we live in an experimental laboratory of gender assignment. We were determined to do better than our parents, in allowing our son the gender flexibility not afforded the previous generation. We really want to provide our boy a place to be himself without the constraints of a "normal" heterosexual model. We expose Zack to a variety of choices in toys, clothes, games, and anything that might be remotely associated with varied gender expressions. Our family is also a mixed-race family, with each of its members of a different race. As a matter of course, we expose Zack to a variety of cultural expression as well, such as photographs and stories of African-American inventors, writers, artists, or Asian sports figures, activists, and leaders. We hope he'll realize that he has a wide space for becoming himself, and that he'll make good use of that space.

Two lesbian mothers raising a boy who appears bent on fully expressing his seemingly hardwired masculinity is indeed one big adventure! Seriously, what crazy cosmic power in the universe arranged for the world's most masculine boy to be raised by us? Fortunately, we wholeheartedly embrace masculinity. My partner relates to masculinity in her own body, in her own gender presentation. Though more feminine in my gender expression, I am attracted to multiple masculine identities, especially in women. I find these women's independence and internal strength endlessly interesting, particularly my partner's. There is no one kind of masculinity and it can be embodied by men or women. We believe gender expression can be nuanced and individual and we hope our boy will benefit from such flexibility.

We entered motherhood with eyes wide open, ready to forge new territories away from the restraint and dysfunction of the gender conceptions in our own families. Personally, I wanted to make a family that was more elastic, fun, and experimental than the one I grew up in. My family was a typical 1960s mixed-race family intent on homogenization in class and race issues, whereas gender expectations were steeped in the rigid roles of such examples as *The Jetsons* or *I Love Lucy*.[1] Which things would we end up repeating and to what extent would we be able to shape our own inclusive, free, open, and fun family? As with all parenting situations, we really couldn't know without trying. We wondered, of course, whether we would lose control to the greater context of our culture, a culture that still celebrates and rewards only stereotypical manifestations of gender-manly men and girly girls.

Zack's Sensitivity

With Zack as our test pilot, we were happy to find that his biological maleness was not in itself a deterrent to his ability to afford space for other expressions of gender. Sensitivity grew in our boy. For example, Zack was aware of femininity in his friends of both genders in varying degrees. He accepted these expressions as individual styles and choices and didn't assign positive or negative weight to any particular expressions. To him, they were just qualities in his friends that made each unique. At preschool age, masculine and feminine qualities flowed in all children effortlessly.

Zack had a friend at preschool, the son of an artist who was driven to draw anything and everything he could. He drew all his class members when he was four. He specialized in princesses and lovingly curled the ends of their hair, making extra long torsos and legs so he could decorate their elaborate clothes with curled details, flowers, and carefully chosen colors that indicated various jewels. Even the boys in the class were drawn elaborately with fancy flaps and coats that were reminiscent of the 1960s or the Victorian era. Zack was invited to this child's birthday party and when we asked him what to get for this talented boy he suggested a purple pony or a princess doll. Zack knew that this boy who wouldn't be interested in Legos or balls or the things he himself might desire. Zack suggested this gift without skipping a beat, without a laugh or even a smile. He saw this as appropriate to his friend in light of his individuality.

Years later, this child's mother told me her son was desperate to wear dresses to elementary school, and that she discouraged him for fear of social alienation. I was sad for the boy. The fear of social pressures and ridicule by peers is a serious issue. Parents aim for some social conformity in their children, at least enough so they won't struggle too much socially. However, this goal raises the question of whether fitting in is worth the cost. Kids are negotiating the balance between satisfying their own desires and trying to determine whether or not their desires are socially acceptable. Sometimes they care nothing about what others think, and at other times they are intensely motivated to win everyone's approval. Where is the balance? On one hand, conformity brings the confidence that one's child can be a success within the social order. Even those of us living exciting lives outside the mainstream hunger for safe areas where we can feel accepted and respected. On the other hand, we don't necessarily want to be like everyone else. Many gay people reject the notion that we are exactly like our heterosexual counterparts as parents. Our respective subcultures can be nurturing and creative at the same time, creating, for example, happy and safe spaces for feminine boys to wear girls' clothes if they want to. In the Bay Area of California there are heterosexual families who are also part of this subculture of acceptance. Where are the other safe places for kids like this? Is it geographic or psychological? Perhaps the moment has arrived to embrace elastic ideas about gender expression in children and a similar flexibility of standards regarding successful parenting as we help our children find a balance between authenticity and acceptance. One hopes her child will be invited to play dates and birthday parties, and will thus have some semblance of a social life. There is a terror and a tragedy associated with any failure on the part of the social life of one's child. What parties was he not invited to? Who is and is not willing to reach out and become close to my child, giving him opportunities for play and learning? Zack befriending or being befriended by a friend with a different gender presentation is cause for celebration. Happily, with children, difference can triumph as an arena for bridge building.

Zack's Race

> *Most black males are bombarded in early childhood with the message that they are inhabiting an all-powerful universe that not only does not want them to succeed but wants to ensure their demise.*
>
> bell hooks[2]

No black boy is born into this world without the sharp waves of the world breaking around him like a rocky sea. These are huge, dangerous waves of difficulty, heartbreak, and limited opportunities. Even in the most politically progressive communities in the United States, such as in our town of Berkeley, California, experience can make one pause. When we realized that diagonal lines drawn on the map from the upscale hills to the more modest flats created our public school system, we were happy. This formal gesture of cartography should have allowed for a race and class integrated environment in the schools. Quickly, we saw how idealistic our optimism was, for a large number of Caucasian kids would go to private elementary schools. These private schools would be nearly entirely Caucasian, engaged in a struggle to find children of color that could afford their institutions. The irony of this situation is poignant. If even in such a politically and socially "conscious" community there is a situation where race and class divide children, how can we expect to dismantle hierarchies anywhere?

Having an African-American son, I quickly perceived that the racism specter was much more overwhelming than I imagined. Zack's race seemed to be the sum of his identity – his large body, his brown skin, and his spicy temperament provided circumstantial evidence that he was guilty of something. He fit neatly into the bottom of a predictable, racist, and dangerous social hierarchy. Our mothering action plans would fundamentally be challenged by this perception at every turn; we had to be ready. His blackness would often enough prompt others to imagine he was violent. Many times we noticed parents gathering up their children and moving them away from him at the park or pool. These experiences stung and we hoped that Zack would be oblivious to them. Was he? Hopefully, but we weren't. I could barely contain my rage in such situations. I became a mother tiger, refusing to restrain myself from meeting such actions with a precise response. After all, I had grown up as a mixed race child and had easy access to my own vivid memories of racial epithets being hurled at me by random children in my neighborhood. My well-meaning parents assured me that I was "not different" from these kids in any way, and that homogenization was the rule of the day. I knew I never wanted to deliver that message to my own child, but what should a mother do? Mothering Zack would require vigilance against negative social expectations and experiences and a passionate celebration of the joy, beauty, and triumph of African-American identity and of our unique family.

Race differentiation happens early. The first thing children notice is actual skin color, such as "Mommy, you seem to be yellowish-brown, I am chocolate colored, and my other mommy is pinkish." Associations attached to color and gender identifications are less apparent, but quickly begin to form as kids begin to take note of many implications of differences during their school years. When Zack was in elementary school, we noticed that the black boys were most often the ones found sitting in the principal's office. Why is it that the majority of the kids in trouble are black boys? Race is part of this picture, but we should also wonder why the majority of the kids in trouble are boys. Are we failing our boys in how we educate them?

Zack's Desire

Although being a certain gender does not imply that one will desire a certain way, there is nevertheless a desire that is constitutive of gender itself and, as a result, no quick and easy way to separate the life of gender from the life of desire.

Judith Butler[3]

Watching Zack's desires develop was illuminating and endlessly fascinating. At first, it was easy to see what he wanted because his "affect" (as child development specialists informed us) was high. In other words, Zack was dramatic. He let you know exactly how he felt about things – about his choices of clothes, toys, sports, computer games, board games, food, books, movies, and anything else he wanted. More often than not there was a gendered quality to these choices. It first showed up in clothing. He was not going to feel comfortable putting on pink, puffy animal print pajamas. Even yellow, the assigned gender-neutral color, was off his list. He only wanted stereotypical "boy" colors, shapes, and textures in his clothes: blue, black, gray, and green. Definitely no pastels. Red, well, red is interesting. For Zack, red was an acceptable color because his favorite soccer teams wore red jerseys, and many football, basketball, and baseball teams donned red. Red became a color of desire for Zack, which in turn opened a space for him to explore femininity. There is a joy and flexibility in red as it affords a creative in-between space. I am always happy to see him in red.

Zack's toys are also freely chosen. We gave him many options, putting before him many male and female dolls, animals, and books, including those that girls are typically expected to enjoy. Why should our son be limited to traditional male toys? Alas, at each and every age he rejected playthings marketed to girls. His desire was inextricably located in what are sometimes called "all boy" choices: trucks, Hot Wheels, Thomas the Tank Engine trains, remote controlled cars, Bionicles, Legos, Bakugan Battle Brawlers, and the likes. Perhaps it was the cumulative effect of these choices that got to me, more than any one of them.

We continued to present Zack with boy dolls of color, with creative ways to make pictures, with things to take apart, and with objects that reflected his own identity as an African American. As our son has grown, the area in which he's most comfortably and enthusiastically explored gender cross-over has been with books. An avid reader, Zack will happily read stories about girl protagonists. However, she has to be a particular kind of girl, an active tomboy or a clever detective who will capture his attention. The window to a more gender-complex world was opened through books and we are making the best of it.

Zack also loves to play team sports. He wants to be with his teams as much as possible, whenever possible. Recently, we had the joy of cheering his baseball team on to win the division championship. Despite the fact that neither of us spent time on teams ourselves, we grew very involved with Zack's teams. Our son happened to be a big kid with a lot of physical strength and watching him smack the ball way out to make a home run or a triple play was a profound joy for us. We learned how much fun parenting this masculine ball of fire on the sport's field could be. Masculine desire guided his everyday play, like throwing rocks or running hard on the playground. He especially liked to push other children on the tire swing, especially when the swing would return to crash into him and knock him over. He passionately enjoyed that! As Zack's behavior inevitably seemed to involve risk, a kind of internal gesture of "letting go" was required from his mothers. Perhaps this "letting go" is the mantra needed in parenting in general.

Of course, there are masculine choices or behaviors that might not be all positive. For example, our son does not like to tell us how he feels. When he does, it is after waiting so long he can no longer avoid it. Is this gender based? Putting feelings into words is a developmental skill, but he continues to struggle with describing his inner thoughts and feelings. He would rather us play a guessing game.

Avoiding discussion of feelings is common for men of my father's generation. In fact, males of his Depression era generation are surrounded by a deafening silence about virtually all personal issues. Is it really that difficult for the male gender to describe matters of the heart? What keeps their emotions on lockdown? What makes revealing the intimate nuances of internal psychological mechanics so difficult for some and so easy for others? This can certainly be influenced by external environment. We are highly wound mothers who can blow off emotional steam with gusto. Creating a high-keyed emotional environment might not be the best for our child, a boyish boy. To our dismay, we began to see that the emotionally charged family environment was a perfect setting in which masculine repression could grow. The stoic responses of our son lead us to think that if we wanted to raise an emotionally sensitive man, we better take a hard look at our own behaviors. Emotional resiliency comes from internal strength and flexibility. These can be gendered both ways. Humor, fair mindedness, and flexibility are things that we seek for ourselves and we dedicated our efforts to helping our son cultivate these tools as well.

Zack's Violence

Having "high affect" gave Zack a face of big emotions. When he was sad he was very sad, and when he was angry, he was scary. His aggression was surprising when it first developed. He kicked and hit and bit us. He was wild at times. Passers-by would gasp at the sight of his tantrums; once, someone called the police, thinking we must have done something horrendous to evoke such a reaction. We had to determine what might set him off and learn how to head that off at the pass. Could the cumulative effect of two women foil a potential for violence? It seemed that one woman might not be a good match for our son, but two promised to balance out the spicy behavior of our little drama queen.

A particularly troubling side effect of his demonstrative anger was the fostering of our own. This was something that felt familiar to me, as it was a dynamic present in my heterosexual family of origin. (My parents were akin to Martha and George in the movie *Who's Afraid of Virginia Woolf?*)[4] Our efforts to deflect, curb, and calm Zack became our full focus for many years. Eventually, we hoped he would do this for himself, and we tried various configurations of rewards and incentives appropriate for his age. Our efforts focused on helping him thrive socially on play dates, at the park, the pool, preschool, and, now, in elementary school. Our relentless efforts paid off. By the time he entered preschool, he was able to control himself emotionally. This was a real triumph, perhaps the pinnacle of our parenting: the taming of the wild man inside every toddler, inside every boy.

When Zack's brewing sense of anger and violence wells up, and I *can* see it coming, his intonation changes, he grips his fist. It's as if he is an actor in a play, overplaying his emotions. Thus far our son has not shown any tendencies towards violence in school. Will this hold into middle and high school? One hopes, and time, of course, will tell. At home, things are different. Many times we have had to pin him down and wait until his crying and lunging would stop. We are charged with remaining calm, and loving the violence out of our boy. If we can love him consistently and demonstratively in the wake of his anger, maybe we have a chance.

Music

Having experienced Zack's other gendered choices, it wasn't surprising when we began to see that his choices in music followed some familiar patterns. Can one define music or sound as having a quality of gender? Or rather, why not think of sound quality as it surrounds gender? In watching Zack acquire and refine his musical taste, I began to have an even deeper understanding of his innate nature as a boy. His music allowed me to appreciate his masculine qualities in an aesthetic framework. Zack began to find much joy in hip-hop. His preference for hip-hop required vigilance on our part as mothers, as we sought to screen out developmentally inappropriate songs. He loves percussion, and the bass notes, the "boom boom boom" of the *Black Eyed Peas*, for example. He had been listening to hip-hop exclusively up until the time one of his baseball teammates gave him a CD to pump him up for the championship game. It was fascinating to me to see the role of music as a tool to charge up our young warrior to do battle on the ball field. The CD was made up of the theme from *Rocky*, Black Sabbath's "Iron Man," and selections from heavy metal.[5] These songs have become favorites of Zack, as he has moved his taste from purely hip-hop to a larger variety of compositions that have a definitive bravado or masculinity. I understand that this music has appeal to women as well, myself included. Regardless of gender, many of us mimic air guitar and want to make those electric bass gestures to get at our own ya yas.

Conclusion

We are used to calling our son spicy and beautiful – a boy's boy. We watch him develop and greet each change with a sigh and smile. We are lucky to have him and he us. What more could lesbian parents, could *any* parents, ask for? The differences between all of us nurture loving and fertile relationships while forging an arena of gender reaffirmation and experimentation. Our son, without knowing it, changed our notions of raising children – indeed, of human nature. His boyness, or his masculinity, is strong, hardwired, and beautiful. Societal and political forces are undeniable and overwhelming at times, but so too is the force of biology. We work daily to parent Zack as best we can. At the end of this big adventure we hope to have raised a good man.

NOTES

1   *The Jetsons* was a space-age themed, primetime animated cartoon produced by Hanna-Barbera and originally ran from September 1962 to March 1963. *I Love Lucy* was an Emmy award-winning classic American situation comedy, starring Lucille Ball, Desi Arnaz, Vivian Vance, and William Frawley. The black-and-white series originally ran from October 1951 to April 1960 on CBS.

2   bell hooks, *We Real Cool: Black Men and Masculinity* (New York: Routledge, 2004), p. 80.

3   Judith Butler, *Undoing Gender* (New York: Routledge, 2004), p. 1.
4   *Who's Afraid of Virginia Wolf* was a 1966 American film directed by Mike Nichols. The screenplay by Ernest Lehman is an adaptation of the play of the same title by Edward Albee. The film version stars Elizabeth Taylor as Martha, Richard Burton as George, George Segal as Nick, and Sandy Dennis as Honey.
5   *Gonna Fly Now*, composed by Bill Conti for the 1976 movie *Rocky*, a film written by and starring Sylvester Stallone and directed by John G. Avildsen. "Iron Man" is a song by British heavy metal band Black Sabbath from their second studio album, *Paranoid*, released in 1970.

PART II

LABOR PAINS

The Work and Wonder of Being a Mom

CHAPTER 5

DAYS AND NIGHTS OF A NEW MOTHER

Existentialism in the Nursery

When I was raising my children, nothing was meaningless, although at the time so much seemed mundane, ordinary. All of it was sacred.
Mary Hood Hart[1]

I distinctly remember a turning point in my first few weeks as a new mother. It happened late one night in a moment of desperation. It goes without saying that I was deeply exhausted, more so than ever before in my life. I felt like I had reached and surpassed all of my limits. I collapsed into a chair, ready to sob, and then – of course, predictably, you know what comes next – the baby began to cry. AGAIN. And my baby was not the kind to muster a gentle little whimper. For the first four weeks, she screamed a furious, red-in-the-face, whole-body tense, accusing, and demanding cry.

Just when I felt like I couldn't go on, she called for me. And in that moment, the full meaning of my new identity as "mother" sunk in. I realized: in this moment, it does not matter that I'm exhausted, I haven't showered, my c-section incision aches, I haven't eaten, I'm depressed, my newly nursing breasts are swollen and stinging, at their worst even cracked and bleeding, and all in all I'm a mess. What matters is that this infant is crying, she is hungry, she needs milk, a clean diaper, and love; and right now I am the one and only person here who can care for her.

I experienced a devastating loss of self. I felt like I had forever lost the freedom and self-centeredness of my youth – in a very concrete way, in this moment my own needs did not matter. In fact, I imagined that they would never matter in exactly the same way again. I now had a second heart. For better and for worse, I would never be alone in my cares again.

But in the same moment, I also recognized that a profound commitment had taken root inside of me, and it was beautiful. I felt a duty that ran deeper than any I had known before. I had lost my old self, but in return it felt like I gained a life imbued with new meaning. There was something almost sacred in the self-sacrifice that I felt was required of me as the mother, caring for this child. Everything was meaningful in a new way, and I was changed.

But I was also still myself. Though sometimes in the exhausted, intimate enmeshment of the earliest weeks, it felt like my individual identity had washed away in a sleep-deprived haze, I still knew at some level that being a mother didn't completely define me. Somewhere beyond the every-two-hour routine of feed-diaper-sleep, I must be more than "mommy."

How can we make sense of this maternal experience, in which the mother is so intensely bound together with another being, and at the same time a free and separate individual self? Maternal theorist Andrea O'Reilly has written that we should be "truthful and true to [ourselves] in motherhood."[2] But who exactly is the "self" of the mother to whom we should be true? And what is it that we should be truthful about?

The experience of motherhood raises the philosophical problem of the relation of the individual and the social in a particularly interesting way. Simone de Beauvoir, a twentieth-century French existentialist, explored the complex relation of the individual and the social in her book *The Ethics of Ambiguity*. Existentialism is often accused of taking a decidedly negative attitude towards the social, and it's true that this reputation is not helped by Jean-Paul Sartre's famous claim that "Hell is the other."[3] One might suspect that, in emphasizing the freedom of the individual, an existentialist would interpret the loss of freedom experienced in motherhood as tragic, and the willing self-sacrifice of a mother as masochistic. But Beauvoir's existentialist portrayal of the human condition in *The Ethics of Ambiguity*[4] provides us with conceptual tools that can be helpful in an attempt to re-envision the complex relation of the individual and the social in general, and the experience of mothers in particular.

The Maternal Condition: Freedom in Situation

From the perspective of existentialism, the most important thing about being human is that each of us possesses a fundamental freedom to make choices. Here we are not yet talking about a practical freedom exercised in the world, but rather a primal freedom of consciousness that is central to the very definition of a human being.

Beauvoir was an atheist, and she believed that in the absence of a God there is no such thing as an objectively true value. Humans are the creators and givers of meaning, and all values are ultimately human creations, the products of human choices. Things, events, identities – none of these have objective meaning or value. Apart from humans, they exist in a value-neutral way, and it is we who enter upon the scene and pass judgment. As she explains, "It is human existence which makes values spring up in the world on the basis of which it will be able to judge. . . . Freedom is the source. . . . It is the original condition of all justification of existence."[5]

It is not the case that we simply have the *option* of choosing our own values – from an existentialist perspective, the central fact of human existence is that we are free to choose, and in order to live, we *must* choose. Even to refuse to choose is to have made a choice. To look outside of ourselves for direction and to follow another is still to have freely chosen which other to follow.

How can this help us to understand the meaning of the identity "mother"? In *The Second Sex*, Beauvoir's groundbreaking study of "the woman question," her existentialist approach to gender leads her to conclude that there is no such thing as an essence of true womanhood or an "ideal feminine." Similarly, we can conclude that there is no such thing as an essence of the "ideal maternal." If all values are ultimately human creations, then the values and expectations that we traditionally associate with being a mother do not represent an immutable objective truth. The "ideal mother" is revealed to be a social construction, and one that varies historically and culturally. For example, in the past, an ideal (wealthy) mother would have her children nursed by wet nurses. After the advent of formula, the ideal mother was supposed to move away from the "unhygienic" practice of breastfeeding altogether to use formula instead. Today's ideal mom is expected to breastfeed her child exclusively.

The second most important thing about the human condition is that this freedom is always *in situation*. We never possess pure freedom without limits; freedom is always within a specific context that sets the boundaries of possibility. For example, my current situation is made up of factors such as where and when I was born, my height, all my past experiences and choices – all the things that are beyond my control right now – and these set the context for and limit my freedom. It is within this situation that I have the freedom of consciousness to interpret and to respond. Existing between the two extremes of pure freedom and complete determinism, humans occupy what Beauvoir refers to as an "ambiguous" space.

A crucial element of our situation is that we are always in relation to others, in one way or another. Beauvoir pays particular attention to the fact that we are fundamentally social – we affect each other, depend on each other, struggle with each other, hurt each other, and need each other. We also live and move within the social realm via the languages and cultures that give us the tools for understanding ourselves and the world. Beauvoir explains that other people "give me the world," in the sense that the social sphere supports and sustains me, through culture, language, and real supportive relationships. But others also "take the world away" from me – since I am always in relation to others, the world is not mine alone, and this limits my freedom. This is another source of ambiguity in the human condition. We are never completely alone as individuals, but we are also never completely lost in the social – the reality is in the tension of experiencing both at the same time.

In *The Second Sex*, Beauvoir writes that to be a woman is not everything, but neither is it nothing. Ambiguously, it is both. We can apply this same description to the identity of "mother." To be a mother is not everything, in the sense that it could never completely define a person. Because of our fundamental freedom, we are always more than and other than the identities we possess and the roles we play. We are not mothers in the way that a stone is a stone, for example.[6]

But neither is being a mother nothing – the category of "mother" cannot be dismissed as simply meaningless or pure fiction. While the image of "mother" may be a construction, it also plays a real role in our daily existence. There are the physical realities of mothering. In discussing gender, Beauvoir remarked that while possessing a specifically female anatomy does not fully determine a woman in an essential sense, as many have argued over the years, the human differences in anatomy surely do influence the ways we experience the world. For biological mothers, there are specific physical experiences of pregnancy, birth, and perhaps nursing, and for all mothers, the physical realities of caring for a child.

ELIZABETH BUTTERFIELD

There are also the social realities of being a mother. To be a mother is to be socially positioned in a specific way, within a specific social context in the world. This context presents us with expectations for how a "good mother" should behave, and there may be real advantages and disadvantages – socially, emotionally, materially, and physically – associated with the extent to which one follows or veers from the stereotypical script.

So the identity of "mother" is also ambiguous. To be a mother is to live in a situation that is determined in real ways. And yet, while I am mother, I am also always more than and different from mother. I am never completely, essentially a mother, in the way that a stone is a stone. It is up to me to choose what being a mother will mean to me, how I will respond to the prescribed social scripts, and how I will live this identity. To be a mother is to possess an identity that is always in progress, both at the individual level, as I figure it out for myself, and at the larger social and cultural level, as meanings are maintained or created anew throughout time.

Beyond the "Ideal Mother": Creating Our Own Identities

Freedom is not always easy, and the responsibility that accompanies it can be intimidating. To be in a situation is also to be in relationships with other people, in which our choices take on the weight of consequences not just for ourselves, but for others as well. This brings us to a third existentialist observation regarding the human condition – that in response to our fundamental freedom, our responsibility, and the ambiguity of our situation, humans experience *anxiety*.[7] For example, the task of finding a way to justify our own existence is so overwhelming that we sometimes crave the comfort of absolutes – if only there were some objective values that could tell us what to do, so that we could escape this freedom and simply follow instructions! But as much as we crave them, according to Beauvoir, these absolutes simply don't exist. Ultimately, the only option is to make our own choices and to create our own values, and this can be overwhelming. Thus it is not surprising that Jean-Paul Sartre, another leading existentialist and Beauvoir's life-partner, claimed "we are condemned to be free."[8] Sometimes freedom can feel more like a life-sentence.

Beauvoir observes that in response to these feelings of anxiety, it is common for people to attempt to flee their own freedom. She describes a character who does this by looking outside of himself for a set of values and then pretending that the values he has subjectively chosen possess objective truth. Beauvoir calls this character the "serious man," presumably because he chooses a set of values to take *seriously*. He then uses these "absolute" values as a foundation for his identity, and they provide him with a sense of meaning in life. He is now on a defined mission, serving a higher purpose. He no longer sees himself as a person – he is wholly "Father," "Boss," "Church Member," or "Member of the Communist Party."[9] He tries to convince himself that this new identity defines him entirely. It is as if the ambiguities of his existence have been erased – it is now clear to him what he will believe and how he will choose.

Why does the serious man choose this attitude? According to Beauvoir, he is desperate to abdicate the responsibility of justifying his own existence, so he looks outside of himself in search of someone else to do this for him. She explains that he "forces himself to submerge his freedom in the context which [he] accepts from society. He loses himself in the object in order to annihilate his subjectivity."[10]

What can Beauvoir's example of the serious man teach us about motherhood? By definition, the "serious mother" would be one who takes the identity of mother *seriously*, as if it could completely define her. However, in the case of motherhood (and of many other social identities as well), in addition to the basic human existential anxieties that lead us to crave absolutes, there are also myriad social pressures that try to *persuade* us to adopt the ideology of "the good mother" as an absolute. Judith Warner refers to this contemporary phenomenon as "the American Motherhood Religion," in which motherhood is "unmoored from reality and turned into theology . . . made into an overdetermined thing, invested with quasi-ecclesiastical notions of Good and Evil."[11]

What is particularly interesting about the case of motherhood is the content of the "normative-stereotypical-expectations of motherhood"[12] we encounter. The ideal of "the good mother" proclaims that "a 'natural' mother is a person without further identity . . . [T]hat maternal love is, and should be, quite literally selfless."[13] The ideal teaches us that a mother should always put the needs of her children before her own, and that being a mother ought to fulfill all of a woman's own needs and desires. It is as if when one becomes a mother, the free, separate, individual self is naturally supposed to dissolve under the all-encompassing identity of mother – and anyone who is not completely satisfied with this new position should be shamed as selfish or unloving. In sum, the message of ideal motherhood pushes women towards sacrifice of the individual self for the sake of service to another.

For many women around the world, of course, there are real and dangerous material, physical, and social consequences to be faced if one chooses to reject or rebel against the socially prescribed script of the good mother. But for now, let's consider the case of a woman who is, materially and socially speaking, relatively free to refuse the script, but who subjectively chooses to adopt the values of the "good mother" and to set them up as absolutes. Why might she choose to hold herself to such a standard and submerge her own freedom?

Just as the serious man experiences relief when he is freed (temporarily) from the anxiety of a freedom which plagues him, the serious mother may initially find relief in adopting motherhood as her singular purpose. As a mother, she is now on a clearly defined mission, and this can provide a sense of objective meaning in life. This is not all bad – she may feel important and even heroic in the self-sacrifices of mothering, and this may be positively reinforced by society. Difficult as mother-work is, it can also be beautiful and enjoyable, especially when paired with an intense love for the child.

Beauvoir identifies several problems in the serious man. She finds the serious attitude fundamentally dishonest, since she believes that we are all pre-reflectively aware that objective values don't exist. In fleeing his freedom, the serious man is avoiding precisely what it is that defines him in his humanity. She remarks upon "the absurdity of a life which has sought outside of itself the justifications which it alone could give itself."[14]

The serious mother is vulnerable to the same problems. First of all, she is in the absurd position of freely choosing to deny her own freedom. As the serious mother attempts to lose herself in the work of caring for her children, she now has an excuse to avoid all the messy and difficult aspects of being a free individual. In response to issues that were previously sources of anxiety for her (career? relationships? health? personal development?), she may say that she no longer has time for things like that, or that they no longer matter. But the serious mother is doomed to failure. It is impossible to live up to the standards of ideal motherhood, which require selflessness. We are told that good mothers have no needs or desires beyond mothering, and that they should be completely fulfilled by the experience. But as fulfilling as it may be, at a fundamental existential level, this selflessness is simply impossible. Again, one can never be a mother in the way that a stone is a stone.

Second, Beauvoir observes that the serious man's goal of escaping anxiety is doomed to failure as well. In fact, the serious life often ends up in a state of constant worry. He has made himself, his very identity, and his sense of purpose and meaning in life, dependent upon something ultimately outside of his control. Beauvoir explains, "Everything is a threat to him. . . . Despite all precautions, he will never be the master of this exterior world to which he has consented to submit, he will be constantly upset by the uncontrollable course of events."[15]

Similarly, the woman who defines herself exclusively as mother puts herself in an extreme state of dependency. Any changes in her role as mother then take on the weight of threatening her very identity and the very justification of her existence. In this way, her initial attempt to flee anxiety ends up resulting in a state of constant worry. With her own needs repressed and unmet, and her only hopes for fulfillment invested in living up to a standard that it is impossible to meet, the serious mother is doomed to a precarious emotional existence and seldom has any peace.

Finally, Beauvoir cautions that the serious man may be dangerous. Since he has chosen to sacrifice everything to the higher purpose he has established as absolute, there is a possibility of fanaticism. As he is willing to sacrifice his own subjectivity to this higher cause, he may be willing to sacrifice others as well. She gives the example of a colonial administrator who believes so fully in the colonial ideology of progress that nothing else seems to matter. In his case, if the ideology of progress requires that the new highway be built, then it must be built, no matter the cost in human lives and suffering.[16]

Just as the colonial administrator is willing to sacrifice the wellbeing of others for the sake of a higher goal, the serious mother may be willing to sacrifice the subjectivity of her family members in order to meet the standards of ideal motherhood. She believes she will be judged on the basis of her children, so the pressure is intense. After all, if the children don't "turn out well," then she, as a mother, will be seen as a failure. And if being a mother is all she has to live for, this failure could be devastating. Beauvoir addresses this in *The Second Sex*, when she is critical of mothers who try too hard to shape their children's development, instead of recognizing that these children too are humans who must justify their own existences for themselves.

In *The Ethics of Ambiguity* Beauvoir argues that instead of attempting to flee the fundamental ambiguity of our human condition, we should face this ambiguity directly with honesty and courage. So in contrast to the serious man, she presents a character she calls the "genuine man," who refuses to recognize any values from outside of himself as absolutes. Instead of looking to others for a justification for his existence, he realizes it is up to him to make his life meaningful. The genuine man understands that "it is not a matter of being right in the eyes of a God, but of being right in his own eyes."[17] He resists the pressures of the normative expectations he encounters in society, as he tries to find his own way. The key word for the genuine man is *responsibility* – he takes responsibility for his free creation of meaning, and he recognizes that his actions have consequences for other beings.

Likewise, a genuine mother doesn't seek a guarantee of her existence outside of herself, and doesn't accept the ideal of the good mother as an absolute value. Rather, like the genuine man, she realizes that it is not a matter of being right in the eyes of God (or the in-laws! Or other mothers! Or anyone!), but rather, of being right in her own eyes. She resists the script of the good mother, refusing to wear the "mask of motherhood," and refusing to "partake in . . . 'the national game of Let's Pretend' where we're all supposed to be perfect."[18] While she is bound in love to the care of her child, the genuine mother also realizes that she has "a life, a purpose and identity outside and beyond motherhood."[19] It is an honest acknowledgment of the fundamental freedom of being human.

Mommy and Me

On a daily (if not hourly) basis, mothers have to make choices about how to negotiate this overlapping terrain of individual and social. We are constantly challenged to find a way to be "me" and "mommy" at the same time. The case of motherhood is unique because of the special intimacy between mother and child, which is different from that of any other relationship. As Adrienne Rich describes the experience, "To suffer with and for and against a child – maternally, egotistically, neurotically, sometimes with a sense of helplessness, sometimes with the illusion of learning wisdom – but always, everywhere, in body and soul, *with* that child – *because that child is a piece of oneself*."[20] For biological mothers, in the physical experience of pregnancy and birth, in nursing, and for all mothers, in the hormonal connection, the physical closeness of carework, and the bonds of love, there is a unique intimacy.

This is not just any relationship – the mother and child are (sometimes even literally) one being and two at the same time.

Adrienne Rich has observed that while scholarship on the psychological process of individuation traditionally has been understood as the *child's* drama, with the mother assumed as a fixed given (or even an obstacle to be overcome), we should come to recognize that in the experience of mothering, a woman undergoes her own drama of individuation. Rich writes, "the mother, too, is discovering her own existence newly. She is connected with this other being . . . in a way she can be connected with no one else. . . . And she, too, needs to struggle from that one-to-one intensity into new realization, or reaffirmation, of her being-unto-herself."[21]

We should reject the concept of mother as a naturally selfless being with no needs or interesting issues of her own, and replace it with the more realistic account of the mother as always also a work in progress. Mothering is one of *many* factors in her own narrative of development. Just as the child moves from the intense togetherness of infancy, to grow into a mature individual self, the mother too is recreated in this relationship. As Mary Hood Hart describes her own experience of mothering, "Swept up in the wonder of their childhoods, *I was re-created*."[22] She explains that even in the mundane care work of raising a child, such as the cycles of feedings, baths, bedtime stories, and comfort in feverish nights, "I was the blessed one, . . . the recipient of graces I am still coming to recognize."[23]

We also require a new understanding of the maturity that results from this process of individuation. Traditionally, maturity has been presented in terms of the developing child's break with the mother and her world in order to venture out on his own as a separate, independent individual. However, what we learn from an existentialist perspective on the human condition is that purely separate and independent individuals don't exist. We are always both individual and social, free and determined, and facing the ambiguities of our human condition is something that is never finished. It is an ongoing process, and it involves constant negotiation and renegotiation.

As we have seen, the same can be said for motherhood. In the relationship between mother and child, there is no ending.[24] The dynamic of the relationship is renegotiated again and again throughout our lives. Like the mother herself, the mothering relationship should be understood as a work in progress. For better and for worse, then, a mother's work is never done.

ELIZABETH BUTTERFIELD

NOTES

1 Mary Hood Hart, "Everyday Graces: Lessons of Motherhood," *Southern Cross* (San Diego), February 19, 2009.

2 Andrea O'Reilly, "Feminist Mothering," in *Maternal Theory: Essential Readings*, ed. Andrea O'Reilly (Toronto: Demeter Press, 2007), p. 805.

3 Spoken by the character Garcin in Jean-Paul Sartre's play *No Exit*, translated by Stuart Gilbert (New York: Alfred A. Knopf, 1948).

4 In this essay, for the sake of brevity, I will draw primarily upon Beauvoir's *Ethics of Ambiguity*, occasionally referring to *The Second Sex*. But I believe that the philosophical framework underlying this presentation of the human condition can also be found in an immature form in Sartre's *Being and Nothingness*, and is later very well developed in the more mature social philosophy of Sartre's *Critique of Dialectical Reason*.

5 Simone de Beauvoir, *The Ethics of Ambiguity*, trans. Bernard Frechtman (Secaucus: Citadel Press, 1948), pp. 15, 24.

6 ". . . in the way a stone is a stone": this is a reference to language commonly used by Sartre to describe human identities. In "Existentialism is a Humanism," he claims that we are not our identities in the same way as a cauliflower is a cauliflower.

7 The roots of this term can be found in Kierkegaard's Danish *Angest* and later Heidegger's German *Angst*, adopted by Sartre and translated into the French *angoisse*. It is commonly translated into English as anxiety or despair, and in this context it refers to a fear of the open-ended nothingness of our freedom.

8 Jean-Paul Sartre, "Existentialism is a Humanism," trans. P. Mairet, excerpted in *Existentialism*, ed. Robert Solomon (Oxford: Oxford University Press, 2005), p. 211.

9 Beauvoir, *The Ethics of Ambiguity*, p. 48.

10 Ibid., p. 45.

11 Judith Warner, "The Motherhood Religion," in Andrea O'Reilly (ed.) *Maternal Theory: Essential Readings* (Toronto: Demeter Press, 2007), p. 706.

12 Andrea O'Reilly, introduction to *Feminist Mothering*, ed. Andrea O'Reilly (Albany: State University of New York Press, 2008), p. 5.

13 Adrienne Rich, "Anger and Tenderness," in Andrea O'Reilly (ed.) *Maternal Theory: Essential Readings* (Toronto: Demeter Press, 2007), p. 12.

14 Beauvoir, *The Ethics of Ambiguity*, p. 52.

15 Ibid., p. 51.

16 Ibid., p. 49.

17 Ibid., p. 14.

18 O'Reilly, "Feminist Mothering," pp. 804, 805.

19 O'Reilly, introduction to *Feminist Mothering*, p. 11.

20 Rich, "Anger and Tenderness," pp. 11–12; emphasis added.

21 Ibid., p. 22.
22 Hart, "Everyday Graces"; emphasis added.
23 Ibid.
24 I would argue that even after the death of either mother or child, the remaining member of the relationship continues to be in relation to the other. The possibility of new interactions and experiences together may be gone, but the meaningfulness of the relationship remains, the influences continue to unfold, and the understanding of the other continues to grow and change.

CHAPTER 6

MINDFUL MOTHERING

How Feminist Buddhist Practices Enhance
Experiences of Beauty

"Pain is inevitable: Suffering is optional" is one formulation of the first noble truth of Buddhism. Any mother will tell you that as a mom, she experiences pain. Whether it is the pain of childbirth or the pain of witnessing a child's first social rejection, the pains involved in mothering are numerous. Some of the pains occur because of the fleeting nature of so many of the stages of childhood. Infants may only wear an outfit a few times before they've outgrown it. The stroller is replaced by the wagon which in turn is replaced by the bicycle with requests to borrow the car the next step. Each stage comes with its own special brand of worry about the child's wellbeing or with regret about how things could have gone differently . . . if only. All of these moments arise when the mind is not fully present. The pain is inevitable; we frequently experience suffering.

The aim of this essay is to examine three of the noble truths of Buddhism from the perspective of a contemporary mother: (1) pain is inevitable; (2) pain arises from cravings and attachments; (3) the end of suffering is possible. The path to enlightenment (as realized by becoming increasingly compassionate and kind) is not only available to monks who endure long periods of silence, but also to us mothers in our everyday experience as mothers. It is my belief that looking at some typical experiences in light of these truths enables one to see the beauty of the world, and especially the beauty of the experiences inherent in mothering.

Pregnancy and the First Noble Truth: Pain is Inevitable

Pain is inevitable – this means that life is difficult and painful. Much pain stems from the fact that there is a gap between the way the world is and the way we want it to be. Sometimes we get what we want but are nevertheless disappointed, and other times we desire what is impossible or otherwise unrealized. Perhaps even more frequently we crave easy decisions; however, many major life decisions are anything but easy.

When I turned 30, I thought it was time to decide whether or not to have children. This was not a decision that I was making alone, as I had been married for some time. In fact, my father-in-law frequently wondered aloud whether he would have to settle for a four-legged grandchild (in our dog named Barkley). My husband Michael and I set out to find good reasons we should have children. We aimed to make this decision rationally. We weighed the advantages and disadvantages: on the one hand, children are expensive, time-consuming, and constant sources of worry; on the other hand, we thought children might be fun. We ached for a clear and convincing answer to the important, life-changing question of whether or not to become parents; we wanted a clear yes or no. We discovered that there are no such clear answers to such important, life-changing questions. In the end, we found no rational reason to have children. Nevertheless, we decided to give it a try. Pain is inevitable. In the absence of clear and convincing arguments, we had to make a life-altering decision either to have children or not. The pain does not stop with that decision, but continues onward.

The sexual education that I received in high school was heavy on fear and shame, although it did manage to teach the biological facts with an emphasis on the risks involved in any and every sexual encounter. So much emphasis was placed on the risk of getting pregnant that I was confident

SHERYL TUTTLE ROSS

getting pregnant was easy. We figured that if we did the things that we were told that we should not do in health class, the rest would pretty much take care of itself. Many months later, there were nothing but minus readings on the home pregnancy kits.

Pain is inevitable – the world did not conform to my desires. Nevertheless, suffering is optional. Once I realized that my health teacher was not telling the whole story, and that even though I desperately wanted to have a child despite not having an overwhelming reason to do so, I let go. I decided that life would be okay without a child and that there were other ways we could go about having one, such as adoption. My over-whelming focus on this one desire was making me, and, for that matter, my husband, miserable. Within those trying times, that we *chose* to see our suffering as optional.

What does that mean? Often times we get so caught up in what we want that we forget there are other options. Realizing there is a difference between the experience of life itself and how we evaluate it allows us to see that frequently our evaluation is the cause of suffering. It does not have to be that way. In each life, some rain will fall. Things will happen which bring us physical, emotional, and even existential pain. Acknowledging this pain as an inevitable part of the human experience helps lessen its intensity. Indeed, it might be that feeling the pain intensely is part of what it means to be human, so that experiencing it fully is actu-ally beneficial if not pleasant. However, when we resist the pain, pretend that it does not exist or really hurt, it actually causes more pain. This runs contrary to one prevalent strain of ethical reasoning. Jeremy Bentham thought that humans naturally embraced pleasure and avoided pain. People, he believed, are motivated to try to maximize pleasure and mini-mize pain. Moreover, he thought that we should construct a whole sys-tem of morality based on the fact that humans don't like pain. He considered actions right in so far as they minimize pain and maximize pleasure and wrong in so far as the pain they produce outweighs the pleasure.

Buddhists have a very different take. Although most Buddhists don't say humans actually like pain, Buddhists simply believe pain is an inevi-table part of the existence we call human. If we are going to really experi-ence happiness, Buddhists believe we'd better be prepared for the pain that will inevitably come our way. One way of dealing with the pain is to identify how it arises. The pain and an understanding of its causes help engender compassion for ourselves and for others.

The Second Noble Truth: Pain Arises
from Cravings and Attachment

This is a fairly tricky truth, particularly since it seems that the very essence of motherhood, if there is indeed such an essence, is attachment. We love our children and we want them to love us. This love seems to be a key component in their developing worthwhile relationships – both friendships and, later in life, romantic partnerships. It is hard to see all pain as simply arising from attachment and cravings. Think, for example, of the physical pains involved in pregnancy, childbirth, and the basic care and feeding of very young children. These do not seem to be related to any desire or craving, but rather to be brute physical facts. Other examples of pain that does not seem to be related to attachment are the painful embarrassment one experiences when her child throws a nasty tantrum, the mental pain that comes in the form of the sheer boredom of re-reading the same children's story over and over and over again, and the painful guilt many of us feel because no matter how hard we try we never feel like good enough parents. The demands of our lives can feel overwhelming. Last summer my daughter said to me, "Mommy, sometimes I feel like you like your job more than you like us." Ouch! That hurt.

One pain of attachment is that we want those we love to be free from suffering, especially the suffering that we cause. However, no mother can be continuously available to meet all the desires of a child, nor would it be beneficial to either mother or child even if this were possible. Attachments cause suffering when we want things to stay just as they are forever or when we become so in love with an idea of how things should be that we can't accept anything else. The idea is perfect; reality is messy. My daughter wants me to be constantly available to her and sometimes I have to be available to write papers and teach classes or serve on committees. The cravings that cause pain do so because we want things to be different than they are. We do not want to accept the reality of the present moment. We do not want our child to throw herself on the floor, screaming wildly. We do not want to read *Brown Bear, Brown Bear, What Do You See?* yet again. We want our child to go to sleep, now! We want the toys to magically pick themselves up. We want the siblings to stop fighting and for summer vacation to be over already. We want, we want, we want. We crave what is not present and in that absence, we suffer. Sometimes this is because we refuse to acknowledge that fundamentally things are ever changing or because reality provides a stark contrast to our ideas of how things should be.

The Third Noble Truth: The End of Suffering is Possible, or How to Be a Feminist Buddhist Mommy

Step 1: Breathe

This first step seems quite simple enough. After all, in order to live, we as humans must breathe. But there is a difference between simply breathing and breathing mindfully. One way to pay attention to the breath is by engaging in a formal meditation practice sitting on a cushion, straightening the back, closing the eyes, and focusing all of one's attention on an aspect of experience such as the breath. "Breath is the bridge which connects life to consciousness, which unites your body to your thoughts. Whenever your mind becomes scattered, use your breath as the means to take hold of your mind again."[1] We do not need to make a special time to focus our attention on the breath: one can pay attention to the breath in the line at the grocery story, stopped at a red light, or while sorting the laundry.

The breath serves as an analogy to life itself. During the course of most of our lives we breathe without paying attention to the very fact that we are doing so. More generally, we live without noticing that this is in fact what we are doing. There is a habit of living life on autopilot. Our attention can be scattered from memories to fantasies and packed to-do lists waiting to be checked-off. However, when we pay our full attention to the breath we are right here, right now, living in the present moment. To be present to the moment is to truly live, because there is no other place to be. As Thich Nhat Hanh puts it:

> While washing the dishes, you might be thinking about the tea afterwards, so try to get them out of the way as quickly as possible in order to sit and drink tea. But that means that you are incapable of living during the time you are washing the dishes. When you are washing the dishes, washing the dishes must be the most important thing in your life. Just as when you are drinking tea, drinking tea must be the most important thing in your life.[2]

When washing the dishes or changing the diapers, our minds may be making plans. The point here is not that we, as mothers, should never make plans, but rather when we are planning we should do so mindfully, that is, fully aware we are planning. By being present even in the planning, we are able to be present likewise in the doing.

The breath represents change. We can't hold our breaths for very long – what comes in must go out. With every inhalation and exhalation, one breath comes into and then goes out of existence.[3] If we pay attention to the rhythm of the breath, we can be reminded that this too shall pass. This includes us, and we are also reminded we are impermanent. The self that many of us think we are, some unchangeable golden nugget, cannot be found. Instead, we are ever changing; we are our breaths, the content of our experience. This no-self idea can inspire a certain amount of fear. The fear might say, "Wait a minute, there is no 'I' there? No 'I' here? What about Descartes, who famously philosophized that 'I think, therefore I am'?" The Buddhist notion of no-self does not imply that we don't have bodies, thoughts, feelings, and experiences, but rather that the self that has those things is always changing. By noticing the sometimes subtle changes of the breath we can become better acquainted with the subtle changes in our selves.

There is no doubt that mothering changes us. Our bodies change if for no other reason than sleep deprivation. Our thoughts change as we take our children to be a fundamental concern and source of joy. The memory of my son's first raspberry picking adventure where his bowl is empty but face smeared in purple never fails to bring a smile to my face. What we choose to experience changes because we are mothers. Those choices in turn change who it is that we are. If we can first become aware of the subtle changes of the breath, we can become aware of other aspects of our present-moment experience, including how we experience our selves as mothers.

Step 2: Become aware

Paying full attention to each and every breath is difficult. It can be dis-couraging at first because very soon after starting this meditation the mind is likely to begin to wander. In a formal meditation the eyes may be closed but the mind far from the breath – maybe wrestling with some huge issue at work, rehearsing some recent conversation with a friend, or wondering if the present back pain will ever stop. During the grocery line meditation, we may focus on our breath only to be distracted by the candy aisle or juicy tabloid headlines. If there is time for the meditation to continue, we can counter this mental wandering. When we realize that our attention has wandered away to thoughts, feelings, or other sensa-tions, we can recognize this and gently invite the mind to focus on the breath again. We invite the mind to grow ever more curious about the actual qualities of this breath right here, right now. The way in which we invite the mind to return to the breath is vital. I remember when I first began meditating how critical I was of these moments of not paying attention. The internal voice I used with myself was not a voice I'd ever want to use with my children. Mare Chapman, who teaches Vipassana meditation, instructs us to cultivate an attitude of kindness, sometimes referred to as Metta, toward ourselves in these distracted moments and, indeed, in all moments. Metta might be described as a motherly compassion for the fragility and imperfection of our humanity.

We can also use this attitude in our actual meditations; in this case the nature of the meditation changes to include awareness of thoughts, feelings, and sensations. We start with an awareness of the breath that invites relaxation, then expand the field of awareness to include any sensations, thoughts, and emotions, softly naming any of those experiences "thinking," "fear," "song on the radio," and so on. The aim is to become very curious about the relationship between what we notice and our judgments of it. Chapman instructs: "When you notice that you are judging, resisting, avoiding or trying to change what you experience, be soft and gentle and kind to yourself . . . practice companioning what is occurring . . . accepting the direct experience of the present moment."[4] The act of companioning the breath and all direct experience amounts to creating a certain amount of spaciousness. Chapman writes: "Spaciousness is the sense of inner openness of internal vastness, of inner space around the object of attention. . . . In the habitual judging and attachments of the conditioned mind, there is very little spaciousness, and thus our minds are very unstable, erratic; we are easily knocked off balance and swept up into a train of thoughts and feelings."[5]

When we experience this spaciousness, I think we also open ourselves up to the experiencing of the sheer beauty in the ordinary. I began this sort of practice when my children were very young. The experience of mindfully pushing my son on the toddler swing at the park is still vivid in my memory. I was present to the feel of the small stones beneath my scandals, the moderate air temperature, the weight of the swing, the quality of the sunlight. I was present to the connection between myself and my son. The smile on his face, the way he gulped for air when he laughed at the motion. It seemed as if my son had no choice but to be present. I had to make that choice, but by paying attention, I did not miss what was in front of me. The experience of beauty is not limited to so-called pleasant experiences like pushing swings. At times, I have paid close attention to whiney tantrums or the bored lamentations of my now

8-year-old son. Paying attention with spaciousness allows us to experience pain without suffering. It is as if we are saying to ourselves that this is part of the package of life and, moreover, this too shall pass. I think this experience can count as a beautiful one if we appreciate the form and the experience of the pleasure or pain without necessarily identifying it as a possession: "it's mine." The experience's ephemeral quality combined with the view that all life is precious lead Buddhists to claim that being present to the moment is to appreciate its beauty.

This does not mean we are simply observers of our life's experience or that we give up agency. It does mean that when we are present to direct experience with an amount of spaciousness, we do not have to react to whatever situation is at hand. Rather, we can take appropriate responsibility for the experience itself and what we do with it. Part of figuring out that responsibility is identifying how our experiences are conditioned.

Step 3: Recognize the role that social scripts and conditioning play in how we experience our lives as women

Allison Pearson's popular novel, *I Don't Know How She Does It*, aptly depicts the contradictions inherent in contemporary ideas of motherhood.[6] The main character, Kate Shaddock, stays up late making store-bought pastries look home-made by applying extra powdered sugar. In another scene, she appears before what is called the Court of Motherhood. Pearson writes:

> There she was, all the arguments on the tip of her tongue, the perfectly good reasons why she went to work . . . the way it benefited both her and her children, the killer quote from Gloria Steinem about how no man has ever asked advice about how to combine fatherhood and a career. And the minute she was standing on that dock, the justifications went to ashes in her mouth.[7]

Mothers who work outside the home are expected to fulfill all of the unrealistic demands of a stay-at-home and be the perfect employee. Feminists have labeled this "the second shift," as women who work outside the home still do the majority of household tasks and planning. Studies have shown that this has led to a decrease in leisure time for women, an increase in stress, and a sense of dissatisfaction with one's lot in life.[8] This dissatisfaction often manifests itself as guilt. Kate

Shaddock confesses at the Court of Motherhood: "All right, you really want to know the truth? Guilty, unbelievably, neurotically, pathologically guilty. Look, I'm sorry, but I have to go. For heaven's sake, just look at the time."[9]

Kate may be guilty, but under the current social scripts all mothers are guilty! I know that I am guilty. I have been late picking up my kids from school. I have been too tired to read stories to my children before bedtime. I have (gasp!) even missed my children's choir concerts because of work. I have been dismayed at how my children treat each other on occasion, and even more dismayed at how I've handled these mistreatments. But if all mothers feel consistently guilty then current social scripts are absurd. Recognizing the absurdity of these scripts is one big step in becoming a mindful mommy. This step might be described as feminist. Guilt in general arises when we break a rule or agreement. These rules can be written or unwritten; agreements can be explicit or implied by social conventions. One of the basic problems with contemporary motherhood's rules is that they are impossible to abide by and therefore create guilt in people who are not in fact guilty.

The first step in dealing with these unrealistic, guilt-inducing expectations is to identify them, to simply notice them. This is not as easy as it sounds. Here, paying attention to the breath, noticing where the mind wanders, and creating spaciousness and kindness around this wandering are instrumental in identifying the social scripts and breaking free from their oppressive coloring of our experiences. So when our minds turn to the same Court of Motherhood that Kate visits, where the expectations are that good mothers provide home-baked goods for school bake-sales and kids receive calming and cleansing bubble baths every night, we can know that even Martha Stewart served prison time and give ourselves a bit of space.

Step 4: Wise and kind response

We are not perfect and we never will be. Many of us are sailing in relatively uncharted seas. I was something of a maverick in my graduate program, as none of my female mentors in graduate school had children, and only a few of my graduate student colleagues were moms. I am incredibly thankful that I do have children because they have enriched my life. I think they have also made me a better philosopher and a better person. I wish I could say that I am always a mindful mommy who takes responsibility for the experiences she has and provides the perfect environment for her children. Alas, I am not.

More frequently, I am filled with self-doubt about my roles as a professional, a mother, a wife, and as a member of my extended families. The balm I apply on that self-doubt is to allow myself to experience it. I need to be present with it. I need to identify the social scripts that are informing any current suffering. The choice becomes mine. I can choose what scripts I agree or disagree with and act in accordance with the value system that *I* choose.

Breath serves as an anchor. As I notice how social scripts color my experience, I ask more about the experience right here, right now. What else is really here? That is, the practice of mindfulness requires us to go beyond the social scripts to inquire about the reality of our individual lived experience. Ultimately, this mindfulness practice includes the creation of our own scripts that include being aware of the present moment and dedicated to the relief of suffering for all.

Mommy Meditations

I would like to conclude this essay with three mommy meditations: one where the experience is pleasant, another where it is unpleasant, and the final one is a Metta meditation for the benefit of mothers everywhere.

A pleasant experience: for me, this was the practice of walking to school. This is a simple task, one we take for granted and, more often than not, one we forget to enjoy. I make a daily meditation practice of walking the kids from the car to their preschool and from home to their elementary school. In the earlier years, I would make the children hold my hands as we walked together. I would take a breath in, noting how small their hands were in comparison to my own. I would breathe out, trying to see my breath in the air on cooler days. I would notice the quality of sunlight and how it would cast shadows. I would engage my seeing, hearing, touching, tasting, and thinking. Once I check in with each of these senses I feel present in the moment and truly alive.

The meditation consists in asking ourselves: What am I seeing right now? What am I hearing right now? How does my experience of touch feel right now? What am I smelling right now and how does that interact with what I am tasting right now? What am I thinking about and is this something that I truly believe?

One unpleasant experience is that of the temper tantrum. Of course, temper tantrums can happen at any age, but they change their contours with the age of the child. Ironically, this meditation invites us to answer all of the same questions as we do in the meditation while holding hands with our children. It invites us to be present to the tantrum as if it were a friend. But it also invites us to ask the question: What else is here? It invites you to notice the special lines of your child's face, the tone of the voice, the color of the walls or the grass. This meditation invites you to check in with yourself so that when you respond to the tantrum you are not doing so from a tantrum yourself. This is easier said than done. However, I have started with the basic physical experiences. In one recent tantrum meditation, I noticed that as my son wrinkles his nose in disgust, his nostrils flare. He accomplishes the loud stomping noise he makes on his way to his room by lifting his knees incredibly high and uses his arms on the sides of the walls for extended balance. He glances back every so often to make sure that I am taking note of his displeasure. He slams the door (something we are still working on). The sounds of rearranging the furniture emerge. Finally, a tired silence descends as he settles into the time-out. Throughout this display, I note my own heart-rate and whether I can smile and not smirk. I use the time-out to remind myself that humans have instincts, including the flight or fight instinct, and this is simply my son's exercise in managing his fight instinct.

The last meditation is a Metta meditation or a form of well-wishing to all. The Metta meditation can be part of a formal meditation process or more informally as we focus on our breath throughout the day. The Metta meditation that I propose wishes the following: may all mothers unconditionally love their children. May all mothers experience patience and spacious mindfulness with their children. May all mothers know the beauty of their children and the world.

I wish all of this for you.

NOTES

1   Thich Nhat Hanh, *The Miracle of Mindfulness* (Boston: Beacon Press, 1975), p. 39.
2   Ibid.
3   Sylvia Boorstien, *Pay Attention for Goodness' Sake: Practicing the Perfections of the Heart – The Buddhist Path of Kindness* (New York: Ballantine Books, 2002).

4   Mare Chapman, "Cultivating Authenticity through Mindfulness," Vipassana Workshop Handout, Madison, Wisconsin, February 2002.

5   Ibid.

6   Allison Pearson, *I Don't Know How She Does It* (London: Anchor Books, 2003).

7   Ibid., p. 70.

8   Arlie Hochschild and Anne Maching, *The Second Shift* (New York: Penguin, 1989).

9   Pearson, *I Don't Know How She Does It*, p. 71.

CHAPTER 7

A FACE ONLY A MOTHER COULD LOVE?

On Maternal Assessments of Infant Beauty

Beauty and love are concepts that play prominent roles in our social lives, but the connection between them is complex and often obscure. Nowhere is this more evident than in our relationships with infants. Encountering an infant can inspire positive feelings of tenderness, affection, and love, and the words that come most naturally to one's lips when meeting a newborn are aesthetic ones: "She's so beautiful!" Yet it isn't so clear exactly what these words mean in this context; nor is it obvious how we should think about this strange and powerful confluence of love and beauty. In this essay, I attempt to shed some light on it by exploring mothers' experiences of the beauty of their own infants, focusing particularly on the influence of love upon those experiences.

Mothers on Baby Beauty

To some, it may seem just obvious that most mothers perceive their infants as being more beautiful than others do: in general, babies look more beautiful to their moms. After all, who hasn't heard the cruel adage, "He has a face only a mother could love"? But we can love things – an old pair of jeans, for example – without finding them beautiful. Perhaps maternal love, expansive as it is, is like that. How do we know that babies are more beautiful to their mothers? An initial piece of evidence that they do is the fact that mothers *say* that they are. In one experiment, mothers were found to rank photographs of their own children as cuter than observers unfamiliar with these children rated them.[1]

Since this study measured rankings of cuteness, and not rankings of beauty, a word or two is in order here about the relationship between beauty and cuteness. "Beauty," in the sense I have been using it so far, refers to pleasing physical appearances, or what is commonly known as "good looks." In this sense, to say that a person is beautiful is to say that their physical form is pleasant to look at, for its own sake. This is what is sometimes called the aesthetic sense of the word "beautiful." The word also has a second sense in which it means simply "excellent" or "great." This is the sense in which one might exclaim "Beautiful!" when a choice parking spot suddenly appears. Used in this way, "beauty" doesn't indicate an appearance that is pleasing for its own sake. It is merely a metaphorical way of saying that something is good, for whatever sort of reason. This linguistic fact makes it difficult to study people's assessments of what is beautiful in the aesthetic sense: when a person says that X is beautiful, does this mean that she finds its appearance pleasing, or does it just mean that she thinks it's good?

For this reason, empirical studies of beauty tend to employ more specific terms such as "cute" and "attractive," instead of "beautiful." These words belong to a class of terms, also including words like "striking" and "handsome," that typically express more or less the same concept as "beauty" used in the aesthetic sense. That is, they typically refer to an appearance that is pleasing to behold for its own sake. However, these other terms differ from "beautiful" in being less ambiguous and somewhat more specific. Thus, someone with striking looks, for instance, is someone whose physical form is pleasing in virtue of bold or conspicuous features, and someone who is cute is someone whose form is pleasing in virtue of features such as large eyes, a large face, and a soft rounded body.[2]

GLENN PARSONS

These features are characteristic, of course, of human infants, and all infants have these features to some extent, but some possess them to a greater degree than others: these babies look especially babyish and for that reason we find them particularly pleasant to behold. Thus, we can think of cuteness as one sort of beauty, or pleasing physical appearance, the kind most applicable to infants and children. Correspondingly, the fact that mothers rank their own children as cuter than others would rank them supports the hypothesis that mothers perceive their infants as more beautiful than others do.

However, this is far from conclusive. It may be that mothers *say* that their infant is cuter than the competition, but don't actually *believe* this to be the case. People often make appraisals that are false, for all sorts of reasons. Sometimes we utter falsehoods as a way of communicating something else that we want to express. For instance, a loyal sports fan might earnestly chant "The Leafs are number one!" in spite of the fact that they are in last place. Fans like this aren't ignorant of the standings (quite the contrary); rather, they are expressing their undying faith in their team by saying something that everyone, including the team, knows is false. In other cases we tell white lies or stretch the truth to spare someone's feelings ("That jello salad was really tasty!"), to show gratitude or affection ("You're the best coach in the whole world!"), or to encourage our friends to further efforts ("Boy, your bagpipe playing is really coming along!").

Perhaps, then, the fact that mothers rank their own babies' cuteness higher than others do doesn't reflect what mothers really believe about their infants' looks. Perhaps the mothers are simply stretching the truth in order to express their love. Alternatively, the difference in rankings might just reflect the mothers' desire to be perceived as loving and unconditionally supportive parents by other people (such as the scientists conducting the ranking study).[3] Thus, in addition to our hypothesis, we have before us a number of alternative interpretations of this bit of maternal behavior. Which is correct?

The existing empirical evidence doesn't directly test these different alternatives, and it would probably be very difficult to distinguish between these different motives in a psychological experiment or study. However, there is some empirical evidence that might be thought to favor the view that mothers *don't* actually believe that their own infants are cuter. This evidence consists of some rather disconcerting studies that show that mothers treat their newborns less affectionately when those newborns are rated as less cute by strangers.[4] These differences in treatment are not extreme: this study found that even babies scoring low in cuteness were adequately cared for. But those babies did receive less verbal stimulation, close holding, and direct eye contact from their mothers. This might suggest that, regardless of what mothers say, their behavior suggests that they in fact don't see their infants' appearance differently than others do, since their treatment of their infants lines up with how others rate their appearance.

However, we shouldn't let this consideration convince us that mothers don't really believe that their own infants are cuter. What this study shows is that mothers unconsciously or instinctively behave in a way that is at odds with this belief. Generally speaking, however, we can behave unconsciously or instinctively in ways that conflict with what we believe. Consider the belief that if you fall backwards, I will catch you. This is a very common sort of belief. Yet even if you had this belief (say you trusted me completely) the odds are that, when falling backwards in this sort of situation, you would still flinch or turn around at the last instant. This doesn't mean that you don't believe I will catch you. It's just that you are "hardwired," as it were, to respond by flinching automatically, regardless of what you believe. Something similar might be true in the case of maternal behavior: perhaps mothers really believe that their infants are super cute, but yet instinctively or unconsciously treat them otherwise.

So we seem no closer to answering our question: do mothers perceive their infants as more beautiful (that is, as cuter) or do they merely say this? When empirical evidence and more philosophical arguments fail to settle the case for us, perhaps it is permissible to turn to our personal experiences for a way forward. In this case, my own experience as a parent conforms to the former view: when I said (as I often did) that my newborn daughter was "beautiful" or "really cute," I think that I believed that what I was saying was true, even if I didn't reflect on this matter at the time. Now experience, as we all know, is a dim lamp, and perhaps my experience is not the norm. I'm also not a mother! The reader should consult her own experience on the matter, but my conversations with other parents suggest that I am not alone in the sincerity of my beliefs. But even if it turns out that some, or even most, mothers don't really believe that their infants are cuter than others believe they are, it will be enough for our purposes if *some* do. And my own experience gives me some reason for thinking that this is true.

Good Mom, Bad Critic?

If what we've said so far is correct, at least some mothers see more beauty, when they look at their infants, than others see. You might also say that, when it comes to their children, moms seem to have slightly different tastes than the rest of us. But then we must ask: whose taste is better? Earlier, I mentioned the view that mothers see their kids as more beautiful than they actually are: they have what psychologists call "positive illusions" about the appearance of their children. If that way of describing the situation is correct, then mother's tastes are defective, or at least inferior.

Some readers will surely recoil at the very mention of defective or inferior tastes. They may say: "Taste, beauty, and such notions are subjective, and the preference or liking of one person is as good as that of another. If a mother sees her baby boy as super cute, and the rest of us find him middling, who are we to say that we are right, and she is wrong?"

This line of thought meshes, in a deeply satisfying way, with modern conceptions of equality. We frown on simply dismissing someone's point of view, or her values, unless some substantial reason can be offered for doing so. And this line of thought is convincing, when presented in the abstract. But when we bring it down to specific cases, it quickly loses its intuitive appeal. This was famously pointed out by the eighteenth-century Scottish philosopher David Hume, who wrote:

> Whoever would assert an equality of genius and elegance between OGILBY and MILTON, or BUNYAN and ADDISON, would be thought to defend no less an extravagance, than if he had maintained a mole-hill to be as high as TENERIFFE, or a pond as extensive as the ocean. Though there may be found persons, who give the preference to the former authors; no one pays attention to such a taste; and we pronounce without scruple the sentiment of these pretended critics to be absurd and ridiculous. The principle of the natural equality of tastes is then totally forgot, and while we admit it on some occasions, where the objects seem near an equality, it appears an extravagant paradox, or rather a palpable absurdity, where objects so disproportioned are compared together.[5]

Hume's examples of writers from his own era are now dated, but we can make his point using contemporary examples. If someone claimed that the novels of Danielle Steel were just as good as Shakespeare's plays, most of us would regard this as an extravagant or outrageous claim. As we are all aware, there are a lot of people who like Steel better than Shakespeare: a whole lot, judging by her sales figures. But most of us simply dismiss the preferences of such individuals as misguided, and their tastes defective.

This point is worth dwelling on a bit. The reader may balk at my suggestion that he regards people who prefer Steel to Shakespeare as having defective taste. The reader may say to himself: "I like Shakespeare better, but that's just me. I wouldn't tell a lover of Danielle Steel novels that she had bad taste. Everyone's taste is equally valid." But this person should consider the full implications of this position. Would he be comfortable with having equal time given to Danielle Steel novels alongside Shakespeare's plays in his kids' English literature class? Has he ever tried to persuade a person who disliked a particular book or a particular film that the book or film in question was actually a good one? If he could put one literary work into a time capsule, to communicate something about our civilization's achievements to future races, would he choose *Season of Passion* or *Macbeth*? If the answer to any of these questions is "yes," then the respondent actually does distinguish between different tastes as better and worse, despite what he or she might say. Hume's point is that, although we are always tempted to say that all tastes are equally valid, it becomes clear that this is not what we really believe when we consider particular cases in detail.

If we do hold that there are better and worse tastes, then our question becomes: of which sort is a mother's peculiar taste in her baby's looks? Again, Hume's discussion of taste provides us with a useful starting point in answering this question. Hume wondered how we could tell good taste from bad, and his answer was that we should look for certain characteristics in people. These are delicacy of taste, or the ability to make fine discriminations between similar things; practice in judging the merits of things of a certain kind; experience in drawing comparisons between different things; freedom from prejudice; and what Hume calls "good sense" or "sound understanding." Good sense is simply the ability to understand what one is attempting to appreciate: for instance, if one is appreciating the beauty of a historical painting, one needs to understand what the painting represents, how it aims to portray the events depicted, and so forth; if one is watching a play, one needs to follow the twists of the plot and correctly assess the motivations of the characters. Hume calls critics with his five qualities "true judges," and if we want to identify verdicts of good taste, it is to them that we ought to look: "Strong sense, united to delicate sentiment, improved by practice, perfected by comparison, and cleared of all prejudice, can alone entitle critics to this valuable character; and the joint verdict of such, wherever they are to be found, is the true standard of taste and beauty."[6]

Drawing on Hume's account of how we can distinguish good taste from bad, we can now rephrase our question: do mothers have the qualities of the true judges when it comes to evaluating the looks of their children? There is no reason to think that mothers who see their children as cuter are deficient in delicacy of taste or good sense. Nor does it seem plausible to think of them as lacking practice in judging the merits of infant looks or experience in drawing comparisons between baby faces: on the contrary, new parents find themselves constantly engaged in both activities. Rather, it is the fourth of Hume's desired characteristics – the freedom from prejudice – that mothers appear to lack. Of this trait, Hume writes:

> When any work is addressed to the public, though I should have a friendship or enmity with the author, I must depart from this situation; and considering myself a man in general, forget, if possible, my individual being and my peculiar circumstances. A person influenced by prejudice, complies not with this condition; but obstinately maintains his natural position, without placing himself in that point of view, which the performance supposes.

Good taste, for Hume, requires that one put aside personal connections to what one is appreciating: that one detach oneself, to a certain degree, from it. If one is friends with the author of a book, it can be difficult to see her production for what it really is, uncolored by one's positive feelings for her. But prejudice of this kind gives us a distorted perception of the work's beauty by causing us to overestimate its virtues and ignore its faults.

A mother's relationship to her infant, however, is the very antithesis of a detached relationship: the mother doesn't "forget her individual being and peculiar circumstances" when she gazes at her baby, nor does she abandon her "natural position." This suggests that, when it comes to the beauty of their children, mothers aren't true judges but poor ones, with a taste skewed or distorted by personal prejudice. To employ Hume's example, the mother is like the friend of a writer who sees more beauty in his friend's works than is actually there – that is, more beauty than better critics, their taste uncolored by prejudicial ties, can find there. Or, to make the analogy closer still, consider the egotistical artist who, despite having some practice in viewing other artworks, is besotted by one of her own paintings: seeing only its virtues, and exaggerating the importance of those virtues, she ignores its flaws.

Of course, there is a difference between the cases. We are apt to look more askance on the failure of taste in the egotistical artist, since her prejudice serves only herself. A mother's prejudice, on the other hand, may turn out to be a great boon to the infant who bewitches her, helping to deepen the mother-infant bond. But from the purely aesthetic point of view, the mother and the egotistical artist seem to be on a par: each may be a good bodyguard when it comes to the object of her affection, but they are lousy critics. Is this really how things stand? Things aren't quite so simple.

Beauty, Love, and Prejudice

To follow up our question, we need to dig a little deeper into the notion of good taste. In particular, we must ask: what is so good about good taste, anyway? Let's say, for argument's sake, that Hume is right in thinking that some people have better taste than others: some people's judgments of what is beautiful and what is not are more likely to be correct than those of others. Let's also grant that Hume is right about who those "true judges" are: those with the five characteristics he listed. Some people – the true judges – see the beauty that things actually have, while others – those influenced by personal prejudice, for example – see beauty where there really isn't any. They see a kind of false beauty. The question is: why should these people *care* that they have bad taste? The true judges get pleasure from things that really are beautiful, but the prejudiced get pleasure from things that they (falsely) believe are beautiful: Danielle Steel novels, perhaps. If the pleasure that they get is the same in overall amount as that which true judges get, what does it really matter, in the end, whether one is a true judge or a poor one? We can apply this line of thought to the maternal case by asking why mothers should mind the fact that the beauty they see in their infants is, in part, an illusion. In the eighteenth century, Joseph Spence noted that, although lovers often see beauties where others can discern none, "to the mind of the lover, supposed Beauty is full as good as real."[7]

In discussing this issue, the philosopher Jerrold Levinson has provided an account of why we should care about not having good taste, and why we ought to try to cultivate it – that is, why we should cultivate the qualities of true judges, including freedom from prejudice.[8] We need not go into the details of Levinson's nuanced account here; rather, we need only note its two principal ideas. First, we all naturally desire to have experiences that are as rewarding and worthwhile as possible. Second, Levinson argues that we have good reason to believe that the pleasures that the true judges experience are more valuable, more worthwhile, than pleasures taken in false beauties. Given these two points, we have reason to turn our attention to what true judges prefer and to attempt to emulate their characteristics – their delicacy of taste, their freedom from prejudice, and so on. For the beauties enjoyed by the true judges yield a pleasure that is more rewarding and more worth having, and to the extent that we can come to share their tastes, we too will have more rewarding experiences of beauty, and, to some degree at least, more rewarding lives overall.

With this account of what is good about good taste before us, we can turn our attention back to maternal illusions about infant beauty. But first consider again the egotistical artist. The egotistical artist might say to us: "So I have 'bad taste.' So what? I get as much pleasure from my personal 'masterpiece' as true judges get from looking at Rembrandts and Van Goghs. Why should I try to change?" Following Levinson, we could respond to him as follows: "You have a good reason to change your tastes, and to abandon your prejudices. The artworks preferred by the true judges provide pleasures that are more worth having, that are more valuable, than those you get from your own painting. Since you, like the rest of us, want to have the most valuable worthwhile experiences you can, you should try to enjoy what they enjoy." To the extent that the egotistical artist "obstinately maintains his natural position," in Hume's words, he is missing out on an opportunity to make his life a little better. The egotistical artist is a lousy critic, and he should try to become a better one.

How do things stand with the case of the mother's taste in baby beauty? It does seem that, like the egotistical critic, a mother is a lousy critic of her own productions. However, unlike the egotistical artist, it *isn't* clear that she has any good reason to care about this, or to try to improve her taste in baby looks. Let's grant that the pleasures that true judges of human beauty would experience are more rewarding, and more worth having in some sense, than the pleasures that a mother derives from the false beauty she finds in her child. And let's grant that, like everyone else, mothers have an interest in having as many worthwhile and rewarding experiences as possible. It will follow that mothers have a good reason to correct their defective tastes, but only if they are actually able to experience more of the truly beautiful things once their tastes switch.

And this is the hitch in Levinson's story when it comes to appraisals of infant beauty, indeed to the appraisal of many sorts of human beauty: the assumption is that you can freely switch what it is that you appreciate, once you improve your tastes. With artworks this is typically the case. If you change your tastes to prefer Shakespeare over Danielle Steel, you can easily switch to spending time with the former rather than the latter. In the case of visual arts like painting the change can be a bit more costly, since good art tends to cost more than bad art. But access to museums and high quality poster reproductions to some extent overcome this problem. When the things being appreciated are human beings, however, the situation is completely otherwise. A parent is not free to drop his or her homely baby like a bad paperback! A mother who somehow managed to ditch her maternal prejudice might try to spend more time admiring the cuter productions of her friends, or leafing through the airbrushed photos in baby magazines, but anyone familiar with the amount of time one must spend watching an infant will quickly see the absurd hopelessness of such maneuvers. No, unlike art lovers, mothers can rest easy with the distortion of their taste by parental love, for, unlike art lovers, they have no good reason to correct it, or even to regret it.

It is, perhaps, worth stressing the strength of our conclusion here. As we noted earlier, mothers have a very strong practical reason not to worry about their distorted tastes: their positive illusion, distortion of taste though it may be, may strengthen their bond to their children. But, as I have argued in this section, even when we put such practical considerations aside and restrict ourselves to aesthetic matters, mothers have no reason to regret the mingling of love and appraisal. There just is no payoff to improving one's taste, when it comes to your child's looks.

In fact, our discussion might even make us wonder whether it is apt to call a mother's taste "distorted" or "defective," or to describe her as subject to "illusions" about her child's looks. For the mother who fancies her own infant the cutest has cultivated her tastes in just the appropriate way, given the situation. For her, prejudice is not a hindrance or obstruction to the proper exercise of taste, but a means to it. If this seems odd, it is because our thinking about such matters continues to be so focused on the inanimate artwork as the paradigm object of beauty and taste. While mothers' experiences of baby beauty are interesting in their own right, as a part of the rich activity of mothering, they also remind us that beauty looks very different in the more complex realm of human relationships.

NOTES

1 Katherine A. Hildebrant and Hiram E. Fitzgerald, "Mothers' Responses to Infant Physical Appearance," *Infant Mental Health Journal* 2 (1981): 56–61.
2 The classic characterization of the features involved in cuteness is Konrad Lorenz, "Part and Parcel in Animal and Human Societies" in *Studies in Animal and Human Behaviour*, 2 vols., trans. Robert Martin (Cambridge, MA: Harvard University Press, 1970–1), Vol. 2, pp. 115–95. A nice discussion of cuteness in relation to beauty in general is John Morreall's "Cuteness," *British Journal of Aesthetics* 31 (1991): 39–47.
3 Hildebrant and Fitzgerald, "Mothers' Responses to Infant Physical Appearance," p. 60.
4 Judith H. Langlois, Jean M. Ritter, Rita J. Casey, and Douglas B. Sawin, "Infant Attractiveness Predicts Maternal Behaviors and Attitudes," *Developmental Psychology* 31 (1995): 464–72.
5 David Hume, "Of the Standard of Taste," in *Essays Moral, Political and Literary*, ed. Eugene F. Miller (Indianapolis: Liberty Fund, 1987), pp. 230–1.
6 Ibid., p. 241.
7 Joseph Spence (under the pseudonym Sir Harry Beaumont), *Crito: or, a Dialogue on Beauty* (Dublin: George Faulkner, 1752), p. 43.
8 Jerrold Levinson, "Hume's Standard of Taste: The Real Problem," *Journal of Aesthetics and Art Criticism* 60 (2003): 227–38.

CHAPTER 8

KEVIN, COMING INTO FOCUS

On Getting to Know My Son

Even now, as I sit down to write this, I try to imagine you as a 17-year-old reading this essay. Today, you are throwing yourself in my arms and screaming, "Catch," and laughing. What will your 17-year-old self be like? Will you read this with pride that you'll conceal with scorn? Will you be embarrassed? Will you be at all interested?

Conception

On March 27, 2007, I got "The Call." After applying to an international adoption agency in August of 2006, and running the daunting and

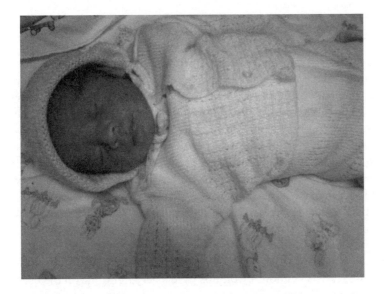

seemingly endless paper chase to put together my dossier, my adoption coordinator called to say that they had a referral for me of a little boy from Guatemala.

My partner Pat and I had returned home from a happy hour with people at work to find a message from my coordinator on my voice mail. She sounded very happy and excited. It was close to 5 p.m. when I got her message, and I immediately called the agency, praying that she was still at the office and that this was news of my referral. She was and it was.

"His name," she told me, "is Kevin Estuardo. He was born on January 23, 2007. I'm looking at his picture right now. They have him dressed in a cute little yellow sweater. He's sleeping, and his arm is stretched out. I'll send you the photos by email right now and send hard copies in a packet this weekend. Are you near a computer?"

My computer at home is over ten years old and any picture displayed on its monitor shows up dark and hazy. I wanted my first glimpse of my new son to be on the best computer to which I had access, so my partner and I drove to the university where we teach to view the pictures on my office computer. I remember feeling flushed and excited sitting in the parking lot before going up to my office, fully aware of the historic importance of this moment.

You are my son, you are my son. Sleep well. What is inside of that small head of yours? I wish I could see your eyes, but it's okay. Sleep well, and we will be together soon.

Gestation

My coordinator informed me that Kevin was staying in a foster home with one other child who had also been referred for adoption by the agency. The foster family consisted of a single mother in her forties and two teenage boys. As our case ran through the never-ending trail of red tape from bureaucratic office to bureaucratic office in two different countries, Kevin would stay with this family until he could finally come home for good. Pictures of Kevin would be taken monthly and sent to me via email along with the measurements for his height, weight, and head circumference. In this way, I could stay informed about his growth and development. I could also send care packages to Kevin and his foster family, including disposable cameras so that they could take pictures during this time that we were apart.

My coordinator also told me about an online support group for parents who were adopting from Guatemala with the agency who communicated via a list serve. The monthly photos were a very hot topic on the list serve. Each month, around the time that the pictures were due to come out, prospective parents on the list serve would begin inquiring, "Has anyone received their pictures yet?" Others would answer, "I talked to my coordinator, and she said they wouldn't be out until early next week."

When I received my pictures of Kevin, I'd be in seventh heaven. I would often just sit and grin at the photos. The experience of receiving the photos helped make the whole adoption experience seem more real to me and helped me feel more in touch with Kevin. I could see how he was growing and changing. Kevin was with his foster family for nine months, and I received six sets of monthly photos from April to September of 2007. There were usually about five or six pictures each month, and I would scrutinize them down to the most minute detail.

> What are you thinking? What are you feeling? What are the people around you doing to get the kinds of reactions and expressions you exhibit in the photos? Were you in a good mood when this picture was taken? Were you tired or cranky? Are you feeling well physically? Are you in good health? How have you changed from the last set of pictures? What is your personality like? Are you funny? Are you smart? Will you be well behaved? Will you be mischievous? Are you active and energetic? Or are you more passive and laid back? And, my gosh, you've got some big hands!

All of this information was a lot to expect from five or six two-dimensional images, but like all prospective parents I had certain expectations. I wasn't

hoping that my child would be a genius or that he would be extremely attractive. I just wanted a child who was good natured, kind, well liked, and, odd as it may sound, wasn't afraid of hard work. The first set of pictures I received came in April. This is one of my favorites from that group.

You look exactly like the ideal image of my child that I had in my mind. You look like a "Player" in the best sense of the word, and like someone who would understand the irony of a 3-month-old baby having a "Star Player" shirt on. If I had to write a caption for this picture it would have you saying, "Me, a star player? Nawwww" in a modest, come on guys, kind of way.

In May, I received another packet of photos which caused me to adjust my impression of Kevin. In these pictures, he looked like a little choirboy. With his hands folded, his eyes like large brown liquid pools, and his little pink bow-shaped mouth, he looked nothing short of cherubic. I began to suspect that the "player" aspect of last month's pictures might have had more to do with the fact that he couldn't hold his head up too well than with anything else.

Oh, my angelic child, it will be my responsibility to keep you safe and to protect this purity of spirit I see before me. How will I ever be worthy of you?

Around this time, a message came across the Guatemalan adoption list serve from a couple who were adopting a little girl they named Sienna. They were asking about the foster mother that their daughter was with, and it turned out that Kevin had the same foster mother. I responded immediately, and this proved to be a very beneficial alliance for a number of reasons. I was a little reticent about calling Kevin's foster mother in Guatemala, especially because I assumed there would be a huge language barrier. They were not so reticent, and they found out that the foster mother's sister who was often present in the home spoke fairly fluent English.

I called and got one report on Kevin by phone from the foster family. Kevin's foster mother's sister told me that he was very active, that he had been sleeping through the night, that he liked music and liked to dance, and his favorite song seemed to be "Don't You Wish Your Girlfriend Was Hot Like Me?" by the Pussy Cat Dolls. She also said that the past couple of nights he had woken up crying in the middle of the night and that her sister was going to ask the doctor about it at his next visit, but they thought he might just be teething.

In June, Sienna's adoptive parents went to Guatemala to visit her. I chose not to visit Guatemala before I picked Kevin up, for two reasons. First, I couldn't afford two trips to Guatemala; and second, I knew it would be harder to leave Kevin once I'd actually been with him in person

06/18/2007

for several days. When Sienna's parents returned home from Guatemala, they sent me an email containing the following:

> We invited our foster mother and her sister to dinner our last night there. Lo and behold a handsome young man arrived with them in our foster mother's arms whom she has nicknamed "prince" (aka your little Kevin!). We were able to take some pictures of Kevin and we will mail them to you once we get them organized. We saw MANY little baby boys on our visit, but both my wife and I thought that Kevin was the cutest ever! He is very perky and appears very healthy and strong (loves to use legs to bounce up and down on lap). Our foster mom is top-notch and both babies respond well to her. She really has a great heart and you can tell that she truly cares for her foster babies. She says that Sienna and Kevin hold hands sometimes when they nap. (How cute.)

The pictures that they sent once again forced me to reevaluate my preconceptions about Kevin. Out of all the pictures of Kevin I received, these were the most meaningful. I was thrilled with the monthly pictures from the adoption agency, but seeing Kevin in these informal snapshots taken by private individuals from the United States made the whole experience seem so much more real. Moreover, Kevin himself looked different and more at ease somehow. The agency pictures were always of Kevin by himself. These showed him in an everyday context with the only family he yet knew. There were several pictures of Kevin with his foster mother

ON GETTING TO KNOW MY SON 🐎

and her sister, and there were several of Kevin alone. In all of them, he was extremely expressive, striking a variety of engaging poses.

Who is this thin, impish boy with the big hands and toothless grin who looks like he's the life of the party in every photo? You seem to relish being out to eat and being the center of everyone's attention. What is Sienna doing? You look so happy and confident with your foster family. Do you have any sense at all of the major changes that are about to swoop into your life? Can you be as happy with me as you seem to be with them?

I received the last set of pictures in September of 2007. Kevin was eight months old. I was stunned by these pictures because Kevin seemed so much older than in the previous set of photos. He had grown bangs, for heaven's sake. He was dressed in a jean jacket, and he looked tired and sad to me in every photo, even the one that seemed to be taken outside on a porch.

You look like you too are tired of waiting and are ready to come home. I feel like it needs to be soon, before you become too conscious of your surroundings and circumstances. It's time.

Labor and Delivery

On August 24, 2007, our case was approved by the PGN, the centralized Guatemalan agency in charge of adoptions at the time. Our final interview at the United States Embassy in Guatemala was scheduled for October 12. I would finally get to hold Kevin in my arms on October 11, 2007. Pat and I made our travel arrangements. He was the perfect person to accompany me on this pick-up. Not only is he naturally calm and reassuring, but he has two children from Korea whom he adopted in his previous marriage. So he had been through this kind of thing before.

Once we landed in Guatemala, things were pretty chaotic. Our hotel had arranged for a shuttle bus to pick us up. There was such a crowd and so much confusion in the baggage claim area that the van driver who found us there practically swooped us up and smuggled us out before I even got a good look around. Once we arrived at the hotel we were informed that our room wasn't ready yet. I called the agency representative in Guatemala to tell her we had arrived. After several confusing phone calls back and forth, it was decided that we would meet the agency representative and Kevin and his foster mother in the hotel lobby at 4 p.m.

Our hotel room became available before then, and hotel staff brought a portable crib and a bottle warmer into the room. I remember noticing how easy it was for the bellhop to set up the crib. There was nothing left for Pat and me to do but wait. So, at 3:15, we decided to walk to McDonald's for a bite to eat. There was an armed guard at the front door of the McDonald's. The warnings from the agency that we should exercise caution while moving about in Guatemala City began to make more sense. I can't remember what I ordered at McDonald's. For some reason, I feel like it was something I had never ordered before and haven't ordered since. I do know I didn't finish it. As soon as we sat down, I started telling Pat we had to go back. I didn't want to be late for this most important meeting of my life.

We arrived in the lobby a few minutes before 4 p.m., but no one else was there yet. At what seemed to be about 4:30, a young, stylish-looking woman in sunglasses came in with a baby and checked in at the reception desk. I have to confess that when I heard the term *foster mother* I pictured a stout and dowdy, but loving, maternal older woman. This woman was a knock-out. She walked over to us and introduced herself. The baby in her arms was asleep, and she was in tears about handing him over to us. After all, she had been his mother for the past nine months.

Once she sat down, it quickly became apparent that she knew very little English, and we knew very little Spanish, so our ability to actually have a conversation was quite limited until the agency representative arrived and could translate for us. I began to study the baby in her arms. He was just starting to rouse from his sleep. He was wrapped in a blanket and was wearing a little cloth cap, shorts, a t-shirt, a little jacket with a basketball hoop on it, and black converse high top gym shoes with designs on them that we later discovered lit up. I was in shock. Being a bit reticent, I didn't reach for Kevin right away. His foster mother handed him to Pat, and so he was the first one of us to hold him. I got the feeling that his foster mother was relieved that I wasn't all by myself in this. When I introduced Pat to her, she practically sighed with relief and said, "Oh, Papa!" We took some pictures of all of us with Kevin and waited for the agency representative to arrive.

Kevin's foster mother brought all of the clothes we had sent for him with her, although she wasn't required to do so and we weren't expecting them. She also brought enough diapers for our trip and a can of formula mix and a can of cereal which she had been mixing with the formula. She tried several times to explain something to me about the nipple on the bottle that she had brought with him, but I couldn't understand. I had two years of Spanish in high school, and I'd read a couple of English/Spanish preschool books to Kevin on tapes I had sent, but I'm really not fluent at all. She kept pointing to the top of the nipple and using the Spanish word for "cup" from one of the books I'd read on the tape in Spanish, but I still couldn't understand. Later, in the hotel room after way too many unsuccessful feeding sessions in the middle of the night, I understood all too well what she meant.

The agency representative arrived and began to translate for us. One might think we would have a lot to say, but the rest of the meeting went fairly quickly. Kevin's foster mother described his feeding and sleeping schedule in Spanish, and the representative would repeat it for us in English. At one point, they were discussing solid food, and the representative said something like, "Maybe a little chicken every now and then," which I took to mean, God save me, that at this point in his development solid food was optional. All too soon, the agency representative and Kevin's foster mother got up to leave. Before they left, Kevin's foster mother asked if she could come back and see Kevin one last time before we departed for the United States. We invited her to join us for breakfast on our last morning in Guatemala.

The three of us, Kevin, Pat, and I, returned to our hotel room. I have to say I must have still been in shock. It had nowhere near sunk in that this was my son who would be with me for the rest of my life. I think it might have been a survival mechanism not to dwell on this. I set about trying to keep Kevin happy and satisfied one minute at a time. I held him. Pat held him. We played. We cuddled. The last baby I'd spent a lot of time with was my niece, and she was now eight years old, and that night I probably played with him in ways that were too old for him. We changed his diaper. We decided it might be time for him to go to bed, but he wasn't going to sleep. I held him for about ten minutes and rocked him, and he did drift off, but only for about a half an hour.

I kept thinking how scary this must be for him to be taken from his source of care and security for the past nine months and left in a hotel room with these two complete strangers. I vowed to do the very best I could to make him feel safe, comfortable, content, and, if possible, happy. It was a very long night, and the first of several, in that small hotel room. Kevin's feeding schedule called for him to be fed every three hours. One of us would get up in the night, prepare the bottle, and sit in the only armchair in the room and try to feed him. Repeatedly, this proved to be a very unsatisfying process. Where we would expect him to fall asleep, he would only cry longer and harder. On the second night, it dawned on me, new parent that I was, that there was something wrong with the bottle. The formula and cereal mixture was too thick, and the nipple had some kind of obstruction. I cleared the nipple obstruction to the best of my ability, and this helped the eating problem to a certain extent, but the sleeping problem continued.

When I was at home looking at his monthly pictures, I couldn't wait to see Kevin in person. I thought that then I would really *know* him. If I knew anything with certainty those first few nights, it was that that assumption was absolutely wrong. I remember we had him lying on a blanket in the hotel room with some toys around him, and it dawned on me to suggest to Pat that we just let him wander as he please to see exactly what he was capable of in terms of movement and coordination. It turned out he was capable of a lot more than we were giving him credit for. He could crawl really fast, and partially pull himself up on things, and wait for people outside of the bathroom door. It was astounding, all that he could do.

The next day was our interview at the embassy. There were several other parents from the United States adopting Guatemalan children there. I remember telling some of these parents that we'd had a rough night and inquiring into their night. Pat and I were very proud because Kevin seemed to be the best-behaved child there. It may have been exhaustion because Kevin certainly made up for his good behavior at the embassy on the plane ride home.

We stayed in Guatemala for six days. Through time, the feedings would take longer and longer and be less satisfying, even after I thought I'd fixed the obstruction in the nipple. Kevin would get very cranky at times, and he rarely slept through the night. On the third day, we went to a small grocery store nearby and bought supplies. I bought some "first step" solid baby food, a yellow ball with a picture of Sponge Bob on it that said *Bob Esponja*, and a HotWheels car. I bought little spoons for the baby food in the hotel gift shop and tried to feed Kevin the baby food. He loved it. He, literally and figuratively, ate it up. This is when it occurred to me that the poor child was starving. "Maybe a little chicken sometimes" didn't mean solid food was optional. I had gained another very important piece of knowledge about Kevin.

We tried everything to get him to sleep at night. I'd hold him. Pat would hold him. We'd rock him. We'd stroll him. We'd feed him. We'd put him in bed with us. Nothing worked. Finally, on our last night, out of sheer exhaustion, we just let him lay in the crib until he cried it out. And, lo and behold, he fell asleep and slept through the night.

Our last day there, his foster mother met us for breakfast, and her presence made Kevin more relaxed than he'd been the whole week with us. She was so good with him. She popped pieces of scrambled egg into his mouth, and pressed on his nose and said, "Beep, beep," and he smiled. We tape recorded a message from her for him when he gets older, and she wrote me a six-page, double-sided, handwritten letter documenting all the developmental landmarks in his life up to this point. Her 18-year-old son had drawn him a picture of a blue rose with the word *Principe* ("Prince") on it. They had also put together a slide show to music they said Kevin liked with pictures of him playing the guitar dressed like a pirate, helping his foster mother make pasta, and visiting a parrot. Kevin looked so happy in those pictures. I hoped that he wouldn't look back on those nine months as his halcyon days. My anxiety aside, I could not have wished for a better foster experience for Kevin. He was well loved and well cared for. He came to us happy and healthy.

After breakfast, we departed for the airport. Kevin's good behavior out in public that started at the embassy continued until we sat down in our seats on the plane. Then, he began crying and screaming. Nothing either of us did could console him. The young man from Guatemala next to us was very patient and understanding. The flight from Guatemala City to Charlotte, Virginia took six hours; Kevin cried through five of them. Suddenly, he became silent, and we all breathed a sigh of relief. At which time we noticed a particular odor coming from his diaper. We thought maybe we could wait to change him until the plane landed, but our second breath proved this idea untenable. Pat, Kevin, and I went to the airplane bathroom. With Pat and I standing, and Pat holding Kevin vertically, we changed Kevin's diaper. Then, we all gave each other a look like, "What next to entertain the other passengers?"

When we arrived in Charlotte it was as if a white glow were emanating from Kevin's head. He suddenly perked up and became extremely happy and excited. I don't know if it was just getting out of the cramped airplane, but I like to think it was because he'd arrived in his new home. We pushed his stroller and he smiled and waved to virtually everyone he saw. When we went through customs, the women working there held him a five minute party with balloons and streamers, all of them exclaiming, "Welcome, Kevin," "Welcome to the United States!"

Home

As an adoptive parent, I'm very concerned with questions of "realness." As a philosopher, I know that the question of what is real is intricately bound up with what we as human beings are able to know. I tried so hard to know Kevin through his pictures, but all of my interpretations turned out to be fuzzy and incomplete. He's very dramatic, and hence was able to embody all of the characteristics I'd perceived in his pictures. As a bonus, although of course I may be biased, he's extremely intelligent and attractive to boot.

Now that he's been home for almost two years, I have a montage of memories and experiences of him upon which to draw. I remember the day (before he was even one) when we let him out of his stroller at the museum in Louisville and he began spinning on his knees and doing an improvised crawling moonwalk on the polished wooden floors to impress another little boy who was out of his stroller too. I remember how after that he would choreograph crawling dance routines for us when asked. He also executes a surprisingly large number of yoga poses (his favorite is downward facing dog) with no formal instruction. I've observed with delight how in the past several months he's taken to saying "Slally, Mater" in a sad and sympathetic voice during the poignant part of *Cars*, his favorite movie. We laughed so hard when the first three words he strung together were "No way, baby!" when I asked if he wanted to stand up in our boat by himself. He used to run around shouting "Blue-lellow!" like it was a battle cry. When I informed him that it was all right if he didn't know his colors yet, he proved to me he did know them by very deliberately pointing to four different things and correctly identifying them as "white, red, blue, black."

I know he likes to clean and scrub and put things away, and he has from an extremely young age. I know he loves cars, trucks, trains, and anything with wheels. If it doesn't have wheels, he can usually find a way to pretend it does. I know he has a half-brother in Indiana who is a year and a half older than him. I've watched them interact and have been amazed at their similarities and their recognition of each other, in spite of the fact that they didn't meet for the first time until last summer.

But, I still don't feel like I know him. I find myself asking how much I project onto his presence and behavior as I projected thoughts and feelings onto his photos. Beyond that, I find myself wondering how much of his personality (i.e., how he acts, how he talks, etc.) is due to my influence and how much is just who he is. Then there's the fact that he's always growing and changing. Is it the case that Kevin appears blurry to me because he hasn't yet resolved into who he's going to be? Or is it sometimes that he's outgrown my image of him and I need to update my perceptions?

In the *Republic*, Socrates tells us that the two-dimensional image of an object is inferior in being and truth to the three-dimensional physical object of which it is an image. The three-dimensional object, on the other hand, is inferior to the metaphysical form or concept of that object. The soul, like the forms, belongs to what is immortal and unchanging. Therefore, it contains more being and truth than the physical body or its image.[1] Unfortunately, because we are bound to these physical bodies, the soul is also much harder to know. This, perhaps, is part of the human condition. Biological or adoptive child, child or parent, friend or stranger, we may never really know each other. I may never really know Kevin, but that's all right because he may never really know me, either.

I picture your 17-year-old self looking at the picture of us together and thinking, "That was my mom. She looks so young. What was she thinking? What was she feeling? What were the people around her doing?" Your gaze imbues my image with a sense of gravity and grace it's never had before even though you may never really know me.

NOTE

1   Plato, *Republic* (Indianapolis: Hackett, 2004), pp. 287–8.

PART III

MOM'S MORALITY

Ethical Issues in Mothering

CHRIS MULFORD[1]

CHAPTER 9

MAKING CHOICES

The Ethics of Infant Feeding

A human baby placed skin to skin, prone between its mother's breasts, is "hardwired" to seek a nipple and begin suckling in the first hour after birth. Swedish midwives published this observation in 1986[2] and produced a video (*Breastfeeding is . . . Baby's Choice*) in 1993. In 2007 a *Breast Crawl* video from India was posted on YouTube for all the world to see.[3] I am the mother of two breastfed children. Through the 1980s I assisted at scores of births as a suburban community hospital nurse. Every year about 1,000 mothers at that hospital chose to breastfeed, yet I have never seen a newborn baby, not even my own, do the breast crawl. Mothers and babies are the actors in the newborn feeding story, but evidently other people, other forces, also influence the script.

We see heroic examples of mothering in other mammal species. Rat mothers fiercely protect their young and resist being separated from them. A dog may lose up to 10 percent of her non-pregnant body weight while nursing her puppies despite taking in three times her usual number of calories.[4] A marsupial or primate mother carries her baby until it can keep up with her troop. Human mothers have the same basic anatomy and physiology, the same hormones, as other mammal mothers, but our clever brains and hands have come up with an array of choices for mothering our young. Writing this essay gives me the chance to ask what philosophy might tell us about making those choices.

Specifically, I want to think about the feeding relationship, when a lactating mother's body is linked with her child's body over and over again, rendering her quite a different creature, hormonally speaking, from her pregnant or non-pregnant, non-lactating self. This embodied role may affect how she finds a balance between her needs and her child's needs. Also, I want to investigate the role that the rest of us play – the mother's partner, her other support people, and the wider community, including policymakers and the world of commerce – in facilitating breastfeeding.

A Riff on Infant Feeding

For mammals, early feeding is essentially a nutritional transition period. Milk is the bridge between intrauterine life, when the fetus gets nourishment directly from the mother's bloodstream, and weaning, when the youngster no longer needs milk and can eat what the mother eats. Compare this to the typical bird family, in which both parents depend on what the neighborhood offers to feed their nestlings. (There are exceptions to this rule. Google *pigeon milk* to learn about one.) In the USA we generally call baby feeding *breastfeeding*, but in many places it is called just *feeding*.

The word *breastfeeding* refers to what both mother and baby do. The one word encompasses a complex system of feedback (no pun intended) that begins with a signal from one partner, usually the baby. The other partner responds by getting ready to feed. Even before the baby connects with the breast, the interaction turns physical as well as social. Both partners experience a surge of hormones that affect their perceptions, feelings, and behavior. The baby sucks. The breast releases milk, giving the baby water, nutrients, and immunoactive substances. The baby's sucking pattern responds to the milk flow rate, and vice versa. As the breast is drained, it prepares to make milk for next time. Typically, the baby falls

🐾 CHRIS MULFORD

asleep or lets go to look around and play, leaving a third of the milk behind. This scenario is repeated thousands of times in the normal course of breastfeeding.

Breastfeeding is an extraordinary relationship – interactive, yet asymmetrical. One partner is an adult – rational, verbal, and able to exercise choice. Her body is engaged, as well as her mind. The other partner is immature, a baby at first, non-verbal but assuredly vocal. At birth the mother must learn her baby's language, and over time the baby learns to speak the mother's language. Babies learn moral lessons at the breast, too – "Don't Bite Mama!" being one of the first.

The feeding relationship begins at birth and continues as the baby grows. The World Health Organization (WHO) characterizes *optimal infant and young child feeding* as six months of exclusive breastfeeding (100 percent mother's milk),[5] then continued breastfeeding along with complementary foods (foods that provide nutrients needed in greater amounts as the baby grows, but not supplied by mother's milk) until age two or beyond.[6] Anthropologist Kathy Dettwyler asked the question "how far beyond?" She extrapolated from the weaning ages of other large primates, using physical standards like *age of attaining 1/3 of adult body weight* or *age at eruption of first permanent molars*, and arrived at some time between 2.5 and 7 years.[7]

But humans are more than large primates. We are inventors and communicators. Our ancestors, if faced with a motherless baby, sought another lactating woman to rear the baby. (Wet nursing probably rivals prostitution for the title of "world's oldest profession.") If no lactating woman could be found, they tried hand feeding a variety of mixtures from a variety of containers. Most of these methods were unsuccessful. It was only in the late nineteenth century that babies started to survive hand feeding, after Pasteur developed the germ theory of disease. The glass and rubber industries came up with a feeding bottle and teat that could be sterilized, and scientists realized that the young of different mammals receive a species-specific balance of proteins, sugars, and fats in their mothers' milk. The medical specialty of pediatrics developed partly in order to study and improve artificial feeding.

What choices are available for infant feeding nowadays? As alternatives to breastfeeding when necessary, the WHO lists milk expressed by the baby's mother, milk from a healthy wet nurse or human milk bank, or a breastmilk substitute. These can be fed by bottle and teat or by cup.[8] Readers of this book probably live in countries where people believe they can use formula and bottles safely, having access to the sanitation, safe public water supply, refrigeration, food distribution system, and child healthcare that make up the infrastructure needed by families who don't breastfeed, or who wean babies from the breast earlier than age two. However, even under these conditions, rates of illness and death are higher for babies who are not breastfed.

A recent addition to the list of choices is pumping. A few mothers supply milk but never put their baby to the breast. Others settle for bottle feeding pumped milk after an unsuccessful effort at direct breastfeeding. Many women express milk if they are away from the baby and breastfeed when they get back together. With sufficient support, lactation scarcely limits the possible range, both in space and time, of a woman's physical separation from her infant. There are stories of flight attendants who pump between international flights and soldier-mothers who send milk home to their babies from Afghanistan. Even wet nursing was back in the news recently. When a Michigan man's wife died of an amniotic fluid embolism after giving birth, a family friend recruited two dozen lactating women. They have been nursing baby Moses in rotation for six months and plan to keep it up until he turns one.[9]

All these options increase the complexity of infant and young child feeding. When it comes to feeding human babies, someone has to be responsible for making the choices. If the biological mother is involved in her baby's care, she gets to decide whether to use the natural resource that her body provides for her baby, or to let her milk dry up and use replacements. However, this is not the only feeding choice to be made over the course of caring for her baby. The mother (and any other caregiver) will make dozens of decisions every day, deciding whether and how to respond each time the baby indicates a need. If the mother has chosen to breastfeed, then giving the baby her breast will remain one of her options until the child has weaned. In practical terms, the *choice* of whether to breastfeed is not a "one-off" but a mode of caring that a mother repeatedly will choose – or not – to retain in her caring repertoire. Can philosophy offer her any help in making these choices?

Ethical Questions about Infant Feeding

An ethical system is a theory that provides a framework for classifying actions, for example as right or wrong, good or bad, forbidden, permitted, or obligatory. An ethical system assigns values to actions and includes

🐾 CHRIS MULFORD

a way of getting from values to endorsements of action. Thinking about ethics and breastfeeding, several questions came to my mind, and I considered them along the way to asking my key questions: How should the actions involved in infant feeding be classified? Who is responsible for those actions?

Question 1: Are there rights or duties related to infant feeding?

A duty is an obligation, whether to oneself, to others, or to a higher power. We have the duty to act in certain ways regardless of the cost to ourselves. For example, people who run recreational programs for children have the duty, as far as possible, to protect the children from harm, even though the costs of screening and training staff are considerable. Under most human ethical, religious, and legal systems, parents have a duty to care for their children.

Along with duties come *rights*. A person's right, for instance to own an item, is related to other people's duty not to steal it. In the twentieth century, human rights, including the specific rights of women and children, were codified in several UN conventions. Nations that ratify the conventions then have the duty, through their governments, to respect, protect, and fulfill the human rights of their citizens. The UN Convention on the Rights of the Child (CRC)[10] calls on governments to help parents meet their responsibility for raising their children.

After the CRC was adopted, an international group met to develop a consensus statement on the nutrition rights of the infant. Some members wanted to say that babies have the right to breastfeed, and others were concerned that claiming that right for babies would saddle each mother with a duty to breastfeed instead of supporting her right to make her own decisions. The group's final position is that the mother and child, *together*, have a right to *protection from interference* with breastfeeding. Thus, "children have the right to be breastfed, in the sense that no one may interfere with their mothers' right to breastfeed them." Furthermore, "women have the right to social, economic, health, and other conditions that are favorable for them to breastfeed or to deliver milk to their infants in other ways" and "States . . . have an obligation to . . . facilitate the conditions of breastfeeding." Conditions that facilitate breastfeeding, such as accurate information, accessible skilled healthcare, community support for families, and maternity protection in the workplace, would in turn benefit all mothers, including those who choose not to breastfeed or who wean early.[11]

Question 2: How do we decide whether a particular feeding choice is good?

Surely it's "good" to produce food in a hungry world, yet breastfeeding is seldom recognized for its value as food production, as small scale "agriculture" on a par, say, with growing tomatoes in your garden. Yet in aggregate, national milk supply figures are impressive. Economists estimated that counting human milk in Mali, even at the (very low) value of US$1.00 per liter, would increase GDP by 5 percent.[12] Although food production was not on my mind when I was a breastfeeding mother, I once estimated that, nursing two children long term, I probably made a ton of milk. How is it fair that those years when I was contributing to the US food supply are the same years that show up on my Social Security record as zeroes?

Mothers have duties not only to their children but to themselves – to maintain their own health or to develop their potential, for instance – and to other people – partner, other children, parents, etc. In a non-supportive social setting, the barriers to breastfeeding may just be too high. The USA lacks national paid maternity leave or family leave, sharing this dubious distinction with only three other nations: Swaziland, Papua New Guinea, and Lesotho. US mothers also lack the right to paid nursing breaks when they go back to work[13] and few employers offer on-site or near-site childcare. Employed US women pay a large "income penalty" for motherhood. A woman who reduces her paid workload when her children are small risks missing out on training opportunities and professional advancements such as tenure or being made partner at a law firm. Recent research found that non-black employed women who breastfed over six months had a bigger loss in earnings than other women, and it was still affecting them ten years after birth.[14] No matter how a woman might *prefer* to feed her child, she might have to *choose* bottle over breast in order to meet other goals.

Health authorities agree that breastfeeding is the best choice, but to tell the truth, it doesn't always feel like it. It can be hard for many of us to learn. The discomforts of the first weeks are legendary. Some women just never feel emotionally comfortable making their breast available to that little critter even though they "love her to bits." An in-depth survey of 25 Australian first-time mothers found a range of reactions to breastfeeding.[15] All of the women were committed to breastfeeding prenatally. For about 35 percent, breastfeeding was a wonderful experience that powerfully connected them with their babies; 40 percent reported mixed feelings; and 25 percent were "disappointed and distressed." These women were in stable relationships with the baby's father, and they lived in a country where breastfeeding gets better community support than in the USA. Even so, most of them did not attain "Breastfeeding Nirvana," as they may have hoped. (Note, however, that 80 percent of them stuck with breastfeeding for three months, and 72 percent were still nursing at 6 months, the end of the survey.)

Although there is ample evidence that breastfeeding is life-saving under developing-country conditions, the epidemiological evidence of better health outcomes for breastfed individuals in developed countries is modest.[16] Periodically, critics of breastfeeding question the science behind health-based recommendations for breastfeeding.[17] Still, there's nothing else like breastfeeding. Human milk contains a wealth of immunologically active components and living cells.[18] These are not available in a can, and never could be. The milk "delivery system" is also unique, a relationship in which each mother-baby dyad develops its own "nursing style," changing as the baby grows and changes.

At the practical level, there are a host of reasons for the individual decisions each mother makes at the dozens of moments every day when her baby frets. She is probably not recalling the economic value of her milk or the statistics on breast cancer and childhood ear infections. She is doing what will get her through the day – or the next five minutes.

It might seem that the breastfeeding mother is doing all the work and the baby is getting all the value. But the lived experience of breastfeeding is more of an ongoing "win-win" negotiation. Baby mammals and birds make a repeated high-pitched distress call that seems designed to motivate a response from adults. Lactation consultant Diane Wiessinger suggests that a mammal mother may be acting out of self-interest when she offers her breast to her fussing baby; she does it to hush the baby's annoying noise. Suckling releases maternal hormones that promote relaxation, satiety, and affiliation, so giving the breast may also result in maternal pleasure. It can be a refreshing pause for both partners by day and the easiest way to settle a wakeful baby at night.

Question 3: Do people have different roles and responsibilities in infant feeding?

Until recently, philosophy was written by males, a sex that doesn't breast-feed and traditionally hasn't done much caregiving. Some feminist writers argue that women learn empathy through the experience of caregiving. This "female" value contrasts with the "male" value of objectivity, the ability to follow the rules of trade and government without becoming emotionally involved. Beginning in the 1940s, psychologist Niles Newton explored the central role of the hormone oxytocin in the interpersonal acts of coitus, birth, and breastfeeding.[19] Recent studies have shown the key role of oxytocin in other social interactions, including caregiving, pair-bonding between mates, social recognition, social memory, and affiliation.[20] Mothers' greater exposure to oxytocin, in childbirth and especially when breastfeeding, may provide one physiological explanation for gender differences in perspective.

A female critic of breastfeeding recently wrote "it just felt so selfish. My . . . husband and my mom . . . had to sit there tapping their feet with lust to get at those luscious babies who spent most of their time latched onto me like lovely little leeches."[21] Another critic quoted a Canadian friend who chose to bottle-feed because breastfeeding "creates an unequal dynamic."[22] Some women, after fighting for equality with men in public life, strive to follow that strategy in their private lives as well. After the manifest inequalities of pregnancy and birth, it seems to them that it's time for Dad to step up and do his part. Since what new babies mostly want is to eat, breastfeeding doesn't seem to leave enough for him to do.

But sharing responsibility doesn't have to mean that tasks are divided with mathematical exactitude. Parenting, like reproduction, is an asymmetrical and reciprocal partnership. It can be unequal and still be equitable, not exploiting either partner. Babies do need to be carried, amused, and settled, as well as fed. Surely, in the intensity of raising a baby there's enough work to go around without abandoning breastfeeding.

It is a truism that children are our future. Biologically, they carry on their parents' DNA, and ethically, parents hope their children will carry on their values. Children's future productivity will provide their elders' old-age benefits. The state takes a great interest in the health and education of its future citizens. Insofar as breastfeeding contributes to raising healthy and capable children, we all have a stake in supporting it.

Closing Thoughts on Classification and Responsibility

The vulnerability of human babies is noteworthy. Our young have the longest period of dependency of any mammal; several years elapse between birth and the time when they can find and prepare food for themselves. Babies' survival depends on being fed, and their development as full human

CHRIS MULFORD

beings depends on their forming a close attachment with the person or persons who care for them, with feeding playing a central role. So it is easy for me to conclude that to feed babies and young children is *good* and *right*, and indeed *obligatory*. Because we are mammals, our biological norm is breastfeeding – simultaneously a food, a relationship, and a method of care. Because life has its mishaps, humans have invented alternative feeding methods, and these work pretty well, given a supportive infrastructure. But several historic trends have converged to put breastfeeding at risk.

The industrial revolution offered women a wider choice of jobs. The women's movement helped us organize for equal rights and equal opportunity. The medicalization of birth and infant feeding substituted science for women's traditional wisdom. The invention of breastmilk substitutes, baby bottles, and breast pumps separated feeding from mothers' bodies and allowed them to share the tasks of mothering with other caregivers; the commoditization of infant foods and feeding devices introduced a profit motive for the provision of these items. In 1960s America, not one mother in five even attempted to breastfeed. Four decades later, that number has edged up to near 75 percent, but breastfeeding duration is still pitifully brief. The alternative feeding methods that were invented to be a safety net when breastfeeding didn't work have spilled out of the First Aid closet and threaten to take over the field, crowding out the biological norm. It doesn't help the situation that somebody is making money when this happens.

It seems clear to me that if anyone has a duty toward breastfeeding, it is not exclusively or even primarily mothers. It is all of us, collectively. An individual woman has to make the choices that seem right for her. However, she chooses within an environment that limits or expands her options, both by influencing what she thinks and by putting assistance or obstacles her way. Just as artificial feeding requires an infrastructure of public sanitation and food distribution, so too breastfeeding requires an infrastructure of support for women and families, gender equity, and public information, if it is to survive in the modern world.

For millennia, human reproduction has comprised four dyadic stages: coitus, gestation, birth, and suckling. Whatever it is that we value about breastfeeding – attachment, maternal and child development, short- and long-term health effects, food security, its irreplaceable immunoglobulins, its economic, environmental, or aesthetic value – there is a role for all of us bystanders to support breastfeeding through public discourse, policy decisions, budget appropriations, hands-on help for families, and general cheerleading.[23]

NOTES

1 I would like to thank my son-in-law Bijan Parsia and my sister Margaret A. Robinson for their critical help and helpful criticism.

2 A. M. Widström et al., "Gastric Suction in Healthy Newborn Infants: Effects on Circulation and Developing Feeding Behavior," *Acta Pediatrica* 76, 4 (1987): 566–72.

3 Available online at www.youtube.com/watch?v=zrwfIcPB1u4 (accessed August 8, 2009).

4 Gail Kuhlman, "Feeding the Gestating and Lactating Dog," available online at www.gundogsonline.com/Article/feeding-the-gestating-and-lactating-dog-Page1.htm (accessed June 28, 2009).

5 Medicines, vitamins/minerals, and small amounts of culturally determined ritual foods are also allowed within the definition of *exclusive breastfeeding*.

6 WHO/UNICEF Global Strategy for Infant and Young Child Feeding (2003), available online at www.web.archive.org/web/20071129082404/ http://www.who.int/gb/ebwha/pdf_files/EB109/eeb10912.pdf (accessed August 13, 2009).

7 Katherine Dettwyler, "A Natural Age of Weaning," available online at www.kathydettwyler.org/detwean.html (accessed August 13, 2009).

8 The WHO recommends cup feeding over bottle feeding because an open cup is safer than a bottle – easier to clean and less likely to sit for prolonged periods holding milk at temperatures where bacteria can proliferate.

9 K. Jahnke, "Two Dozen Nursing Moms Come to Aid of Baby Boy in Marquette," *Detroit Free Press* online, www.freep.com/article/20090726/FEA TURES08/907260333&template=fullarticle (accessed August 13, 2009).

10 The USA and Somalia are the only members of the United Nations that have not ratified the CRC.

11 George Kent, "Child Feeding and Human Rights," *International Breastfeeding Journal* 1, 27 (2006), available online at www.internationalbreastfeeding journal.com/content/1/1/27 (accessed June 28, 2009).

12 Anne Hatloy and Arne Oshaug, "Human Milk: An Invisible Food Resource," *Journal of Human Lactation* 13, 4 (1997): 299–305.

13 About 70 percent of other countries provide nursing breaks for at least some of their workforce. They are most common in Europe. See www.waba.org. my/whatwedo/womenandwork/mpstatus.htm.

14 Phyllis Rippeyoung and Mary Noonan, "Is Breastfeeding Truly Free? The Economic Consequences of Breastfeeding for Women" (2009), available online at www.paa2009.princeton.edu/download.aspx?submissionId=91391 (accessed August 14, 2009).

15 Virginia Schmied and Lesley Barclay, "Connection and Pleasure, Disruption and Distress: Women's Experience of Breastfeeding," *Journal of Human Lactation* 15 (1999): 325–34.

16 Two recent studies that demonstrated significant positive effects associated with breastfeeding were forthright in their acknowledgment that some of the effects were modest. The differences include, for older children or adults: lower mean blood pressure, lower total cholesterol, lower overweight/obesity and Type 2 diabetes; higher performance on intelligence tests; for babies, fewer ear infections, less diarrhea, fewer severe lower respiratory tract infections, less atopic dermatitis, less asthma in young children, less obesity, less Type 1 and 2 diabetes, less childhood leukemia, less Sudden Infant Death Syndrome, and less necrotizing enterocolitis; for women who breastfed their babies, less Type 2 diabetes, less post-partum depression, less breast and ovarian cancer. See Berndardo Horta et al. (2007) *Evidence on the Long-Term Effects of Breastfeeding: Systematic Review and Meta-Analyses* (Geneva: World Health Organization), available online at www.who.int/child_adolescent_health/documents/9241595230/en/index.html; S. Ip et al. (2007) "Breastfeeding and Maternal and Infant Health Outcomes in Developed Countries," *Agency for Healthcare Research and Quality* (2007), available online at www.ahrq.gov/downloads/pub/evidence/pdf/brfout/brfout.pdf.

17 Debra Dickerson, "We Over-Privileged Bitches Who Dare Not To Breastfeed," *Mother Jones* (March 15, 2009), available online at www.motherjones.com/blue-marble/2009/03/we-over-privileged-bitches-who-dare-not-breastfeed-0#comments (accessed March 17, 2009); Hanna Rosin, "The Case Against Breastfeeding," *Atlantic* (April 2009), available online at www.theatlantic.com/doc/200904/case-against-breastfeeding/3 (accessed August 14, 2009); Helen Rumbelow, "Benefits of Breastfeeding 'Being Oversold by the NHS'," *Timesonline* (July 20, 2009), available online at www.timesonline.co.uk/tol/life_and_style/health/article6719696.ece (accessed August 3, 2009).

18 M. H. Labbok et al., "Breastfeeding: Maintaining an Irreplaceable Immunological Resource," *Nature Reviews/Immunology* 4 (July 2004): 565–72.

19 Niles Newton, "The Role of the Oxytocin Reflexes in Three Interpersonal Reproductive Acts: Coitus, Birth and Breastfeeding," *Clinical Psychoneuroendocrinology in Reproduction: Proceedings of the Serono Symposia*, Vol. 22 (London: Academic Press, 1979), reprinted in *Newton on Breastfeeding* (Seattle: Birth & Life Bookstore, 1987), pp. 7–14.

20 Inga Neumann, "Brain Oxytocin Mediates Beneficial Consequences of Close Social Interactions: From Maternal Love and Sex," in *Hormones and Social Behavior* (New York: Springer, 2008).

21 Dickerson, "We Over-Privileged Bitches Who Dare Not To Breastfeed."

22 Hanna Rosin, "Mother's Milk" (video), available online at www.theatlantic.com/doc/200904/case-against-breastfeeding (accessed August 14, 2009).

23 Economic development specialist James Akre has proposed the organization of a vast "International Breastfeeding Support Collective," quite a doable task given the possibilities of the Internet. See James Akre, *The Problem with Breastfeeding* (Amarillo: Hale Publishing, 2007), available online at www.ibreastfeeding.com/catalog/product_info.php?products_id=55 (accessed August 14, 2009).

CHAPTER 10

LACTATIONAL BURKAS AND MILKMEN
On Public Breastfeeding and Male Lactation

Gloria Steinem once asked how our culture might be different if men could menstruate.[1] We might ask a similar question about how culture might be different if men could breastfeed. No doubt men would brag about how much milk they produce. There would be lactational sports clubs furnished with breastfeeding booths equipped with a sea of televisions. There would be "workman's lactational leaves," and companies offering benefits packages including membership to gyms where men could pump milk and iron at the same time. Suits would come with leak guards. Commercials admiring the size of a man's breasts would sell supplements promising to increase one's supply. Most certainly the meaning of breastfeeding as an intimate act with sexual connotations would come to be seen as an act as mundane as dining at a restaurant and come to be as eagerly accommodated as is any hungry man. This shift would bring about diverse and specialized spaces for breastfeeding, and the spectacle of nursing men would bring new meaning to the phrase "skins vs. shirts."

This thought experiment may be far-fetched, given that evolutionary biology seems to have designated women as the producers of the species' milk supply. But, in fact, men can lactate, both with and without hormonal supplements, posing questions about why this bodily capacity has not been further developed in men, and why women should exclusively bear the burden of breastfeeding. When pointed out that with some effort it is possible for them to lactate, it is common for men to ask "why would we want to"? Given that most men currently seem unwilling to develop this capacity, the main question I wish to explore is how maternal equality is tied up with the public accommodation of breastfeeding, but this question invites serious contemplation of the proposal that men ought to ease maternal burdens by sharing the labor of breastfeeding.

Here I use a feminist ethic of care to argue that breastfeeding is a natural function that is intimate but not obscene, and is a practice that ought to be widely publicly accommodated. I propose that we understand the push for women to cover up while breastfeeding in public, or worse, to remain exclusively in private spaces, as having the effect of imposing "lactational burkas" on women. Pursuing this argument leads me to consider lactational burkas as a maternal burden, the potential obscene and intimate aspects of breastfeeding, the pressures to breastfeed or not, and the ways in which lactation might be reciprocally accommodated in part by developing this biological potential in men.

Lactational Burkas, Lactational Burdens

The United States considers itself to be progressive in women's rights and shows consternation for Muslim cultures where women's bodies are considered so overtly sexual that they must wear burkas in public and remain isolated in their homes. However, lactating women in the US have their freedom similarly restricted in being pressured to breastfeed in private and under conditions of induced modesty, imposing what could be called "lactational burkas." Just as actual burkas come in different varieties – with some being more restrictive than others – lactational burkas come in many guises, from blankets or garments used to shield women from the public gaze, to spatial arrangements where breastfeeding women are quarantined from the larger public while they feed their children. In characterizing these restrictions as akin to burkas, I mean that they are based on understandings of the female body, specifically the breast and nipple, as essentially sexual and intimate, and thus subject to norms of modesty that can be extremely conservative and inconveniencing to women. As feminists recognize that when freely chosen, a Muslim burka or hidja (headscarf) can be an authentic religious expression legitimately rooted in a desire to avoid sexual objectification, likewise a feminist care ethic gives less reason to be critical of lactational burkas when they are freely and authentically chosen, out of recognition that some women prefer privacy when nursing their children. What is problematic about lactational burkas is not their existence as such, since women may freely choose to breastfeed their children modestly or in privacy for any number of legitimate reasons. Rather, problems stem from the imposition of lactational burkas and the burdens they induce.

In addition to the difficulties associated with caring for an infant in general, given that babies feed as often as every two hours in the early weeks, and every three or four hours for months, lactational burkas require that women alter their normal public lives with scarce public provision for clean and spacious facilities for breastfeeding. Women who breastfeed in public may be harassed as immodest, increasing the burdens associated with motherhood more generally. For example, on October 13, 2006, after hours of delay, Emily Gillette was finally seated in the plane, nursing her daughter as their Freedom flight prepared to leave Burlington International Airport in Vermont. She and her daughter were seated by the window in the next-to-last row, with her husband seated next to them in the aisle seat. Although no part of her breast was showing, a flight attendant asked her to cover herself and her nursing daughter with a blanket. She declined, telling the attendant that the plane was overly warm, and she had a legal right to breastfeed. Soon after, she and her family were removed from the plane.

This story is just one of many incidents of nursing mothers being ejected from public places like restaurants, shopping malls, movie theatres, and swimming pools. Although public breastfeeding is legal in over 34 states, women in the US are often harassed for breastfeeding in public on the grounds that it violates public decency standards.[2] Affirming the idea that public breastfeeding is obscene, Facebook recently removed all photos of nursing mothers, citing violation of their obscenity policy. Despite strong government endorsement for breastfeeding, governments do not always affirm breastfeeding as a right that extends to corporate settings, sometimes sanctioning against lactating mothers. For example, the Ohio Supreme Court recently upheld a lower court ruling in favor of the Totes/Isotoner Corporation after they fired LaNisa Allen for taking unauthorized bathroom breaks to pump her breastmilk.[3] While the dissenting judge found that the lower court had failed to consider why Allen's need for bathroom breaks was different from those of other employees, the winning opinion ruled that the breaks were unauthorized and that her termination did not violate the state's pregnancy anti-discrimination law. Shouldn't we question why greater public accommodation for lactation and breastfeeding is not viewed as part of pregnancy anti-discrimination law? Beyond the disturbing fact that women often resort to pumping breastmilk or breastfeeding in bathroom stalls, Allen's case reflects a general dearth of public accommodation for maternal work, despite its status as a vital human activity.

For example, mothers with infants are commonly inconvenienced by a lack of facilities for changing diapers (and when facilities are provided they are often only in women's and not men's restrooms!). Although parents flying on planes may do so with their child on their laps, sparing them the expense of a separate ticket, this proves to be a very challenging endeavor if a parent (typically, the mother) wishes to eat, drink, use the restroom, or even pick up a dropped item. Successfully accomplishing any of these tasks with a child on one's lap is to a great degree contingent upon the cooperation and patience of fellow passengers. Taking a line from *A Streetcar Named Desire*, we can say that mothers have always depended on the kindness of strangers. Mothers with infants find their ability to occupy public spaces severely curtailed, making it difficult to attend conferences, public talks, or any other public event not specifically designed to be "family friendly." As for those who use a wheelchair to achieve mobility, a baby in a stroller can pose public access problems in buildings without elevators or ramps, or in small, crowded spaces. Being forced to nurse or pump breastmilk in a restroom stall, which is cramped, under demand, lacking in basic amenities and comforts, and sometimes smelly or dirty, is not only an inconvenience, but an indignity to mothers and children. The effects of these spatial arrangements are, as disability advocates have argued, issues of equality of opportunity and civic inclusion. Prompted by a desire to make breastfeeding more convenient for women and the irony of these actions in a society where sexualized images of breasts are regularly visible in public spaces, "lactivists" have organized in support of public lactation, challenging the idea that breastfeeding in public is obscene.

Breastfeeding as Obscene

I remember as a child of five or six when my neighbor explained to me that I could not go shirtless like the boys because, as she said, "girls have boobs that need to be covered and you could be arrested for not wearing a shirt." Even then, this explanation seemed blatantly unfair, especially as there was no real difference between my physical appearance and that of boys at the time. This initial lesson in social modesty took root, though, such that when I became a mother struggling to dutifully breastfeed while still having a life, I found myself preoccupied with preventing breast exposure, not because I was worried that I would be arrested (although in my head this was always a possibility), but because I recognized it would be considered by many, including some in my own family, to be obscene.

But why should public breastfeeding be considered obscene, and for that matter, why should the exposure of a female breast more generally be considered obscene? Historically, women's breasts, lactating and otherwise, have been iconic. Compared to most other contemporary liberal societies, the US alone exhibits extreme prudery when it comes to the female breast, exemplified by the scandal that following Janet Jackson's "wardrobe malfunction" during Superbowl halftime events in 2004. But throughout Europe women's breasts are readily visible on public billboards and beaches (the London newspaper the *Sun* features a different topless woman every day on the third page, known as the "page three girls"), with little consternation, except perhaps by American tourists. Although the exposure that may come with breastfeeding in public might offend some people throughout the US, should it be considered obscene?

One way to determine whether it is justified to consider public breastfeeding as obscene is to subject it to the Miller test, the standard test used to determine what material counts as pornographic and thereby subject to state action. The Miller test, named for the landmark 1973 Supreme Court case *CA v. Miller*, cites three criteria which must be met for an image or act to count as obscene: the image must appeal to a prurient interest, be patently offensive, and fail to exhibit any serious literary, political, or scientific value. Applying these standards, there does not seem good reason to consider public breastfeeding obscene to the point of warranting social sanction. For example, in the case of Facebook, the Miller test fails to demonstrate that all photos of breastfeeding women are obscene, because as a class they do not appeal to a prurient interest in terms of being designed to sexually stimulate, and they do exhibit political and social value as expressions of identity and conviction. Although such photos might be offensive to some, this condition alone is not enough to justify prohibitions of public breastfeeding. No doubt the depiction of many things, such as public displays of affection between interracial couples or same-sex couples, offends some, but are not for this reason legitimately prohibited in public. It is important to examine the underlying reasons and assumptions beneath the offense taken to public displays of breastfeeding to determine whether such offense is warranted.

In fact, offense taken to public breastfeeding is not warranted because it reflects a demonization of the body that is hypocritical, subject to pernicious sexual double standards, and rooted in flawed biological reductionism. Being offended by public breastfeeding is hypocritical given that while nursing a child a woman's breasts are typically no more exposed than when she wears a bikini or evening gown. While there is potential for nipple exposure (the body part which seems to cause the most concern) in most cases such exposure is fleeting and evident only to a prolonged gaze, that is, only to someone who *wants* to see the nipple. Further, there is also reason to question why it is consistent to view the female nipple as singularly and innately sexual, when male nipples are not so considered. Men in America go shirtless without much public consternation, yet the exposed female breast is considered inherently sexual and taboo, even as it is readily visible in a variety of sexualized settings. Likewise, even though men's breasts equally qualify as erogenous zones, men's "chests" are not reduced to their sexual contexts. The view that women's "chests" are inherently sexual oversimplifies the biological picture, making it difficult to recognize female breasts as multifunctional. As Monica Casper observes, squeamishness over public breastfeeding in part has to do with the non-sexual nature of lactation: "Given that we are bombarded constantly by pornographic and suggestive displays of women's anatomy, I suspect discomfort with breastfeeding has more to do with context than content . . . . What unsettles people about lactating breasts is being forced to observe these repositories of fantasy in a context that is decidedly non-sexual."[4]

While Casper is right that many women find it absurd to consider breastfeeding a sexual act, it is less certain that it is utterly desexualized. What may be equally disturbing to some about public breastfeeding is a sexual suggestion of incest. But more interesting is Casper's observation that "something else is going on, too: need . . . a hungry baby *is* raw need in motion, nature carried into the nursery, trailing dirt and entrails, or rather, projectile vomit and yellow poop." Thus, perhaps the indecency of public breastfeeding has less to do with occasional nudity, and more to do with a reminder of the needs of human flesh, and a desire to avoid thinking about the vulnerability to which these needs attest. This is especially evident when we consider how public repugnance over breastfeeding increases as nursing children become older and are expected to be more independent. As many have noted, Gillette, the nursing woman ejected from the Freedom flight, was not only breastfeeding in public, but was breastfeeding a toddler, as her daughter was nearly two years old at the time. While it is reasonable to place limits on the age to which children should breastfeed, medical professionals in fact recommend breastfeeding to the age of two, challenging cultural expectations for early weaning and other ideals of independence. Perhaps, however, the problem is not that breastfeeding in public is obscene, but that it is a display of intimacy that makes others uncomfortable.

The Intimacy of Breastfeeding

Even if it doesn't make sense to view breastfeeding in public as obscene, it can still be argued that it is an intimate activity that others legitimately prefer take place in private. Responding to the claim that public lactation is justified because breastfeeding is a natural function of the human body, comedian Bill Mahr once joked that the same could be said of urination and defecation. That is, even if public breastfeeding is not obscene, it could still be viewed as offensive because it is an intimate act best practiced in privacy. The parallel between bodily functions is not exact because most adults do not eat in the privacy of a bathroom stall, but there is some truth in the view of breastfeeding as an intimate act, one that involves bodily contact, a close relationship, and an exchange of fluids. Moreover, it is an act, like a public display of affection, which at times can be awkward to witness. Yet not all intimate acts necessarily or legitimately generate feelings of awkwardness. For example, a surgery or dental procedure may be described as an intimate act involving bodily contact and possible exchange of fluids, and sometimes a close relationship, but not one deemed as something that should always be private. Leaving this aside, what other sources of offense over public displays of breastfeeding warrant privatization?

Perhaps part of the resistance to public breastfeeding is the awkward and embarrassing unexpectedness of it, and the inability of others to know to expect it ahead of time and hence to plan around the possibility of witnessing the act. While some voyeurs may not object to viewing public displays of intimacy, others prefer not to view such exchanges, and would prefer for them to occur more discreetly. However, important distinctions can be made between breastfeeding and other intimate displays of the satisfaction of a bodily need, including the urgency and suddenness of need, and the innocence and non-volition of the needy recipient. Furthermore, breastfeeding is a matter of nutritional intake, an act that perhaps always involves an intimate relation to some living thing, a fact usually ignored as much as possible. Even if vegetarian or vegan, the food we eat is always organic, and almost always representative of a relation of life and death between living things. While dining is often celebrated, great efforts are taken to mask the intimate aspects of meal preparation – from the lives that are lost in the process, to the labor of those who prepare our food. Some of the discomfort behind breastfeeding is probably a reminder of our animality, of the fact that we are mammals, animals that nurse their young. This point was brought home recently in the widespread revulsion to PETA's suggestion that coffee houses replace cow's milk with human milk. But why should it be considered more disgusting to drink cow milk than human milk, when the risks of contamination are equal in both cases, and the nutritional benefits of human breast milk are greater, unless we are uncomfortable with the idea of milking humans, and the intra-species dependencies and intimacies that follow? We do not see the source of food for most mammals to be suitable for humans generally, yet we do not find it odd or intimate to consume the milk of cows, sheep, and goats.

Finally, the offense of public breastfeeding may be intensified by a subconscious idea that it is a kind of regenerative and sustaining canni-balism, resulting in a kind of breast awe, or envy of the maternal body – a feminist flip-side to Freud's notion of penis envy, perhaps. This possibility gains credibility when considering the Christian practice of communion, in which public communion is oriented around the sustaining giving of Christ's body and bodily fluids in a symbolic transference of feminine nurturing abilities: "Take, drink, this is my blood which is given for you." A further tension is evident between religious images celebrating the lactating Madonna occupying the same spaces where actual lactating women are rarely seen in public. Many churches have private rooms where nursing mothers are expected to go to so as to not offend any of the other worshippers. This tension exists despite the predominant pub-lic agreement that "breast is best." Despite the almost universal accept-ance of this adage, a feminist care ethic takes disagreements about the overall merits of breastfeeding seriously.

"Breast is Best"

I have argued that public breastfeeding is appropriate in part because "breast is best" when it comes to meeting the basic needs of young chil-dren. However, this claim is contentious, extending beyond questions about whether breastfeeding benefits children, to questions about whether it benefits mothers, fathers, and others. For example, Hanna Rosin describes being shunned by other mothers when she announced her consideration to stop breastfeeding, and her shock in discovering that the purported benefits of breastfeeding are not as established as we are led to believe.[5] Rosin describes a general disjunction between medical and popular literature, in that the medical texts suggest that breastfeeding is somewhat better than bottle feeding, but that "it is far from the stampede of evidence" suggested by popular literature, such as "IQ scores averaging higher . . . fewer ear infections, allergies, stomach illnesses, lower rates of obesity, diabetes and heart disease . . . 'stool with a buttermilk odor', and 'nicer skin'." Given the pervasive "breast is best" message, it is also startling to learn that breastmilk is the leading lifetime source of exposure to toxic contaminants for infants, and may be undesirable for women because of the real difficulties involved.[6] Beyond the difficulty of combining it with paid work, breastfeeding can also be complicated by extreme pain, lack of milk supply, and non-supportive social environments. On the other hand, benefits of breastfeeding include immunities for infants, lower incidence of ovarian cancer and other diseases in women, endorphin release in both infants and mothers, and more affordability in comparison to formula.[7]

What is left out of the foregoing debate, however, are the ways in which breastfeeding is not entirely up to a mother. As any woman who has attempted it knows, lactation is a practice requiring skill, patience, *and* cooperation. It must be encouraged and accommodated by others in the community, and for some women, nursing may not be possible because of a lack of cooperation on the part the child. Thus, the argument in favor of public accommodation for lactation is not just a matter of vindicating that "breast is best," it is also a matter of securing the willingness and cooperation of all involved. When freely chosen and well mastered, breastfeeding can be understood as both a mother-child and communal accomplishment, but a feminist care ethic also affirms the right of a woman to choose against lactation without feeling she has failed, in part perhaps because breastfeeding is not just up to her.

That reciprocity is an appropriate concept for grounding the accommodation of public lactation is informed by Carol Gilligan's fable of the "mole and the porcupine."[8] According to this fable, a family of moles takes a porcupine into their home to shelter it from a harsh winter, only to find that the porcupine's quills are poking the moles and causing them distress. Gilligan uses this fable to demonstrate the differences between a justice perspective, which posits the right of the moles to eject the porcupine from their home, and a care perspective, which recommends that the moles and the porcupine reciprocally accommodate one another by covering the porcupine with a blanket. Reciprocal accommodation as developed by Gilligan is a useful guide for addressing the issue of public lactation, suggesting that women who desire to breastfeed in public and those who find this activity offensive should accommodate one another, but not necessarily by covering lactating women with blankets. Care ethical reciprocity suggests that those who are offended by public lactation ought to avert their eyes, while lactating women ought to make attempts at reasonable modesty when it is not overly inconveniencing.

Milkmen

A feminist care ethic also gives reason to take more seriously the proposal that men develop their biological capacity to lactate, a capacity that is not well known, but is promoted by lactivist groups who call such men "milkmen."[9] The fact that it is not better known that men can lactate with some planning and effort reflects flawed beliefs that necessarily associate women's bodies with childrearing more so than men's bodies. But indeed men have full mammary glands, and their capacity to breastfeed can be developed to the same extent as women's by using a breast pump for around twenty minutes daily for several months, and by increasing levels of the hormone prolactin. It may seem that these efforts are excessive, unnatural, and unnecessary, given that women breastfeed with comparative simplicity following bodily changes in pregnancy and childbirth. Because the female breasts are larger, it may appear that women may more easily establish a full milk supply and get a baby to latch on than men. But in fact men can establish a full milk supply and learn lactational techniques as do women. There are numerous reported instances of men who developed the capacity to breastfeed after the death of their wives, in response to a hungry child, or as a side-effect of extreme hunger. With technological research and control for unwanted side-effects, male lactation could be as readily facilitated as it is in women, with the availability of supplements to initiate or cease lactation, and to increase or decrease milk supply. For many women, breastfeeding does not come easily, and for many, breastfeeding will involve much planning and even some medical or technological intervention (e.g., in

MAUREEN SANDER-STAUDT

the form of antibiotics to fight infections, supplements to increase milk supply, or breast pumps to express milk while at work or otherwise away from the baby). In these cases, women's efforts to breastfeed are prone to be similar to what men would have to do in order to lactate. That most men are likely to be unwilling or uninterested in developing the ability to breastfeed probably stems from taboos against femininity and reticence to share this difficult work. But if it is true that "breast is best," and if we are committed to assuring that all infants get an adequate supply of human breastmilk, then educating about and encouraging men to breast-feed is one promising option for doing so. Another is the establishment of human breastmilk banks, a proposal that could be facilitated by male lactation through an increase in potential suppliers. Such an endeavor would also likely increase the capacity of men to nurture more widely, and establish early bonding between infants and fathers, two goals that are generally desirable.

Conclusion

Public breastfeeding should be readily accommodated out of recognition that breastfeeding meets the basic needs of children, and that supporting this work promotes the social equality of women. Breastfeeding in public is not obscene, and although it may be offensive to some, relegating it to privacy is equivalent to imposing "lactational burkas" on nursing mothers. To make the work of motherhood more convenient, breastfeeding should be welcome in public spaces, including schools, churches, airports, stores, etc., because the welfare of mothers and infants is a central social good. The lack of such accommodation contributes to the need for women to nurse in places and ways that are undignified and unhygienic. Areas for lactation should be provided in both private and public spaces, in order to avoid the implication that women should only nurse out of public view. While lactating women should use some degree of discretion to minimize cause for offense when breastfeeding in public, those who are prone to take offense should exercise discretion by averting their gaze. Finally, men should be encouraged to develop the capacity to breastfeed to benefit infants and decrease maternal burdens. Certainly, if men lactate there is no guarantee that norms will shift to make public breastfeeding more socially acceptable, but this is one social experiment that is well past its "best before" date.

NOTES

1　Gloria Steinem, "If Men Could Menstruate," *MS* Magazine, October 1978.
2　Melissa R. Vance, "Breastfeeding Legislation in the United States: A General Overview and Implications for Helping Mothers," *LEAVEN* 41, 3 (June-July 2005): 51–4.
3　Associated Press, "Ohio Court Backs Co. in Breast-Pumping" (July 2009), available online at www.news.yahoo.com/s/ap/20090828/ap_on_re_us/us_breast_pumping (accessed August 28, 2009).
4　Monica Casper, "The Edible Parts," *Trivia:Voices of Feminism* 7, 8 (September 2008), available online at www.triviavoices.net/archives/voices.html (accessed May 12, 2009).
5　Hanna Rosin, "The Case against Breastfeeding," *The Atlantic* (April 2009), available online at www.theatlantic.com/doc/200904/case-against-breastfeeding (accessed April 15, 2009).
6　Oskarsson, A., Hallen, I. P., and Sundberg, J., "Exposure to Toxic Elements via Breast Milk," *Analyst* 120, 3 (1995): 765–70.
7　M. Picciano, "Nutrient Composition of Human Milk," *Pediatric Clinicians of North America* 48, 1 (2001): 53–7.
8　Carol Gilligan, *In A Different Voice* (Cambridge, MA: Harvard University Press, 1982).
9　Laura Shanely, "Milkmen, Fathers who Breastfeed," available online at www.unassistedchildbirthcom/miscarticles/milkmen.html (accessed August 29, 2009).

KEVIN C. ELLIOTT AND JANET L. ELLIOTT[1]

CHAPTER 11

ON "CRYING-IT-OUT" AND CO-SLEEPING

To allow a baby to suffer through pain and fear until she resigns herself to sleep is heartless and, for me, unthinkable. . . . I don't believe a baby should be left alone to cry himself to sleep.
Elizabeth Pantley[2]

Often, I will refer to ignoring all crying . . . as the preferred solution to help your child sleep better.
Marc Weissbluth[3]

The most serious sleep problems we've encountered are associated with parents who sleep with their babies.
Gary Ezzo and Robert Bucknam[4]

Most sleep problems can either be prevented or alleviated by sleeping with your baby.
William Sears[5]

What's A Parent to Do?

Helping infants and toddlers fall asleep is among the most challenging and confusing tasks many parents face. The mother of a little girl named Susan recounts her anguish:

> Last summer, Susan's night waking had become so frequent that she was basically awake more than she was asleep. . . . So we were getting up as frequently as she asked and rocking her back to sleep. This happened three or four times a night and often took thirty to sixty minutes. Needless to say . . . my husband and I became quite exhausted and began to resent our child. I knew I was in trouble when I would get up and go into the baby's room and yell at her and then begin crying myself.[6]

Some children cause little trouble of this sort, but others seem to avoid sleep at all costs, and virtually all children present some challenging sleep moments.

Parents are likely to become thoroughly confused when they turn to childrearing experts for advice. Some authors, such as Richard Ferber and Marc Weissbluth, encourage parents to teach 3–6-month-old infants to fall asleep on their own, even recommending that babies be allowed to cry a good deal if necessary.[7] Others, like William Sears and Elizabeth Pantley, argue that it is preferable for parents to go to great lengths to teach their children to sleep without leaving them to cry for extended periods of time.

Our aim is to show how philosophical reflection can help parents to navigate these controversies and in the process hopefully get some sleep. In many cases, there are ethical reasons for avoiding a cry-it-out approach to putting babies to sleep. And, for a number of families, co-sleeping is a promising way to avoid the cry-it-out approach. Nevertheless, the relative merits of crying-it-out and of co-sleeping depend on a variety of contextual factors, including the feasibility of co-sleeping safely, the temperament and age of one's baby, and other family dynamics.

Crying-It-Out

It is difficult to provide a definition for cry-it-out sleep approaches because they vary considerably. For example, Richard Ferber, who resists the "cry-it-out" label for his childrearing strategy, suggests gradually allowing a

KEVIN C. ELLIOTT AND JANET L. ELLIOTT

child to cry alone for progressively longer periods of time while he or she learns to fall asleep independently. In contrast, Marc Weissbluth recommends a "cold-turkey" approach, in which children cry at night for as long as it takes them to fall asleep. We use the "cry-it-out" label for any approach that recommends allowing children to cry alone for extended periods of time to teach them to fall asleep. Admittedly, there is no simple threshold for what counts as an extended period of time, but we, somewhat arbitrarily, will count anything more than 15–20 minutes. Keep in mind that the cry-it-out label encompasses a broad range of positions and that some are more vulnerable to the concerns highlighted here than others.

Consider, as an example of crying-it-out, the story of a 10-month-old boy named Ares, whose parents came to pediatrician and sleep expert Marc Weissbluth for advice.[8] Ares slept for only two hour stretches at night and his mother had to repeatedly go to his crib and nurse him back to sleep. Ares's mother was willing to deprive herself of sleep, but she worried that even her son was suffering from sleep deprivation. Following Weissbluth's advice, she put Ares to bed at 8 p.m. using her usual approach, but she did not come to help him when he started crying at 10 p.m. He cried for 45 minutes but then slept through the rest of the night. For several weeks, he cried for about 45 minutes each night, but once he finally fell asleep he slept for about 12 hours. Eventually, Ares learned to go to sleep without crying and continued to sleep through the night without waking.

Ares's mother acknowledges that it was difficult for her to employ the cry-it-out approach. Regarding his first 45-minute bout of crying, she reports, "I thought I would die. My nervous system went haywire. I cried, my whole body got hot, I was shaking and sweating and my heart pounded. *He's going to think I abandoned him,* I thought. *He will never trust me again.*"[9] Proponents of crying-it-out acknowledge that many parents have these sorts of concerns about their approach. Nevertheless, they emphatically deny that it has any lasting psychological effects on children. According to Ferber, "Allowing some crying while you help your child learn to improve his sleep will never lead to psychological harm."[10] Weissbluth similarly insists that there are crucial differences between the "biological awake mode," during which we feed, bathe, and dress our children, as opposed to the "biological sleep mode," when they go to sleep. He insists that concerns about security of attachment are relevant only for the "awake brain" and not for the "sleeping brain": "Insecurity of attachment as a concept makes no sense when the brain shifts to the sleep domain."[11]

But is there sufficient evidence to assert with such confidence that there are no long-term psychological effects of crying-it-out? It isn't entirely clear.[12] Nevertheless, we want to consider a different worry that has received surprisingly little attention – namely, the immediate suffering that the cry-it-out approach causes to infants and toddlers. The proponents of crying-it-out devote relatively little attention to this significant concern. The extended periods of crying displayed by these infants is evidence of some form of suffering. Admittedly, the conceptual schemes of infants and young toddlers are still limited, so we may not be able to ascribe full-blown feelings of "loneliness" or "abandonment" to them. Nevertheless, when they cry upon being left alone in a crib, they are obviously expressing some sort of distress.

Allowing children to whimper on their own for five or ten minutes is not our concern. Books by cry-it-out proponents are filled with stories from parents who had to let their children cry for hours. In most cases, the length of these extended crying episodes decreased fairly rapidly over the course of several days or weeks, and the parents expressed satisfaction with the overall results of the process. However, these are "success stories." Other parents are less satisfied. According to Amy, the mother of a 10-month-old:

> When we tried letting Christoph cry it out, he cried for two or three hours every night for eleven nights in a row. He became fearful and fussy all day long. Since we gave up that awful idea, we've all been sleeping better.[13]

Or consider Mindy's perspective:

> I did the horrid "cry-it-out" method exactly as described by Weisbluth [sic] with my son for 5 straight days at 6 months and then again at 10 months and his sleep habits didn't improve at all. They only were worse at the end of both terrible experiments and he came down with a bad cold by the end of the week both times. I'm sure it was because he was crying all night, literally, off and on for 5 days and getting at most 6 hours of sleep in a 24 hour cycle.[14]

In cases like these, looking to philosophy can be helpful. Three major contemporary ethical theories, utilitarianism, deontology, and virtue ethics, all regard it as wrong to cause such distress to another individual unless there are overriding reasons to do so. Utilitarians argue that we should act to produce the best consequences (measured in terms of welfare or happiness) for everyone affected by our actions. Obviously, they would regard the suffering of crying infants to be ethically problematic unless there would be greater suffering caused by comforting them. Deontological ethical theories focus on a range of duties that we have to others and deny that our duties

KEVIN C. ELLIOTT AND JANET L. ELLIOTT

are determined solely by the consequences they produce. These theorists insist that we have a duty to alleviate the suffering of others, as long as it can be done with relatively minimal cost to ourselves. Moreover, such ethicists generally think our obligations to assist others are greatest with respect to those with whom we have close relationships, such as our children.

Virtue ethics provides an especially strong case for alleviating the suffering of infants. Virtue ethicists think that we should focus on identifying and developing good character traits rather than on determining rights and duties in specific situations. Obviously, our compassion for others, especially helpless children, is a particularly central ethical virtue. From this perspective, it is noteworthy how difficult it usually is for parents to let their babies cry on their own for extended periods of time. The parents described in Ferber's and Weissbluth's books almost always characterize the experience of listening to their baby cry as agonizing. For example, we saw earlier that Ares's mother thought she "would die," and her whole nervous system "went haywire."

Admittedly, there are circumstances in which virtue ethics would not require responding to a child's cries. Children cry a good deal, and it is not always clear why they do so. Moreover, there are cases in which one has to rein in one's feelings of compassion for the sake of achieving other goods. As parents who used the cry-it-out approach frequently note, they were able to tolerate their babies' extended crying because they knew that their children desperately needed to get a good night's sleep. Despite these caveats, the virtue ethics approach, like the other two ethical theories, clearly places the burden of proof on cry-it-out proponents to show that there is adequate reason to override the generally profound importance of promoting compassion toward suffering infants.

Why has such an obvious ethical problem received relatively little attention from those who defend crying-it-out? After all, leaving an elderly person to cry for extended periods of time without receiving any attention would probably be regarded as an example of serious abuse. Although infants probably do not have as clear a concept of being abandoned or alone as elderly adults, their distress is not thereby made significantly less ethically problematic. Perhaps the widespread insensitivity to the distress of infants in this context stems from unique features of our cultural situation. Contemporary Western culture is somewhat unique in thinking that young children need to be taught to sleep independently of their parents. Given this assumption, and given that it is very difficult to accomplish this goal without some crying on the part of the child (and sometimes also on the part of the parents), we might rationalize the resulting suffering as an inevitable and acceptable part of childrearing.

Those who have attempted to justify the suffering associated with crying-it-out generally employ one or more of three major strategies. First, some suggest that, when performed appropriately, the cry-it-out approach causes relatively little suffering.[15] Second, some argue that the alternatives to crying-it-out (such as co-sleeping) cause significant risks of harm to children, either in the form of poorer sleep patterns or the possibility of physical harm, such as accidental suffocation.[16] Third, some suggest (either explicitly or implicitly) that crying-it-out is often the best way to prevent extensive misery for parents.[17] We respond to the first strategy here and address the second and third strategies when we discuss the details of co-sleeping in the following section.

Assessing the suffering associated with crying-it-out is very difficult because there are many variations of it. Moreover, the ways in which pediatricians and parents actually apply it are even more diverse. In a particularly benign case, Marc Weissbluth tells the story of a little girl named Michelle, who apparently learned to fall asleep on her own after only one ten-minute session of crying.[18] In another case, Richard Ferber describes how he helped a child named Betsy learn to fall sleep by herself after roughly three hours of crying on one night, somewhat less the second night, and very little crying subsequently.[19] He also emphasizes that he allowed Betsy's parents to go in and comfort her periodically, although they were not supposed to pick her up.

In other cases, the cry-it-out approach causes much more distress, as author and parent-educator Elizabeth Pantley summarizes:

> My research has shown that very few parents experience this effortless success [of having their children sleep through the night after only one or two nights of crying]. Many deal with weeks of crying for hours each night. . . . Some babies cry so violently that they vomit. . . . Many find that any setback (teething, sickness, missing a nap, going on vacation) sends them back to the previous night-waking problems, and they must let the child cry it out over and over again.[20]

Most parents are probably familiar with these sorts of horror stories of friends who had to listen to their infants cry for many hours, often over the course of several days, weeks, or months, before the children consistently slept through the night on their own. For that matter, we know parents who bought earplugs so that they didn't have to listen to the hours of crying!

Therefore, the suffering associated with the cry-it-out approach varies dramatically, depending on the ways in which parents implement it and on the temperament of the child. In some cases, it probably causes little suffering. In other cases, however, children appear to experience significant distress. As a last-ditch effort to deny that crying-it-out causes suffering, one might suggest that this apparent distress is merely an illusion. For example, Ferber argues that an advantage of his "gradual" cry-it-out approach over "cold-turkey" styles of crying-it-out is that parents are able to go into their children's rooms periodically and see that they are "not really suffering."[21] This is a strange claim. Of course, the experience of infants and toddlers who are left alone to cry themselves to sleep is different in some respects than that of older children or adults. But surely the crying displayed by these infants usually indicates significant distress of some sort, and of a sort that ethical theories find problematic. Ferber himself waffles when he tries to describe the experience of these children. In one sentence, he says, "Initially, as your child tries to learn to fall asleep a new way, he will be unhappy, but he should not have to feel abandoned or deserted." Immediately after, he admits, "If you come in regularly to comfort him, he will feel *less* deserted."[22]

To be fair, part of the reason for Ferber's contention that the cry-it-out approach causes minimal suffering is because he has purposely *designed* his particular version of it to cause as little suffering as possible. The most recent, revised edition of his book is particularly explicit about trying to minimize unnecessary crying.[23] Mild forms of the approach may indeed produce only minimal suffering in many cases, but that is because they *limit the length of time* that children are left to cry, *not* because the children are free of suffering when they are crying. Moreover, even when the suffering associated with crying-it-out is relatively minor, it can still be reason enough to avoid such an approach if there are sufficiently promising alternatives. As Pantley says, "Many (if not all) parents who resort to letting their baby cry it out do so because they believe that it is the only way they will get their baby to sleep through the night."[24] Our next task is to examine the co-sleeping alternative, which, for many families, may well be preferable to crying-it-out.

Co-Sleeping

Just as crying-it-out is difficult to define precisely, there are multiple activities that could plausibly fall under the label of "co-sleeping."[25] Some parents allow their children to sleep in the same bed with them all night long, whereas others merely provide an extra sleeping bag or mattress in their room in case a child becomes frightened and wants to join them during the night. We will focus on a fairly strict definition of co-sleeping, as the practice of sleeping all night with a child who is either on the same sleep surface or within arm's reach.[26] If we can defend the merits of this practice, then any of the other, less strict varieties of co-sleeping can probably be regarded as defensible as well.

As a starting point for evaluating the merits of co-sleeping, it is crucial to recognize that it has been the dominant sleeping practice throughout most of human history, and it continues to be practiced almost universally in non-industrialized societies. A 1971 ethnographic review of 90 cultures did not find any cases where mothers slept in separate rooms from infants who were less than about 12 months old.[27] Of course, the widespread historical practice of co-sleeping does not guarantee that it is still optimal for children or parents in contemporary Western culture, especially once other options become available. Nevertheless, given that practices like breastfeeding and co-sleeping have been an integral component of our evolutionary history, it seems unwise to dismiss them too quickly. Not only does co-sleeping have the weight of human history and tradition on its side, but it frequently eliminates the ethical problems associated with cry-it-out approaches. Because co-sleeping allows infants and toddlers to be with their parents throughout the night, they do not experience the discomfort of having to fall asleep by themselves.

However, there are still two major strategies for arguing that crying-it-out might be ethically preferable. One approach is to suggest that crying-it-out causes fewer risks of harm to children; another strategy is to show that alternatives such as co-sleeping cause too much discomfort for parents. With regard to the risks to children, for example, Richard Ferber argues that co-sleeping could be psychologically damaging: "If you allow [your young toddler] to crawl in between you and your spouse, in a sense separating the two of you, he may feel too powerful and become worried."[28] This suggestion is both dubious and rather ironic, given his quick dismissal of the similarly speculative psychological hypothesis that children will be harmed by being left alone to cry for extended periods of time. More recently, Ferber backpedals on much of his opposition to co-sleeping, including the notion that it could be psychologically harmful.[29]

Another risk to children is that co-sleeping might result in poorer-quality sleep. Evaluating this claim is complicated. In the first edition of his book, Ferber insists: "We know for a fact that people sleep better alone in bed. Studies have shown that the movements and arousals of one person during the night stimulate others in the same bed to have

KEVIN C. ELLIOTT AND JANET L. ELLIOTT

more frequent waking and sleep state changes."[30] The first and obvious thing to note is that the allegedly poor sleep patterns caused by sleeping with other people cannot be too detrimental, as Ferber does not suggest that spouses ought to stop sleeping together! And, of course, it is worth keeping in mind that humans have, as a rule, been much more likely to sleep together than apart throughout their history, although it is clearly possible that these historical sleeping arrangements were sub-optimal.[31]

Another important point is that, even though some research may indicate that children who sleep with their parents have more future sleep problems than other children, the causes behind this correlation are not entirely clear. As Marc Weissbluth notes, parents may resort to co-sleeping precisely because their children have extra difficulties sleeping at night.[32] As with most claims made by proponents or opponents of crying-it-out, experts differ dramatically over whether co-sleeping actually harms people's sleep. In complete contrast to Ferber, William Sears claims that babies and mothers both sleep better when they are together.[33] Given the state of current research, we doubt that the possibility of increased sleeping problems should count as a decisive consideration against co-sleeping for most parents. Ferber himself has come around to the view that "children can sleep quite well under a surprisingly wide range of conditions."[34]

One might still argue that co-sleeping puts children at other significant risks of harm. Perhaps the most important concern is that young infants could be suffocated if their parents were to roll onto them or if they became tangled in bedding. This worry became especially widespread after the US Consumer Product Safety Commission expressed concerns about bed sharing in 1999 and 2002.[35] In principle, this worry could clearly provide adequate reason to override the ethical case against the cry-it-out approach. It is surely better to allow one's child to experience some temporary suffering rather than to risk killing her. The strength of this argument, however, depends crucially on the actual risks associated with co-sleeping.

It turns out that, under the correct conditions, it appears to pose very little risk. For example, in their 2005 recommendations for preventing Sudden Infant Death Syndrome (SIDS), the American Academy of Pediatrics (AAP) actually recommended that infants were safer if they slept in the same room as their parents but on a separate sleep surface.[36] The AAP did not encourage sharing the same bed, but they noted a variety of factors that appeared to make a significant difference to the safety of bed sharing, including whether the mother smoked or consumed alcohol. Although it makes sense that the AAP did not feel comfortable recommending bed sharing for everyone, other authors have argued that it is actually safer than crib sleeping if appropriate guidelines are followed.[37] In the revised edition of his book, Ferber agrees that co-sleeping can be practiced in a safe manner.[38] Thus, while there may still be some parents who have difficulty engaging in responsible co-sleeping arrangements, there appear to be many cases in which it is unconvincing to defend the cry-it-out approach by appealing to risks of physical harm associated with co-sleeping.

A final strategy for defending crying-it-out against the charge that it causes inordinate suffering is to argue that it is preferable to the misery that parents are likely to experience under alternative childhood sleeping arrangements. This is indeed a legitimate consideration, especially given that mothers are now frequently torn between the demands of work and home life. It is widely reported that, even as increasing numbers of women have entered the workforce, working mothers continue to do well over half of their families' housework.[39] Many other men and women are single parents who have to care for their children without the help of a partner. With this in mind, it seems rather cruel to expect overworked parents, who are likely to be suffering from fairly severe sleep deprivation already, to be jumping out of bed throughout the night in order to try to calm crying children. Thus, one might argue that even if the cry-it-out approach sometimes causes significant suffering on the part of infants, it is generally justified if it can help parents to get a better sleep.

The strength of this strategy depends, however, on the range of alternatives available to parents. If they are faced with a choice between crying-it-out and trekking to the nursery two or three times a night, then there is much to be said on behalf of crying-it-out. However, if co-sleeping is a viable alternative, then the merits of the cry-it-out approach are much weaker. Many co-sleeping parents report that they are able to nurse and comfort their children while experiencing very little interruption to their sleep.[40] Therefore, the argument that crying-it-out is the only way to provide parents with adequate rest loses much of its force once the alternative of co-sleeping is considered.

There are other ways in which co-sleeping might inconvenience parents, even if it doesn't cause them to lose much more sleep than those who employ a cry-it-out approach. For example, one might worry about the effect that it has on the relationship between parents. Not only does it make physical intimacy somewhat more complicated, but many adults in contemporary Western culture seem to resent the idea of having a child in bed with them. Some parents might also experience difficulties convincing their children to move to their own rooms when they are old enough to stop co-sleeping.[41] Nevertheless, these inconveniences vary tremendously based on the dynamics within various families. Many people report that the delightful experience of sleeping with their children is well worth any disadvantages that accompany it.[42] In our own experience, co-sleeping with our children was a welcome solace after harried days of parenting. We also found that one of the best ways to start the day is to be greeted by a beaming toddler crawling over one's spouse. If both parents appreciate the advantages of co-sleeping, the difficulties associated with it can be minimal, and the benefits can be substantial.

Conclusion

In many cases, there are ethical reasons for avoiding a cry-it-out approach for putting babies to sleep. Under the three ethical theories discussed here, it is problematic (in the absence of overriding considerations) to leave young children alone for significant periods of time to cry themselves to sleep. For many families, co-sleeping is a promising way to avoid the ethical problems associated with the cry-it-out approach. Although some proponents of crying-it-out argue for its justifiability based on the notion that the alternatives cause misery for parents and risks of harm to infants, we have argued that these are not always significant problems.

Nevertheless, a central theme in our discussion has been the recognition that circumstances vary widely from family to family, and even from child to child within one family. Many children learn to fall asleep by themselves without a great deal of discomfort. Under some circumstances, it might be unsafe for families to engage in alternatives such as co-sleeping. Furthermore, co-sleeping may not work well if parents feel uncomfortable with it. Providing a one-size-fits-all answer for how to get a child to sleep is not our goal. In our opinion, there are already too many parenting manuals with that tendency. Rather, we have tried to show how philosophical analysis can raise important issues for parents to take into account, thereby enabling them to make decisions that accord with the values and concerns of their families.

NOTES

1   We would like to thank Dionne O'Dell for very helpful advice and Justin Weinberg for generous comments on an earlier draft of this essay.
2   Elizabeth Pantley, *The No-Cry Sleep Solution: Gentle Ways to Help Your Baby Sleep Through the Night* (New York: McGraw-Hill, 2002), pp. 5, 23.

3 Marc Weissbluth, *Healthy Sleep Habits, Happy Child*, 3rd edn. (New York: Ballantine Books, 2003), p. 103.

4 Gary Ezzo and Robert Bucknam, *On Becoming Babywise* (Simi Valley: Parent-Wise Solutions, 1995), p. 58.

5 William Sears, *Nighttime Parenting: How to Get Your Baby and Child to Sleep*, revd. edn. (New York: Plume, 1999), p. 56.

6 Weissbluth, *Healthy Sleep Habits*, p. 56.

7 See, for example, Ezzo and Bucknam, *On Becoming Babywise*; Weissbluth, *Healthy Sleep Habits*; Richard Ferber, *Solve Your Child's Sleep Problems* (New York: Simon and Schuster, 1985).

8 Weissbluth, *Healthy Sleep Habits*, pp. 212–13.

9 Ibid., p. 213, italics in original.

10 Ferber, *Solve Your Child's Sleep Problems*, p. 74.

11 Weissbluth, *Healthy Sleep Habits*, p. xx.

12 See Sears, *Nighttime Parenting*, pp. 34–5, 76.

13 Quoted in Pantley, *The No-Cry Sleep Solution*, p. 7.

14 Mindy's review of Marc Weissbluth's book was posted on May 17, 2009, at www.amazon.com (accessed August 3, 2009).

15 See, for example, Ferber, *Solve Your Child's Sleep Problems*, p. 64.

16 Ibid., pp. 38–9.

17 Consider, for example, that Ferber (pp. 15–21, 38–40) emphasizes how hard it can be for parents when their children don't sleep well, that he expresses a good deal of skepticism about co-sleeping, and that he thinks almost all children can successfully learn to sleep well using his approach.

18 Weissbluth, *Healthy Sleep Habits*, pp. 154–8.

19 Ferber, *Solve Your Child's Sleep Problems*, pp. 63–4.

20 Pantley, *The No-Cry Sleep Solution*, p. 4.

21 Ferber, *Solve Your Child's Sleep Problems*, p. 64.

22 Ibid., p. 67.

23 Richard Ferber, *Solve Your Child's Sleep Problems*, revd. edn. (New York: Fireside, 2006), p. xviii.

24 Pantley, *The No-Cry Sleep Solution*, p. 4.

25 See, for example, J. McKenna, "Breastfeeding and Bedsharing: Still Useful (And Important) After All These Years," in P. O'Mara and J. McKenna (eds.) *Sleeping With Your Baby* (*Mothering Magazine* special edition), pp. 3–10.

26 See also P. Donohue-Carey, "Solitary or Shared Sleep: What's Safe?" in P. O'Mara and J. McKenna (eds.) *Sleeping With Your Baby* (*Mothering Magazine* special edition), pp. 11–14.

27 H. Barry and L. Paxson, "Infancy and Early Childhood: Cross-Cultural Codes 2," *Ethnology* 10 (1971): 466–508.

28 Ferber, *Solve Your Child's Sleep Problems* (1985 edn.), p. 39.

29 Ferber, *Solve Your Child's Sleep Problems* (revd. edn.), p. 41.

30   Ferber, *Solve Your Child's Sleep Problems* (1985 edn.), p. 38.

31   For an excellent historical discussion of bed sharing, both within families and among friends, servants, and strangers, see A. R. Ekirch, *At Day's Close: Night In Times Past* (New York: Norton, 2005), ch. 10.

32   Weissbluth, *Healthy Sleep Habits*, p. 78.

33   Sears, *Nighttime Parenting*, pp. 25–6.

34   Ferber, *Solve Your Child's Sleep Problems* (revd. edn.), p. 41.

35   The reports (Release # 99-175 and Release # 02-153) are available online at www.spsc.gov (accessed June 14, 2009).

36   American Academy of Pediatrics Policy Statement, "The Changing Concept of Sudden Infant Death Syndrome: Diagnostic Coding Shifts, Controversies Regarding the Sleeping Environment, and New Variables to Consider in Reducing Risk," *Pediatrics* 116 (2005): 1245–55.

37   P. Donohue-Carey, "Solitary or Shared Sleep: What's Safe?" in P. O'Mara and J. McKenna (eds.) *Sleeping With Your Baby (Mothering Magazine* special edition), pp. 11–14; P. Donohue-Carey, "Sleep Environment Safety Checklist," in P. O'Mara and J. McKenna (eds.) *Sleeping With Your Baby (Mothering Magazine* special edition), pp. 15–16; T. Kimmel, "How the Stats Really Stack Up: Co-sleeping is Twice as Safe," in P. O'Mara and J. McKenna (eds.) *Sleeping With Your Baby (Mothering Magazine* special edition), pp. 20–2; Sears, *Nighttime Parenting*.

38   Ferber, *Solve Your Child's Sleep Problems* (revd. edn.), pp. 45–6.

39   R. Morin and M. Rosenfeld, "With More Equity, More Sweat," *Washington Post* (March 22, 1998), p. A1.

40   J. McKenna, "Breastfeeding and Bedsharing"; Sears, *Nighttime Parenting*.

41   Ferber, *Solve Your Child's Sleep Problems* (revd. edn.), pp. 48–9.

42   Sears, *Nighttime Parenting*.

CHAPTER 12

NATURAL CHILDBIRTH IS FOR THE BIRDS

Carol Burnett described what labor pains feel like. She said, "Take your bottom lip and pull it over your head."

Bill Cosby, *Himself,* 1983

Childbirth is one of the few biological processes in life for which people will seriously consider just accepting or even embracing the pain involved, often for a preference that the process be "natural." For example, we do not distinguish tooth extractions by whether they are "natural" or not and only the extremely rare individual will consider having a tooth extracted without any anesthesia. As the artist Orlan says of women being encouraged to forgo pain medication during labor and birth, "It's so ridiculous because if we go to the dentist's to have a tooth pulled out, just before going, we don't say: 'Hey, I wonder what it would be like to have it done without a shot? Maybe it would be an experience, maybe it would be interesting, natural!'"[1] Why does the use of painkillers seem to determine whether a birth is or isn't natural, and subsequently, whether or not it is a "good" birth? Of course, a baby is not a tooth. However, the challenge here is to articulate just what is so important and valuable about the pain of childbirth. Advocates of natural childbirth bring up the "naturalness" of the pain involved in child-birth so often that – well, the process has a moniker that reflects as much. Natural childbirth is not so-called because of interventions that impact the mechanics of birth. The difference between a natural childbirth and a non-natural one is often simply the use of a painkiller. This seems a bit odd and worth investigating. In this essay, I do investigate this oddity, considering a series of possible justifications for the seemingly common idea that natural childbirth, understood as birth without the assistance of pain medication, is in some sense superior to pain-managed birth. I conclude that it is not superior; not a more appropriate way to approach birth; not more reflective of a proper attitude towards parenting; and not more moral.

Maybe It's Simple Sexism

The simplest explanation is that sexist convictions lead women and men to think that the pain involved in birth is a natural and proper part of the process. This is quite plausible, given that our cultural inheritance includes the idea that it is good for women to suffer and, in fact, that childbirth was particularly designed to bring this about. Any woman who has given birth will likely agree that if maximizing pain was the intention of the designer, then the process of labor and birth definitely seems like a successful design. One need look no further than the Bible to find a designer confessing to having such a plan: "I will greatly increase your pains in childbearing; with pain you will give birth to children" (Genesis 3:16).

As we all know, it is difficult to rid ourselves of old ideas. Of course, sexism can and does bring about different norms. However, when and how sexism is functioning isn't always obvious. Sometimes an action or practice that looks sexist is actually aimed at overcoming a sex-based injustice. An example will help make this point palpable. Consider the overly quick assumptions that were made about the once common practice of giving "twilight sleep" to birthing women. "Twilight sleep" is a cocktail of morphine and scopolamine which induced a state of semi-consciousness. Debate over whether the practice was sexist or misogynistic was altered when medical professionals who actually worked in the 1950s and 1960s chimed in. Workers from that era maintain that "twilight sleep" was not forced on women motivated by a sexist or misogynistic desire to "control" the messy birthing process, as some critics had contended. Rather, they insist it was given in response to the overwhelming number of women who requested (I've been there, *pleaded for* might be more accurate) painkillers. Doctors, however, were in the habit of denying these and of ignoring the suffering of the women involved. "Twilight sleep" was seen, at the bedside, as a great advance *for* women – as a way to empower them and to reduce suffering. Although sexism provides what may be a partial explanation for the norms of natural childbirth, alone it doesn't provide a sufficient one.

Do Not Go Gentle

Rather than, or in addition to, lingering sexism, a fantastical image or ideal might be responsible for the praise we find for natural childbirth. There is an interesting analogy to be made between birth and death. End-of-life caretakers frequently and passionately bemoan stingy pain-killer policies for the terminally ill. The case of pain management for the terminally ill is similar in some ways to attitudes toward natural child-birth because in both cases something, something quite resilient, seems to trump the numerous concerns we typically have for others. Highest among these concerns is typically the strong desire for them to be out of misery! Maybe behind the judgment that a person should die without ample treatment for the pain they are suffering (not necessarily unmedi-cated because non-pain relieving medications are less of an issue) is some half-baked notion of what death *should* involve behind the judgment. Philosophers have had a great deal to say about how to die. For example, Montaigne takes seriously Cicero's equating philosophizing with learning how to die and tells of his constant, even visceral, awareness of death: "So I have formed the habit of having death continually present, not merely in my imagination, but in my mouth."[2] Along these lines, an awareness of the magnitude of the event, it seems, is a requirement for a proper death, maybe even for a proper life. Whether we think death should be feared or embraced, we get the clear message that our deaths should not be pas-sively experienced. As Dylan Thomas counsels: "Do not go gentle into that good night, Old age should burn and rave at close of day; Rage, rage against the dying of the light." Or, as the philosophical Neil Young puts it, "It's better to burn out than fade away."

One major factor behind the praise of pain in dying, labor, and birth is a strong conviction that these events should be faced soberly and somb-erly rather than finding "easy" and "comfortable" ways to deal with them. But why? What makes the idea of an "easy" and "comfortable" birth uneasy and uncomfortable for so many people? Considering the normative force of calling something "natural" could be illuminating.

Universal Praise for the Natural? What About Natural Disasters?

Maybe natural childbirth is considered a good process simply because, in some important sense, it's "natural." However, the meaning of "natural" is not entirely clear. Philosophers have suggested a long list of possible meanings for the term. In one sense, anything that actually happens is natural, because no laws of nature were violated. Nothing can happen that violates the laws of nature, except miraculous and other non- or more-than-natural occurrences. Given *this* sense of natural, *every* birth is natural by virtue of it happening at all. This very liberal sense of natural is clearly not the one in play when natural childbirth is praised, since some births are considered better than others by virtue of their naturalness.

A second sense of "natural" is a matter of what the non-human world does. This sense of natural helps explain why natural childbirth has such an unusual status. Birth is one of the few things we can do in a manner similar to the form it takes in the non-human animal world. However, when we give birth with the assistance of, say, an epidural, this is quite different from birth in the animal world – so much the worse for epidurals. But does this sense of "natural" do any work to justify this evaluation of some human childbirths as better than others? The mere fact that something happens in the animal world does not mean we have a moral reason to mimic it, for not everything that is natural in this sense is good, not even everything that mothers in nature do. For example, many animal mothers neglect or even eat their newborns, obviously contributing to challenges newborn animals face and further reducing their odds of survival. Surely we shouldn't emulate animals in this way.

In addition, it is strange to focus on just this one feature of a non-human animal's reproductive process – the lack of an epidural. There are so many important differences between births among humans and births among non-humans. Consider the fact that many non-human animals, with their far better hip placement, have a much, much, *much* easier time birthing than most humans do. In ways relevant to the pain of birth, we are very much *unlike* non-human animals. So, comparing our birth process to theirs and considering ours good to the extent that it closely simulates theirs is like considering me a good mom solely because I wear my baby in a carrier that mimics a kangaroo's pouch. Moreover, since many so-called natural childbirths occur alongside the many advantages of modern medicine, those modern medical accoutrements alone would disqualify the births as natural in this sense. Hence, this account of natural is a non-starter for our purposes.

A third sense of "natural" is that which calls an action natural when it accords with our evolutionary history, or at least with our particular (and perhaps laughably flawed) understanding of it. This is the sense of natural that is used to condemn homosexuality as immoral because it is allegedly unnatural – "against evolution." This sense of "natural" is not our best bet, to put it mildly. And it seems to me even dangerously immoral to employ it at all; it doesn't take much imagination to see that extreme and unacceptable policy recommendations could be made based on it. For example, women who need medical intervention to live through childbirth, it might be argued, ought to be left to die. Newborn infants in need of medical treatment could be considered detriments to the gene pool and thus better left to die than be treated. This is a form of social Darwinism that we want to distance ourselves from, as it is neither morally recommended nor possible to recommend without hypocrisy.

Fourth is the sense of "natural" that draws on the conviction that anything that comes about as a result of intentional human activity is not natural. If you need a drawing board to dream something up, it's not natural. If you have a plan, it's not natural. Medicated childbirth is guilty as charged. However, so are most births today, given the common practice of writing a "birth plan" well before the big day. The method by which painkillers are delivered in childbirth is, of course, a human design. Even if some would quibble about the naturalness of medications such as aspirin, which was originally derived from willow bark, epidurals are unlike anything to which our ancient ancestors had access. Is there a moral reason to compliment an undesigned approach to childbirth? This is worth considering and I'll return to this suggestion shortly.

A fifth and final sense of "natural" is explicitly ethical. This is the way we commend processes that are in harmony with nature. The application of this sense to natural childbirth is intuitively appealing. It isn't difficult to see how a natural childbirth might seem ideally harmonious. Such a birth might take place in the comfort of the woman's home, with limited technological interferences, with family members present, and with a supportive midwife and doula at the birthing woman's side. Perhaps the midwife is not laconic like the doctor-stranger delivering the babies at the hospital might be.

Maybe mom feels far more at ease tucked in her familiar space, with familiar people, familiar sounds, and familiar smells. Baby is born into the home in which he or she will live, allowing the family to welcome the baby immediately to the space that is their own. This seems right, peaceful, proper – natural. It does, but I personally possess some hard-won data drawn from my own first birth that speaks against this rosy picture. For the reader's sake, and since I am not an advocate of unnecessary pain and suffering, I shall mention the gruesome details only in passing. To fully consider this understanding of the rationale behind the advocacy of natural birth, we must, however, turn our attention to focus more directly on the pain.

Focus on the Pain

Despite the idyllic picture of a home birth, many "natural" births happen in hospitals; it is curious that today the main factor determining whether a birth counts as "natural" seems to be whether an epidural was administered. Why do we not refer to only home births, ones with no monitors at all, as "natural"? Why do we not refer only to doctor-free births as "natural"? Pain seems to make meaningful the distinction between natural and non-natural births. So let's focus on the pain.

Many medication-free childbirths go beautifully – many women do fine without an epidural. Some new mothers report feeling a rush of endorphins and as a result have little trouble getting through labor and birth completely unmedicated. They will likely say it was difficult and painful, but that the pain was bearable. To keep from making a logical error, it is important to note that births like these can be a distraction from the main issue. If a person has a relatively short labor with no complications and if she pushes for less than a few hours, there is less of an issue with the pain, because there is, literally, less pain. The pain can be born (no pun intended) *sans* epidural. We must set such cases aside for now to keep from accidentally substituting them for all cases of natural childbirth, for not all natural births are this bearable.

Recall the fifth sense of natural discussed above, for it offers a viable reason for preferring natural (painful) to non-natural (pain-managed) birth. The suggestion here is that the pain of childbirth makes for a type of harmonious experience, perhaps by ushering the birthing mother into the right state of mind, one of reverence and humility. If so, then the pain adds something valuable to the birthing experience, or, more accurately, the lack of pain removes something valuable from it, perhaps an appropriate appreciation of the meaning and significance of birth.

Although it is surprising to think of pain as something to be praised, even recommended to others, this is precisely what frequently occurs with natural childbirth. So, what might the pain add that's of such high value that is outweighs the pain itself? Some women say that the pain of childbirth signals something different from typical pain. Normally, we take pain as a sign that something is wrong. In birth, the suggestion is that pain signals the right next move to make, for example, when to push, when to breathe, when to rest, and when to *really* push. Most other pain signals only damage to our system.

Whether this argument holds up depends on whether the pain of childbirth only includes the pressure of labor and not the pain of the tearing so many experience in the process. It also depends on all pain in labor being informative about the biological process underway. But these distinctions don't always hold up. Sometimes, for example, tearing may be the "other," more familiar type of pain – the sort that rightly elicits responses such as, "Someone stitch this up!" "Give me antibiotics!" "Help me!!" This pain is often mixed with the allegedly "good" sort of pain advocates of natural childbirth praise. Given the mixture of pains involved, this case is shaky, for unless there is only one kind of pain in childbirth, the kind that allegedly signals what to do and when and how to do it, natural birth advocates do not have a clean case on these grounds.

Importantly, this line of reasoning also depends on the pain of childbirth not signaling anything fatal. There is a very optimistic account of nature and its relationship to us as childbirthers that I am most keen to call into question. One count of the number of deaths from "natural" childbirth each year is half a million women. In the United States we lose only about 600 women a year. But if it is natural childbirth *per se* that we are discussing, we shouldn't consider only natural childbirth in the highly medicalized and wealthy setting of the United States. Natural childbirth leads to the death of half a million women a year through hemorrhage, infection, hypertensive disorders, and obstructed labor in poorer countries. Historically, about 10 percent of women have died in childbirth. This data has helped me better understand my family tree. My family is chock-full of men with second wives. Many of their first wives died during the birth of their first child, dying as early as 20 years of age. It's my genetic lot. When I had my own traumatic childbirth (that was the *official* label!), I could not help but think that in the not too distant past, I too would have been one of those late first wives, leaving my son only photographs of his mother and a proclivity for narrow birth canals and big babies (marry small, I advise my girls!).

Recommending Pain

It's not surprising that people who have gone through natural childbirth often feel superior to those who opted for painkillers. Weaker grounds for self-perceptions of superiority can be found. People feel superior to others for being born in a city with a winning sports team. People feel superior to others because of the way their hair lays, for having long legs, and for having rich parents. Braggadocios are braggadocios and the praise of natural childbirth should have nothing to do with that. On the other hand, hey, if you've rafted the Grand Canyon, part of your pride involves telling other people, "You have just *got* to raft the Grand Canyon." You did it, and having done so is now such a part of your identity that you can't imagine being without it. Moreover, you're proud that you were able to do it. So, you heartily recommend it to others. Nothing strange here, either.

Natural childbirth becomes a more unique recommendation for other reasons. One is the particularly moral tone it takes. It's not just that people say it is a worthwhile experience; the suggestion is that it is an obligatory one. Part of this, of course, is due to its association with better mothering, which, unlike water adventures, is something all women are assumed to be signed up for and interested in. If you tell me you can't believe I haven't been to the Andes, I just might not care. If you tell me you can't believe I put my newborn at risk by undergoing an epidural to reduce my discomfort, well, those are fighting words. Besides, given the complexity of raising children, the way you delivered them is a point of pride that quickly loses its vibrancy. This dulling moment happens sometime after you let your kid eat something processed or after she bites another child during a playdate. In any case, that fight is boring. Only narrow-minded people start it, and we'd have to wait until the children are in their old age to declare a winner.

What is interesting is what makes the case for "natural childbirth" so unusual. When something (home grown food) is praised for being fitting or harmonious, typically pleasure serves as some of the evidence for the praise. Philosophers have pointed out for millennia that despite our intention to make things easier for ourselves, our cultural contrivances cause much of life's hassle, suffering, and discomfort. If something involves or causes hassle, suffering, or discomfort, it is usually judged negatively to that extent and for those reasons. We don't recommend going to the dentist because it hurts, but rather despite the discomfort involved. With natural childbirth, it is precisely the pain that gives it its moral gravitas. But we are usually suspicious of and uncomfortable with pain-mongers. Think of the lack of sympathy a mother who is deemed a martyr might get for her suffering or consider the flinching reactions to a "cutter" (a person who deliberately inflicts harm on him or herself by cutting into the skin). Sure, we are in awe of the guy who cut off his own arm to free himself from being trapped between two rocks, but if we learned he had the choice of extricating himself in a painless way, we'd be majorly turned off by his self-mutilation.

But there *is* a choice when it comes to childbirth! So what makes our assessment so different? It can't just be potential harm (again, as yet immeasurable) to the baby, because people to whom this thought has never occurred still admire natural childbirth. Moreover, as we have seen from the statistics above, natural childbirth is no guarantee of safe delivery of the baby. For advocates of natural childbirth, the pain involved seems to help make labor and birth more thrilling. Where lies the challenge if it doesn't really, really hurt? Where is the triumph in something that anyone can do? Personally, I don't mind this type of thinking. Find glory where you can. Choosing and enduring natural childbirth certainly deserves a position alongside other thrill-seeking behaviors. But like other thrill-seeking behaviors, the choice to have unmedicated childbirth should be carefully relegated to the "optional and amoral" category of behavior.

Maybe now is a good time to share some of my own story. After days of labor and nearly four hours of pushing, I had level 4 tearing (look it up, or don't). I was cursing nature when I was coherent enough to do so, which I rarely was. I lost my vision from the pain; I literally could not think, which admittedly allowed me to proceed without fear, although I think I would have preferred some degree of coherence. I was not afraid I would die, as my mom says she was through all of her births. I was already dead, in some world of pain that was, already, endless. Let's put it this way: it didn't seem strange to me that some animals eat their young when highly stressed. I was out of mind, and the world did not seem like a safe place to me either (and even that is attributing too much coherence to my horrific feelings at the time). But now at least I know first-hand what the alternative could entail when epidurals are called a cop-out. With all my cursing and screaming (I wonder if there is a Guinness record for the most consecutive uses of the f-word? – or at least a Guinness on tap to help numb the memory), I have nothing to brag about. I was a mess. I am certain I traumatized a room full of medical professionals. I threw up on a nurse and wiped my face on her blouse. I really did. Later, I was given apology after apology because the situation had been so dire. No one had realized the shoulder of my baby was stuck until after I had gone through nearly four hours of pushing. All I could say was "thank you" because I was happy to be alive (my blood pressure had been their main concern). I only wanted to know why three epidurals didn't work. No explanations were forthcoming about that ("It happens"). My doctor told me I gave birth in "'I am woman, hear me roar"-style. But I had no other choice.

Humble Mamas

Above, we touched on the possibility that the pain introduces a great and necessary humility at a great and humbling moment of human life, which is related to the notion that human contriving makes a process unnatural. Avoiding human arrogance is indeed morally important. The pain of childbirth might be considered "natural" and good because it is not right for a mother to feel wholly in control of giving birth. Many philosophers agree that humility is the attitude we ought to develop in response to nature, and I can think of no exception to this moral ideal due to context – not that of a biochemist, an eagle-rehabilitator, or a city planner. I can understand why critics of modern medicine's childbirthing practices grow worried upon learning, for example, of the increasing prevalence of planned c-sections. The fear is that these women and/or their doctors are failing to show temerity before a natural biological process, failing to recognize its rightful control.

Unfortunately, in the meantime, the thought of women making their births convenient seems to bring out some pretty dishonest conjuring. The women accused of having babies in this way are described as singularly selfish and completely lacking in the ability to prioritize what is valuable in life. The image suggested is a caricature of an excessively narcissistic, vain, and selfish person with no redeeming qualities, an image that is unlikely to correspond to any real person. Thinking of people, real people who live real lives, in terms of such overly simplistic caricatures is childish and not to be taken seriously. This kind of pillorying doesn't go on about those who simply take an epidural. These evaluations seem gentler but, interestingly, are usually self-inflicted.

Some women feel very bad about having caved in and taken an epidural. Sometimes they blame the doctor for pressuring them, almost always they report either knowing ahead of time that they could not take the pain or learning that lesson very clearly when labor hit full force. Of course, women feel bad about having c-sections, too. Both courses involve an unwillingness or an inability to give oneself over to the natural course of things, which, in the case of birth, involves pain. However, if natural childbirth is harmonious with nature in so far as it involves humbly submitting to what nature intends, then we encounter a bit of a paradox. This is so because any "birth plan" would therefore disqualify that birth as natural. A birth plan is standard these days, especially in cases of planned natural births, but such a plan smacks of the same arrogance that the pain is supposed to correct. As an aside, it is worth pointing out that medical care is not delivered in a manner that is very empowering. Patients are not calling the shots like they order up room service. In fact, critics of "medicalized" births typically talk of how they *fail* to empower the mother. If so, then it is not obvious that having such a birth involves hubris or will lead to hubris in parenting.

The case for "natural childbirth" being properly harmonious might be better made by the potential thrill of victory in birthing painkiller-free. Mothers who take painkillers may be duped by modern medicine into thinking they can't do what they can. Instead of arrogant, perhaps they are excessively humble and overly afraid. They may not understand that their bodies are capable of delivering the child without assistance, that they *could* have the child with no painkillers. Surely more women could endure unmedicated childbirths than do, but why should getting women to recognize as much be anyone's concern? Is the endurance of pain a moral matter? Let's conclude by considering the possibility of this.

Praise Mama

Not all accounts of ethics give mothers credit for the work of childbirth, but virtue ethics can. A virtue ethics approach can look to the process of giving birth and pay moral compliments to the choices a mother makes along the way. The way the mother reacts to the pain – of whatever intensity (virtue ethics is flexible in this way) – can be assessed, along with every other bit of her behavior, to the extent she is conscious and has her faculties about her. The choice to take a painkiller will be just one of many bits of behavior up for assessment. A virtue ethics approach would not categorically or even generally recommend one course of childbirth over another.

According to most accounts of virtue, virtue has an intellectual, a dispositional, and an affective component. When these components are described separately virtue can seem an abstract and theoretical ideal, but we can recognize the effect of the conjunction of these components through simple examples. The intellectual component of virtue would be a matter of knowing the risks – minimal in a Western nation, high elsewhere – of childbirth. Without awareness of this data and the associated biological facts, virtue ethics would regard the mother as operating out of ignorance. What would need to be understood, in order to give moral credit, would also include an idea of how much care the emerging child could require. Virtue ethics would require that parents be very mindful of the responsibilities having a child engenders. And not all children can fend for themselves at eighteen, or feed themselves at seven for that matter. In this case, the breezy confidence that can be associated with natural childbirth advocates could count against them. Childbirth is an occasion of great moral seriousness, and many examples of admired childbirths are those that include the mother operating out of what a virtue ethic would call ignorance.

The dispositional component of virtue is a matter of how propensities have become second nature. For example, in giving birth there will be some quality the woman has developed, consciously, that is at play during the birthing process without conscious awareness. Someone would be able to say of some aspect of the birthing woman's behavior, "Oh, there's Carol, being so Carol-like," as she labors and births. The affective component of virtue is a matter of doing the right thing without thinking that in so doing you have given up on some guaranteed pleasure. For example, virtuous people do not regret not having stolen money in the past, even if they wish they presently had more money. This is because the pursuit of virtue is transformative and helps weaken pleasure's ability to control the virtuous person. Here we see a clear application of virtue to the pain of natural childbirth. A virtuous person would be able to put the pain in context, to understand what it really means and why it is worthwhile – if, that is, it is. And the Stoics, a classical school of virtue ethics, are well known for their emphasis on how important it is to have the right account of pain. They argue that pain is nothing to us. Obviously, this is supposed to provoke some thought. In the ancient world critics lobbed things at Stoics to see them react to the shock of this "nothing" experience. But their view is actually one that supports my conclusion in this little essay. Pain is not part of agency, pain is not something of moral value, and pain should not be what determines one's behavior in a situation. Rather than encouraging a mother to pursue the most painful course, the Stoics are scoffing at the idea that the pain counts for moral credit. It is nothing, when contrasted to your moral behavior. This is not yet to say the Stoics would care one way or another whether you got an epidural. But let me conclude by suggesting that they might just be for it.

A final criterion for moral credit, according to virtue ethics, is that your moral behavior has to be "up to you." If the pain is sufficient to make a person unable to function morally by making her unable to think, see, or concentrate, as was my experience, then she is not acting morally or immorally; again, we return to the idea that the choice of natural child-birth might be amoral. Virtue ethics doesn't say it is always better to be a candidate for moral evaluation. So, again, if you want to risk the mind-numbing effects of pain, that is of no direct moral consequence. But it does seem possible, on a virtue ethics account, that keeping your wits about you, thanks to an epidural, can be a way to maintain your agency in childbirth. I may not be held responsible for all the cursing I did when I had my son. But I certainly held it together, was polite, grateful, and pleasant, for my next two (medicated) births. And I would have been revealing some flaws in my character if I had not acted this way.

Childbirth was, of course, an amazing experience for me each time. The first time, the *traumatic* birth, gave me clear insight into nature's real plan for me. However, as in other times of stress that have completely exhausted me, I found no moral lesson in the experience or in my survival. Not everything is ethics. Humbly, I submit that childbirth lies outside its reaches.

NOTES

1 Peg Zeglin Brand, "Bound to Beauty: An Interview with Orlan," in *Beauty Matters* (Bloomington: Indiana University Press, 2000), p. 301.
2 Michel de Montaigne, "That to Philosophize is to Learn How to Die," in *The Complete Essays of Montaigne* (Stanford: Stanford University Press, 1958), p. 62.

PART IV

IS MOTHERHOOD EVERYTHING YOU THOUGHT IT WOULD BE? FANTASY MEETS REALITY

CHAPTER 13

THE OFF BUTTON

Thought Experiments and Child Control

A Shared Fantasy

My children are delightful, entertaining little creatures and I love them immensely. Yet it is rare for me to have a day when I don't, at some point, wish that I might easily be able to make them stop what they are doing – e.g., crying, whining, failing to get to sleep, doing anything 100 times or more in three minutes, or insistently repeating "watch me!" In these weary moments, I fantasize about turning them off. (Non-parents may wonder why this off time isn't simply known as "nap time," but most parents will understand that "sleeping like a baby" is really a misnomer.) I wouldn't need to turn them off for long. Just for a moment of peace when I need it, long enough to read the newspaper without distraction, or possibly to run out for a quick cup of coffee with other adults. I'm not a TIVO or video addict, but for the overwhelmed mother, the "pause" feature (and the off button) is truly something to appreciate.

In discussions with other mothers, I've noticed that I am not alone in this fantasy. In fact, I'd say nearly every mother/primary caregiver shares it. No matter how well behaved our children are, we all reach our limits. We have our own lives, after all, and they occasionally require a few minutes of peace when our children are least inclined to oblige. So, what if we could design an off button for children? I'm thinking of something that would be inexpensive and easily medically inserted, would have no troubling physical side effects, and would come with a handy remote control. Turning the child "off" would amount to pausing her, putting her in a sort of stasis.

We might imagine that the child herself would not remember being paused, but would simply "wake up" feeling rested. That is, she would not simply continue with her annoying activities (or start yelling about being turned off again), but would rouse herself and consider anew what she might like to do. I suppose it might feel a bit like narcolepsy to the child herself. In the fullest fantasy, the button would work for lengths of time that might require some sort of sustenance for the child – the two week vacation would presumably require a watering and feeding system – but for most uses, that would not be necessary. We need five minutes here and there, or perhaps a few hours at a time to work on larger projects. Think of it – our productivity, our peace of mind, our sex lives, and our ability to *think clearly* would all improve. Daycare workers could enjoy a much needed break. Overwhelmed grandparents could take a rest. Mothers everywhere would have a chance to put their feet up for a moment. We could take back control of our lives.

Thinking About This Shared Fantasy

It sounds very appealing. It's unlikely that we'll move in that direction any time soon; after all, when have mothers' wishes been at the forefront in shaping research and development, even if the technology were at all feasible? Still, it might be informative and entertaining at least to consider the possibility. Philosophers call this a thought experiment. Rather than enacting actual experiments with real animals or children, we think carefully through what would likely happen *if* something came to be. That is, we use our imaginations to help us theorize, and test our intuitions by imagining the world to be somewhat different than it is.

Historically, Plato asked us to think about what we might do with a ring that makes us invisible – would we act morally, or is our morality held in place simply by fear of punishment? We don't have the ring, of course, but imagining it helps us to think about how we might act if we were sure we wouldn't be caught. Similarly, contemporary philosophers have pondered what is essential for personal identity, and they ask us to imagine people whose memories are copied into other brains, perhaps even into identical cloned bodies. If our memories go elsewhere, but our bodies continue to exist, who is the *real* person, and why? Also, what if we were brains in vats with no bodies, only sensory inputs to give us the impression that an external world exists? Can we know that we are not? If not, what does that say about our ability to know anything about ourselves or the world around us? And the list goes on. We test our intuitions with these thought experiments, and then draw conclusions about what matters most for personal identity.

Philosophical thought experiments provide fodder for stories and film – Harry Potter has a cloak of invisibility, Michael Keaton is cloned several times over in *Multiplicity*, and Keanu Reeves discovers the illusionary nature of the world in *The Matrix*. Perhaps the off button thought experiment would also play well as the basis for a movie. But I think it would likely end up being a dystopian science fiction picture. Once we start thinking through the possibilities for the off button, it becomes rather readily apparent that we'd misuse it, with all kinds of negative consequences, and more importantly, that such a degree of control is contrary to respecting children as developing subjects.

First off, we'd *over* use it. We might pretend that we would only press the button occasionally, when we're really fed up or annoyed or desperate to get something done. But convenience is a mighty attractive motivator. I could, for instance, wait until it is my son's somewhat regular afternoon nap time to start work on writing an article or grading papers, or I could just turn him off a bit early. Why hassle with all that business of getting him to sleep? The same goes for my getting a cup of coffee, taking a shower, and getting to work. Why mess with the possibility of interference or dawdling? The off button would be so convenient, whether the mother in question works outside the home or stays with the kids full time. Our lives are busy and our demands are seemingly endless, so the offer of an easy way to control the kids would be nearly irresistible in a multitude of situations.

Not only would we use it more often than we might think, but I imagine we might leave them off longer than we'd plan. Why stop at one cup of coffee and the headlines if you can drink a pot and read the whole newspaper with it? What starts as a short-term pause may gradually become a two hour siesta. Or a way to avoid the cost of daycare. One of the well-known truisms of motherhood is that you get work done in dribbles and drabbles; if a project can't get done with a burst of effort five minutes here and ten there, it's likely going to remain unfinished. Think of Virginia Woolf arguing that we need rooms of our own. The off button would alter that reality. Imagine the relief we'd feel at having more than a short nap's worth of time to concentrate on something. Let's face it – we love our children, but we also have numerous other obligations and interests, and sometimes we feel like we love them more after a break. Using the off button would not only help us to better serve some of their needs (preparing healthy meals, doing laundry, thinking up riveting stories for bedtime), but would also allow us time to satisfy some of our other urges/appetites/obligations; despite the much lauded image of the completely selfless mother, we do have our needs after all!

Of course, while we were busy making good use of our moments of peace, the children would not be getting any benefit. They might feel rested after an extended pause, I suppose, but that wouldn't bode well for bedtime. And then we'd need that button again. Pretty soon, we might just turn them on intermittently, at our favorite times and places, the ones with the greatest possibility of mother-child harmony (say, at the doughnut shop or for the first few bedtime stories). Noticing how often and how long we'd be tempted to use the button, as well as who would most benefit from its use, suggests that this little fantasy is not arising merely from our minor frustrations here and there. Rather, thinking through how we might use it signals an individual desperation for control and reclaiming our selves, and behind that, a broader truth about the frantic and over-extended nature of our daily schedules.

Judith Warner calls this context "the Mess" in her book *Perfect Madness: Mothering in the Age of Anxiety*.[1] "The Mess" is a combination of individual perfectionism, an ideology of motherhood that expects complete self-sacrifice for one's children and puts full responsibility for their welfare on individual mothers, and market norms that make it difficult for most women to have jobs that allow them to afford good, reliable daycare, or the flexibility to work part time while retaining their benefits. The point about "the Mess" is that it overemphasizes individual responsibility, leading to high anxiety and frustration, all the while ignoring the fact that structural changes in childcare and ideological changes in our thinking about mothering would help to alleviate most of the problem.

More important than over-using the button, we'd likely start thinking of children differently, less as little developing people (with foibles and irritating habits, like the rest of us) and more as objects of our control, and for our gratification. We have children, of course, for all kinds of reasons, including some that emphasize our own ideas about fulfillment in life rather than any desire for their independent wellbeing. But once they arrive, children make it very difficult to continue on the path of selfish pursuits.

SARA GOERING

With the off button in place, our level of control over children would increase drastically. Turning them on and off without their consent would clearly be tantamount to treating them as objects, and our relations with them would become even more asymmetric in terms of power. Of course, children are developing moral agents, and so they can be controlled in ways that would not be appropriate for adults, and we think parents who fail to control their children in at least some respects are doing them harm. But in the typical methods of control – time-outs, withdrawal of treats, threats about the future, bribery – we still must deal with their responses. With the off button, we would control them in a way that is radically more powerful than anything we are capable of doing now. A misbehaving child would not simply be sent to her room for a time-out, but might instead literally have time out of consciousness when we deem it appropriate. In the quick fantasy, we imagine that we could keep everything else the same, and just add in the button. But the presence of the button would change so much else about our relationships with children.

Furthermore, the off button would likely lead to a loss of benefits – opportunities for learning and growing – for children. If children came to understand the power of the button (and how could they not, if they see it used with other kids, or simply start putting together the appearance of the remote control with their missed time and refreshed awakenings), they would no doubt fear us more than they do presently. Sassiness or impertinence are a child's way of testing boundaries, exploring their own power, and figuring out what is acceptable behavior. Our responses to their transgressions help them to see not only *that* but also *why* some actions are not appropriate. And they watch us to gauge the extent of their misbehavior. If we regularly turned them off when they got annoying or when they misbehaved, and then turned them back on when we'd had the chance to calm down or rest a bit, that kind of learning would be lost. Children also learn about self-soothing when a parent enacts a punishment and leaves them alone to cry and think about the reasons for it. In our small house, sending my daughter to her room for a time-out doesn't dampen the sound of the crying or repeated accusations: "It's not *fair*, it's not *fair*, it's not *fair* . . ." With an off button, I'd be tempted to shut her down in those moments, rather than listening to her laments. Even when I know she deserves the time-out and it *is* fair, it's tough to listen to my child cry. But I think we both learn a lot by doing it, working through it, figuring out when I should go in and make peace, and when to wait and listen for the often funny discussions she then has with herself: "Mommy will *not* get to come to my birthday party . . . she can make the cake, but she can't come to the party" or "I will *always* let my kids eat candy and their favorite foods." The punishment gives her time to rage to herself and to think and talk through her responses.

Of course, some losses would also go to the parents. Despite our complaining and our legitimate gripes, I think we do benefit from some of the pressures of parenting, even in some of the most difficult moments. The benefits are less obvious, and they come with lots of wrinkles and gray hair and worry, but they exist. When my husband was out of the country for work, my daughter woke up one night vomiting, and continued to vomit every hour. At the same time, I had a new infant to care for, and he woke up each time to join the chorus of wailing. It was a long night, and it wasn't one I enjoyed, but looking back on it, I learned a lot about what I can do (ignore the disgusting volume and consistency of vomit, at least enough to clean it up over and over; get two wailing children back to sleep, one at a time; make decisions about when to call the doctor and when to call friends and relatives for relief). I survived, and knowing that I can do that is valuable. I'm not ready to advocate a Nietszchean approach to life generally (whatever doesn't kill you makes you stronger), but getting through the difficult patches of parenting is empowering and warrants some celebration. The key is to recognize both that some of the difficulty of parenting is valuable, and that eventually we all need help. As a society, as well as within private families of all forms, we ought to ensure that help is available before abuse or neglect occurs. Parenting teaches us, in essence, important lessons about the limits of any individual's control, and the value of perseverance and acceptance and even a joyful appreciation of the non-ideal.

I don't want to give the wrong impression. Being a mother hasn't exactly taught me how to "surrender" to a lack of control. I still work hard at maintaining some control and fantasize about having more. And I am hopeful that mothers may yet band together to create the impetus for social change that will improve our lives and make it apparent to ourselves and everyone else that mothering does not and should not require the full sacrifice of self. But it has awakened me to the realization that a lot of the things I thought I *could* control are simply not in my power, and really need not be, because when I freak out about control, I typically don't improve the situation *and* I miss the unexpected lessons along the way. For all our hurrying and anxiety, children often simply refuse to play the game, and they show us that generally the world will go on, even if we don't make the deadline or have to miss an important meeting because they are sick, crying, or simply uninspired to rush.

Though it's obvious and bordering on sentimental mush, while mothers are caught in the clutches of the rat race, children do teach us new ways to see the world. They make us slow down because their wobbly legs can't move quickly in the early months of walking. In their dawdling, they teach us to see the beauty in sticks and stones, and the magic of bees pollinating flowers. They help us to hear what we say (and how we sound when we say it) by repeating it back to us endlessly, and often at the most inopportune times.

Of course, one might argue that these "lessons" could be proffered even with an off button, that we could get them during the "on" times, and with less frustration and annoyance. No doubt that might be true. But sometimes the most insightful moments are the ones where we would have preferred not to be in the situation at all (and thus might well have employed the off button), and then some little pearl comes into the picture. Once when I was berating my daughter about being mean, insisting on the importance of politeness, and pretty steamed up about whatever it was she had been doing, I asked her (rhetorically, I thought) if she really wanted to grow up to be a mean and rude person that no one would like. She looked up at me and quietly said, "Mommy, I just want to be *happy*." Of course. It's the kind of thing that makes you reassess the value of politeness, as well as the efficacy of yelling about politeness.

Thinking About Our Thinking About This Fantasy

All this shows that, attractive as the off button might be in our minds at that first, glorious, imagined possibility, it wouldn't really be a good idea. Perhaps the real question is why the thought experiment of the off button comes to mind so easily. Why is *it* our collective fantasy, rather than, say, the fantasy of affordable, quality daycare paired with flexible jobs for ourselves and our partners? Here, I think part of the problem is that we face the difficulties we have with the ideologies and tools of our past, the ones that helped to shape who we are. Given a sociocultural setting that places responsibility for rearing kids on the shoulders of individual mothers in private families, we look for answers that individual mothers can employ in private settings. But instead, we might need to break the frame and think about solutions that give up that ideology – social solutions that relieve the pressures on mothers without necessitating troubling technological forms of control.

Similarly, philosophical thought experiments sometimes rely too heavily on standard ways of thinking. Philosopher John Rawls is widely acclaimed for his book *A Theory of Justice* in which he proposed a thought experiment involving what he called "the veil of ignorance." When we are considering what should be our basic principles of justice, Rawls recommended that we imagine ourselves behind a veil that would obscure many of the details of our lives – our gender, race, class, etc. The idea was to acknowledge that our particular life circumstances – circumstances that are not deserved but merely given – often influence our thinking on fairness and justice. As such, his thought experiment is useful in pushing us to recognize the problem of our biases. But as many feminists have warned, we have to be careful about what work we think the veil of ignorance does. How well can anyone fully discard the biases of his position? We may be interested to learn what individuals would say from behind the veil of ignorance, but we would be wise to acknowledge the limitations of those intuitions (given our limited ability to step away from the details of our own selves). As feminist theorists such as Susan Moller Okin and Seyla Benhabib ask, if we really want principles of justice that acknowledge the unfairness of a variety of positional disadvantages, why not just get a more diverse group of people together to explain and talk about their views and experiences?[2] Who can better explain or imagine the difficulties of being a woman in a sexist society and what principles of justice might address them: a man imagining that he doesn't know his own sex, or a woman knowing her own experience? The veil of ignorance thought experiment is a useful device for pointing out the ways that our particularities may bias our thinking about justice, but we have to be wary of what we conclude from performing it. The intuitions we discover in the thought experiment may not lead to principles of justice that are as fair as we imagine them to be, as we may find when we attempt to translate them back to the "real world."

Similarly, feminist philosopher Susan Brison has critiqued personal identity thought experiments:

> Philosophers . . . have puzzled over such questions as whether persons can survive the loss or exchange of their minds, brains, consciousness, memories, characters, and/or bodies. In recent years, increasingly gruesome and high-tech thought experiments involving fusion, fission, freezing,

🦼 SARA GOERING

dissolution, reconstitution, and/or teletransportation of an individual have been devised to test our intuitions about who, if anyone, survives which permutations.[3]

Having intuitions about such bizarre circumstances can be somewhat difficult. Yet, as Brison notes, philosophers have overlooked the experiences of trauma survivors (e.g., from the Holocaust, rape, etc.), many of whom speak in the language of not being the same person as before, even of the old self as having "died" in the incident. This may well be because "philosophers are trained to divert their gaze from the messy real world to the neater, more controllable, and more comprehensible realm of pure thought."[4]

Indeed, part of the reason for thought experiments is to control what is not otherwise controllable. Without a doubt, thought experiments push our imaginative skills, and help us to think about difficult issues. Their general value is not in dispute. What we need to question are the conclusions we draw from them, and perhaps the reasons we employ them rather than other methods of problem solving. Think about motherhood and child control again. It may seem a bit ironic that as mothers, we are inspired to dream up thought experiments for greater control, even as we learn to recognize and even appreciate what we can't control. The off button thought experiment is useful for considering the extent of our desire for control and free time. But our hypothetical musings have their limitations. Why do we fantasize about relatively impossible solutions rather than working together to create real solutions? The thought experiment can be done easily and individually, and it provides some mental relief for the overwhelmed mother. However, organizing mothers to fight for social change, on the other hand, requires great effort and organization. My point, then, is that thought experiments are valuable in mapping a realm of possibility, but cannot replace the difficult task of working together to figure out what matters and how to create a world that acknowledges that. Our intuitions about fanciful scenarios may not stand firm when they come up against actual people, and our aim, after all, is generally to think more clearly and rightly about this world.

My critic may ask, why are you offering a thought experiment as a way to better understand our impulses toward child control if you yourself recognize the limitations of such experiments for understanding our problems and their possible solutions? What I have done suggests a certain irony, I realize. But my intended point is broader: both mothers and philosophers (and those who wear both hats) might need to recognize the limitations of our attempts at control. The flip-side might be that we need to see the value of muddling through without full clarity or even much control. Whether we are learning to grapple with the constant neediness of children or trying to figure out how to better understand the world and its problems, accepting a certain level of messiness and disorder is advisable. That advice doesn't negate the importance of arguing for social change and better support for mothers.

Once we really think about it, the off button would be desirable for far more than children (just think: the spousal off button, the mother-in-law off button, the drunken uncle off button, etc.). But perhaps what that tells us is that rather than wishing for the multitude of off buttons, we ought to think about realistic solutions to the problem that inspires the fantasy. We don't need to turn off our relatives because we can typically just take a walk and get away for a bit. Babysitters provide the same effect for busy mothers who can find and afford them. Break times do it for daycare workers, at least in organizations that recognize their importance. But we need to make these opportunities to get away more affordable and accessible, not the privilege of the wealthy, or of lucky people with helpful, local family members. We need to make them part of the social structure in which we live, rather than the sole responsibility of the already busy and overwhelmed mother. What philosopher Eva Feder Kittay calls "distributed mothering"[5] – mothering work that is shared by multiple caregivers, state-supported, and cognizant of the fact that good caregivers are emotionally involved and therefore not easily replaced – would allow us to share the burdens of mothering, without guilt and without yearning for the relief of an off button.

I don't mean to suggest that philosophers ought to stop employing thought experiments, any more than mothers should stop fantasizing about having some control over their children. My point is rather that we need to think more carefully about what kinds of lessons we can take from the thought experiments we perform, because what we find, through our mental gymnastics, still needs application to the messy real world. Our intuitions about what is right in the context of strictly controlled thought experiments may not matter much when we think about the ramifications of translating them into the actual world. Similarly, mothers ought to think carefully about the sources and justifications of their desires. We may long for an off button, but still recognize that it wouldn't really be a good idea to implement, even were we to have the technical capacity to do so. Children test our patience and occasionally drive us out of our minds, but in so doing, they show us both the limits of our control over the world and the beauty of that limitation.

NOTES

1 Judith Warner, *Perfect Madness: Motherhood in the Age of Anxiety* (New York: Riverhead Books, 2005).
2 Susan Moller Okin, *Justice, Gender and the Family* (New York: Basic Books, 1989); Seyla Benhabib, *Situating the Self* (New York: Routledge, 1992).
3 Susan Brison, *Aftermath: Violence and the Remaking of a Self* (Princeton: Princeton University Press, 2002), p. 38.
4 Ibid., p. 39.
5 Eva Feder Kittay, *Love's Labor: Essays on Women, Equality and Dependency* (New York: Routledge, 1998).

CHAPTER 14

THE VIRTUES OF MOTHERHOOD

The role of mother is unique – quite unlike any other role a woman can occupy. There is no specific training or formal qualification, but the responsibilities are enormous and the skills required diverse. Before becoming mothers, many women have a very clear idea of the sort of parent they want to be, and believe they will be. However, every mother I have ever talked to has had to eat their words. Before becoming a mother, every woman I know intended to be perfect – they would never let their children have tantrums in the supermarket, their children would always be in bed before 7 p.m., only snack on organic carrot sticks and homemade treats, never eat fast food, and certainly never eat it in the car, and they themselves would never lose their temper, swear, eat the children's leftovers, go back to work full time, not go back to work, have tantrums in the supermarket, or whatever. But becoming a mother brings with it unexpected challenges and inevitable complications, even for those fortunate enough to have a baby that sleeps and eats and doesn't cry all the time. After becoming a mother, our previous conception of how we should act can seem charmingly idealistic and, certainly, largely irrelevant. What, then, is it to be a good mother? What really are the essential characteristics or virtues of motherhood?

This essay takes a light-hearted look at the role of motherhood through the lens of neo-Aristotelian virtue ethics. I reflect on the virtues of motherhood – what they might be, where we learn them, and how we might develop them. I begin by giving a brief outline of the central theoretical commitments of neo-Aristotelian virtue ethics. I then make some general suggestions about the characteristics of "good" mothers – what I am calling the virtues of motherhood – and elucidate three of these suggestions in some detail. Finally, I consider how we can come to know these virtues and how they might be developed.

The Complex Unity

Virtue ethics addresses the question *how should I live?* rather than the question *what should, or must, I do?* It focuses on character development, rather than considering which are right or wrong acts; it concerns itself with being rather than doing; and takes as ethically elementary the *aretaic*[1] concepts of excellence, virtue and *eudaimonia*, rather than the deontic[2] concepts of duty, right, and obligation.[3] In combination, these descriptions of virtue ethics provide a reasonably accurate, albeit brief, depiction of the general theoretical approach of contemporary virtue ethicists. Virtue ethical theory has its roots in the philosophical writings of Plato and, more particularly, Aristotle. In fact, all the ancient schools of philosophy propounded virtue or *eudaimonist* ethics of various kinds, not only Aristotle and the Peripatetics, but also the Stoics and Epicureans. All ancient ethical theories shared certain common theoretical foundations, and the same foundations underpin modern versions of virtue ethics, in particular that known as neo-Aristotelian virtue ethics. Perhaps most importantly, all virtue ethical theories take as primary the question of what it is that will enable the agent to lead a life characterized by *eudaimonia* or, as it is commonly translated, happiness.[4] Virtue theories also assume that an individual arrives at theoretical ethical reflection as an adult – as someone already in possession of a set of moral commitments – so their aim is to provide a person with the means by which she can evaluate her life as a whole and assess her priorities in attaining a life characterized by happiness, or *eudaimonia*.[5]

Furthermore, virtue theories focus on the general question of what it is for an agent to live a good or virtuous life overall, rather than on attempts to adjudicate on specific instances of right or wrong action.

To this end, they suppose that, in working towards her immediate aims, each agent has some final good which drives these aims, and in the light of which they should be assessed. The question of the right and wrong of specific actions, then, is never introduced independently of consideration of the final good for humans; in fact, all questions concerning right action have as their point of reference this final good, which is agreed to be *eudaimonia*.[6] While there is some divergence over how exactly to elucidate *eudaimonia*, virtue ethicists all agree that the final good for humans can be characterized by the term *eudaimonia*, a life of flourishing or happiness which the possessor sees as valuable.

According to virtue theory, the way that we can achieve a life of happiness or *eudaimonia* is through our practice of the virtues, through the simultaneous development of our emotional and rational understandings of the right way to act in a variety of contexts. That is, we develop and train our emotions in the right way when our decisions and our actions are guided by our rationality and practical intelligence. The virtuous person, then, is someone who knows the proper way to act and desires to act in that way, and a virtue is a character trait or disposition that a person needs in order to achieve a life characterized by *eudaimonia* (to flourish, live well, be happy, etc). This claim encapsulates two further and interrelated claims: firstly, that the virtues benefit their possessor as an individual; and, secondly, that the virtues make their possessor good *qua* human being, or that human beings require the virtues in order to live a characteristically good human life.[7] Thus, we might say that what I have called the "virtues of motherhood" are character dispositions that not only benefit their possessor as an individual, but also make their possessor good *qua* mother, and that mothers require such virtues in order for them to live characteristically good lives as mothers. For the purposes of this essay, I will take these claims as the foundation for my inquiry.

Any term or concept that designates a virtue specifies a "complex unity of dispositions to act and feel for certain sorts of reasons, and to see and respond to things in certain sorts of ways."[8] And these must be ways that we *can* be, consistent with our best understanding of human nature, and given human psychology. This complex unity of characteristics and dispositions must be something a preliminary version of which we could recognize in our children and thus develop, expand upon, and correct as part of their moral education.[9] In order to specify the virtues of motherhood, we must attempt to discover, or decide, what this complex unity might be which will dispose us to act towards, and respond to, the myriad of challenging contexts and situations distinctive of the role of motherhood.

Endurance Helps

What, then, are the kinds of character traits and dispositions that make one good at being a mother? What virtues do those who are "good" at being mothers possess and display through their actions and behaviors? By and large, good mothers tend to display the same virtues that good people display – kindness, loyalty, honesty, care, charity, consideration, sobriety, humility, perspicacity, and so on. It doesn't take much reflection to see how these virtues dispose mothers to respond in positive ways to the complex and ever changing set of challenges that motherhood puts in their way. Mothers need to be kind, considerate, and loyal to their children, they need to care for them and be honest with them, and be patient and generous in giving them time. Yet they need to have the perspicacity and sobriety to be able to recognize circumstances where firmness must temper kindness, where straightforward honesty is not the best policy, where loyalty to one's child must take second place to some greater good, and they need to have the humility to admit their mistakes and learn from them. There are other virtues, however, that seem more specific to the role of mother (and, perhaps, the role of parent more generally) – selflessness, endurance, commitment, humor, liberality, moral exemplarity, vision, and wisdom, to name a few. In what follows, I will elucidate three of these more specific virtues of motherhood – endurance, liberality, and moral exemplarity – and show why I consider them to denote a complex set of dispositions characteristic of good mothers.

Perhaps most important is the virtue that I will call endurance. What do I mean by endurance? Endurance, as I see it, is a virtue that combines the more familiar notions of commitment and selflessness with what might be called vision. The need for commitment and selflessness becomes clear from the first moments of having one's first child. I remember well towards the end of my first pregnancy thinking that I was truly exhausted and firmly believing that I had reached the end of my ability to cope with the discomfort and the heat – where I live summer temperatures can reach 100 degrees and above. In labor, I was even more convinced that I had reached the end of my capacity to endure and tolerate pain and exhaustion. Moments before my first child was born, I crossed my legs and said to the midwife: "I'm just too tired. I can't do this. I'm going to go home now and I'll come back tomorrow." Of course, that wasn't an option and, finally, my first child was born. Through the haze of adrenalin and the euphoria of childbirth, I remember thinking that now I had done it, and that my reward would be time to myself to rest and sleep and recover – how wrong I was and how deeply shocked when almost immediately I was asked to breastfeed my daughter. And then, what seemed like moments later, I was asked to do it again, then again. The enormity of the *commitment* I had undertaken began to dawn on me. I suddenly realized that, for the foreseeable future, I may not get sleep when I needed it, and I would have to put another's vital needs before my own. While my exhaustion and need for recovery were important, they were no longer my first priority. Only then did I realize that fulfilling my role as a mother was going to require a degree of *selflessness* greater than I had ever contemplated. Now, this is not to say that a good mother should not have her needs met, or that all of the needs of a child necessarily supplant the needs of the mother, but it is just a plain fact of the first few months of mothering that the baby's vital needs have to be a priority to ensure the baby's survival. For many of us, this is a very rude shock – an awakening to a life where our merest whims and desires no longer even feature, and even our most essential needs, particularly for sleep, rest, and time to ourselves, are often put aside.

Very early on, mothering teaches us about *selflessness* and *commitment*, but even more it teaches us about *endurance*. An analogy with running might help to elucidate how the virtue of endurance combines these characteristics. Some people run short distances or sprints, some run marathons or mini-marathons. The process of mothering includes many episodes that can be likened to sprints – the race to produce a butterfly costume by Wednesday morning without resorting to renting or buying one; the race to feed, bath, dress, supervise the teeth-brushing of, read stories to, and put into bed one child, or several children, in the space of one hour, etc. It also contains many commitments that seem, at the time, like marathons and mini-marathons, beginning with labor and birth, then there are the mini-marathons of sleeplessness in the first six or so weeks of a baby's life where they must be fed every three hours, day and night; the marathon of diapers and toilet training; the marathon of teaching children to read; the marathon of the teenage years; and etc. But really, the whole job of being a mother over the long term is more like an endurance race, like the running done by those who run hundreds of miles, across ever changing terrain. Mothering can be a physically grueling undertaking – a role in which each and every step can be exhausting, and always over new and unfamiliar ground. Mothering is a job that requires a certain mental fortitude, a certain kind of vision in order to be successful. An endurance runner will not constantly focus on the end of the run, in many cases because the end of the run is unknown, or there just is no designated end. The end of the race is not of central importance. The focus must be on enjoying each individual step and on keeping on even when everything tells you to quit. But this must be combined with a *vision* of the entire run – the long view – as the quality of each and every step determines the quality of the run as a whole. In the same way, a good mother does not constantly focus on the end of the job, on freeing herself from the responsibilities and commitments of motherhood. To be able to enjoy each step of the journey of motherhood, and to keep on even when you want nothing more than to walk away, is a key part of the expression of the virtue of endurance. But endurance also requires that mothers take the long view, that they have a vision of each moment and every decision as contributing to the development of a child's life as a whole. Being a good mother over the long term requires resilience and commitment – and the ability to focus on one step at a time, while keeping an eye on the race as a whole.

Motherhood requires endurance because it is a hard task and because it is ongoing. Once you have become a mother there really is no end to the job. Even if you are unfortunate enough to lose your child (at any age) you never stop being their mother. You need to possess the virtue of endurance so that you are tough enough to endure the strains and stresses that being a mother puts upon you. This is not to say that mothering is all strain and stress – any mother knows that that is not so. The physical strains and emotional stresses cannot be underestimated, but what gets a mother through, what makes endurance possible, are the joys of motherhood and the feeling of being blessed and singled out as the mother of the most beautiful child, or children, in the world. Someone, without children, said to me once that all she heard from young mothers when they talked together were complaints about sleep deprivation, stories about diaper changing disasters, and general whining about the hardships of having small babies. Thinking this over, I realized that the reason why these aspects of mothering receive so much attention and get so thoroughly discussed is that they are the things that *can* be quantified. We can easily add up how many nights sleep we have lost and how many diapers we have had to wash or change, and for how many hours our babies cried. Mothers tend not to discuss the good stuff much because it is unquantifiable, deeply personal, even ineffable. The love that we have for our children, the joy that they bring into every moment of our lives, the happiness we feel when they first put their arms around our neck, or first reach a milestone, or first smile or smile for the thousandth time, or write us a card that says "drair mum I love you mor then ool the stas," these things are what makes it possible for mothers to commit, be self-less, have a vision, and endure.

A central aspect of Aristotelian virtue ethics is that a virtue can be elucidated as the mean that lies between a vice of excess and a vice of deficit. The virtue of courage, for instance, can be explained as the mean lying between the vice of cowardliness (the deficit) and the vice of fool-hardiness (the excess). If endurance is a virtue, what then is its excess, what is its deficit? For the virtue of endurance, the excess would be focus-ing too much on the ends and not enough on the means; not enjoying the moments for too much focus on the end. The deficit might be not seeing the big picture of the life that you are responsible for shaping and setting forth. If every action in the present is focused on dealing with the present situation with no vision of the child's life as a whole, with no view to help-ing to form a good person in the long term, it will turn out that we are probably not good mothers. It is very easy as a mother when you are tired and overwrought to give in to your child's demands in order to make life pleasanter in the short term. This is often a mistake because it can set a precedent for both mother and child, which can very quickly erode important standards. If every time a child demands something not good for them we give in to avoid a confrontation in the short term, the long-term picture begins to look more and more problematic. However, there is a mean here: the deficit is giving in to every short-term whim and thus allowing a child to become demanding and spoiled, while the excess is a kind of authoritarianism. You cannot stand on principle about every-thing and unyieldingly maintain every standard. We have all had the experience of eating our words – what may have seemed an extremely important standard from a perspective outside hands-on motherhood can turn out to be largely irrelevant. When children reach the age of per-haps two or three they start to assert their independence and their own desires, and they start to have tantrums when they do not get these desires fulfilled. A mother cannot yield to every single one of these desires, but nor can she deny every desire either. She has to decide what things will make a difference over the long term, she has to have a vision of the future, and to decide which things are worth fighting for. But sometimes there is little to be gained by insisting, as many of our ideal standards turn out on reflection to be dispensable or merely arbitrary whims. Why should my desire to have my son wear jeans overrule his desire to remain in pajamas, on every occasion?

Knowing When to Let Go

This brings me to what I consider to be a second important and intimately related virtue of motherhood: the virtue of liberality, or the virtue of knowing when to let go. A good mother will be liberal with her child, allowing them the freedom to make their own mistakes and live their own life, even from an early age. Of course, a mother has to possess the virtues of perspicacity and wisdom in order to know how to display liberality depending upon the needs and maturity of their child. For young children, the matters about which we need to be liberal are minor and can seem almost insignificant to us. But they are not insignificant to children; to children, the freedom to make their own decisions and to exercise their individual will is very important. What, then, is the vice of deficit and what the excess, between which the virtue of liberality lies? The excess is obvious: giving one's children no boundaries, allowing them to do whatever they want with no guidance and no consequences. There is nothing less wonderful than a small child for whom everything is permitted without restraint or moderation. Unlimited liberality is not only damaging emotionally and socially, it is dangerous. The deficit is also clear: being too controlling, overbearing and authoritarian. Children must be given opportunities to make their own decisions and the guidance to learn how to make decisions responsibly. Children should not be wrapped in cotton wool and over-protected, for how do we learn without experiencing the world for ourselves? Of course, the natural inclination of a mother is to protect her child, but this inclination to protect must be tempered by exercising the virtue of liberality, by knowing when to let children try things out in the world, and how much to let them try, and how much to protect them. The mandate for a mother, and for a parent more generally, is to teach their children and guide them into a position from which they can make rationally informed and balanced choices for themselves, so that they achieve a life of flourishing.

Following Your Example

The role of a mother is to provide a moral example for her children. However, while a good mother's life is intimately concerned with the welfare and development of her children, she must have a life of her own. Rather than letting one's children think that their mother's life revolves around them, it is important to teach them that every person needs to have a life of her own and her own interests to achieve *eudaimonia*. If this is properly understood as a virtue, then the deficit would be not giving one's children enough time through not having enough time to give. Making your own life your priority and expecting your children to always fit in around it is not fair. Because children are unable to fend for themselves and cannot meet many of their own needs, mothers must be, at least to some extent, selfless by making the needs and wellbeing of their children a priority. The vice of excess here might be characterized by a mother living exclusively through and for her children. There are many ways that this excess is manifested; for example, using one's children as an excuse not to fulfill one's own life goals. The mother who spends all her time organizing children's outings and activities without pursuing any interests of her own is not necessarily being a good mother. While many people may think that sacrificing one's own life for one's children is the hallmark of a good mother, I dispute this. If children think that the role and duty of a mother is to sacrifice one's life for them, female children may not want to become mothers and male children may tend to treat females as if this were their only option. Being a parent entails teaching one's children to be good people, to live good and full lives. If you cannot fulfill your own life, if you cannot achieve your own goals and happiness, it is unlikely that you will be able to teach your children to do so. It is one thing to be happy for your children and to share in their achievements and successes, but quite another to make their happiness your only happiness.

Imitation is the Highest Form of . . .

How do we learn these virtues? Largely by example. Children take as a model their parents' behavior. We have to show our children how a good life is lived. There is obviously a balance to be struck here. Mothers have to make sacrifices for their children, but the sacrifices that they make should only be those that they can make with a good grace. A mother who sacrifices everything for her children, and then resents them for what she lost by doing so, sets no good example. A mother who refuses to make any sacrifices for her children, and continues to live her life exactly as she did prior to motherhood, sets no good example either. And there is no good example in a mother who feels that she has not fulfilled her own goals and expects her children to make up for her deficit. I know well a child who by the age of three was learning French, the viola, and taking swimming and gymnastics lessons, as well as attending full-time preschool at a prestigious ladies academy, presumably the very same prestigious ladies academy her mother attended – and failed to learn French and a musical instrument, or become a champion swimmer or Olympic gymnast.

As teenagers we often tend to be critical of our mothers, and our own strong ideas of what mothers should be like tend to be shaped in opposition, rather than in conformity, to our exemplars. However, unless we have had an unusually dysfunctional upbringing, when it actually comes to the point where we have our own children, we end up with a far greater insight into what our parents did right and what, if anything, they really did wrong. Most of us have tut-tutted at the mother in the supermarket who is struggling with a screaming 2-year-old desperate for the candy so helpfully placed at eye level at the checkout. Most of us have thought smugly to ourselves that our children would never behave in such a manner. Becoming a mother puts us in the position of that other mother, not only struggling with a screaming 2-year old, but also having to behave with equanimity, as people around you look judgmental and mildly disgusted. Becoming a mother shows us that mothers receive an unfair share of the blame in the world, and thus teaches us not to be judgmental of other mothers, especially our own. Becoming a mother, we learn that there are many ways to do a job well, and that there are many things that may have seemed essential aspects of a so-called proper upbringing, which turn out to be unimportant. Of course, there is a balance to be struck here. There are some aspects of mothering that are not negotiable – child protection and safety, for instance. However, we can discuss and perhaps agree on what it is to be a good mother – what the virtues of motherhood really are – and we can strive to embody them. But having excellence as a goal does not give us license to judge others against our personal conceptions of what constitutes a good mother.

I have outlined three key virtues of motherhood – endurance, liberality, and moral exemplarity – under the typically difficult circumstances that would be familiar to all mothers. I have written this essay while, for instance, having my hair styled by a 3-year-old, who is also refusing to eat or to get in the bath, in fact refusing to acquiesce to any of my wishes. And, for instance, after spending the day in the role of announcer at a gymnastics competition, having endured the skepticism of a 6-year-old worried that I would not be skilled enough to do her gym hairstyle to the standard of the other moms. I suppose I should not complain, at least I haven't had to go to the supermarket with a 2-year-old. I might also mention that my own mother who, after more than forty years in the role, is still committed and selfless enough to have given up an evening to proofread this essay, without too much complaint. Fortunately for her, endurance is one of her virtues, because she certainly has needed it.

NOTES

1 *Aretaic* means pertaining to the virtues, *arete* being the ancient Greek word for virtue or excellence.
2 *Deontic* means pertaining to duty, coming from the Greek word *deon* meaning duty, obligation, or necessity.
3 Rosalind Hursthouse, *On Virtue Ethics* (Oxford: Oxford University Press, 2001), p. 24.
4 *Eudaimonia* is most often translated as "happiness." While the preceding description is not exactly what we often mean by happiness, it seems that "happiness" is the best available translation of the ancient concept of *eudaimonia*. Other translations have been offered, including "flourishing," "wellbeing," and "success," but for the purposes of this essay and where necessary "happiness" will be used as the closest English equivalent of *eudaimonia*.
5 Julia Annas, "Naturalism in Greek Ethics: Aristotle and After," *Boston Area Colloquium in Ancient Philosophy Proceedings* 4 (1987–8): 149–71.
6 Ibid., p. 152.
7 Hursthouse, *On Virtue Ethics*, p. 20.
8 Ibid., p. 160.
9 Ibid.

CHAPTER 15

THE MEDIA PROUDLY PRESENT

"Lessons" From Celebrity Moms

Meet the Celebrity Moms

Stories of celebrity moms are very familiar. Pregnant celebrities are a focus of magazines, and huge sums of money are paid for the first pictures of celebrity babies. Celebrity moms are routinely categorized as "good" or "bad" and we are aware of how these moms are behaving at virtually any point in time. For example, in 2008, Britney Spears came under intense media scrutiny and was usually represented as having a breakdown. During this time she was widely considered to be unfit to care for her children. Similarly, there was a lot of concern in the media about party girl Nicole Richie's pregnancy and whether she was fit to be a mom. In contrast, celebrities such as Angelina Jolie and Jodie Foster are widely celebrated as mothers. Celebrity fathers, however, are generally not held to the same scrutiny, suggesting that fathers are still not expected to participate in childcare activities and aren't judged harshly when they do.[1] As such, traditional gender roles are arguably still entrenched in the division of household labor and the care of children,[2] with women still being expected to undertake the majority of this work.[3]

Sociologist Sharon Hays argues that to be considered "good," mothers are expected to be selfless, loving and nurturing and to make children their first priority.[4] This means that women in many Western societies are expected to mother "intensively." In short, intensive mothering requires that mothers put their children first. Unconditionally. *If* mothers also participate in paid employment, those efforts and commitments must always be second to caring for children. Fathers are not typically expected to conform to this intensive method of parenting and are instead still widely regarded as breadwinners.[5] In media representations of mothers, the ideal championed by intensive mothering philosophies can be seen very clearly.[6] The media offers mothers a continuous supply of images of primarily heterosexual mothers who excel at housekeeping, managing their looks, pleasing their partners, and caring for their children. Advertisements push products that will give us "softly lit, plug-in scented, flower filled" homes,[7] sitcoms represent mothers as responsible for children while their male partners are the family's sole source of revenue, and magazines give readers examples of good mothers offering advice on everything from the benefits of prenatal music to planning for an infant's future college education.

This obsession with the ideal of the "good mother" is clear in the recent explosion of images of the celebrity mother. These representations let us peer into the lives of celebrity women who become mothers, enabling us to judge *and* idolize them. Articles in popular magazines give us more than we ask for: "How Hollywood Moms Get Thin so Fast"[8] offers tips on losing weight and images of how good a new mom can (and, *ahem*, should) look; "Celebrity Moms Love Mountain Buggy Strollers"[9] tells the rest of us what everyday products are the most properly desired; "Regular Mom Katie Holmes takes Adorable Suri for Fun in the Park"[10] shows mothers how to be relaxed and stylish while caring for their relaxed and stylish children. In these and similar stories, intensive mothering philosophies are reinforced with images of women who either put their careers on hold or somehow manage to have it all, combining motherhood with personally fulfilling lives and careers and, somehow, always managing to put their children first.[11] On the other hand, celebrity mothers who fail to meet this ideal are labeled as "bad" by the media, giving readers the opportunity to judge these celebrities as lesser moms than themselves.

CLEMENCE DUE AND DAMIEN W. RIGGS

How and to what extent are these messages about celebrity moms taken on board by audiences? Do readers receive these messages uncritically, developing opinions about certain mothering practices and certain celebrity mothers based solely on the images and stories they read in glossy magazines or see flickering across the TV screen? Or, are readers more critical, making decisions for themselves about whether the information is enough to label a mother as good or bad?

To study how stereotypical mothering messages in the media are received, students in three of the authors' psychology classes at the University of Adelaide were asked to read four different articles from "glossy" magazines about celebrity mothers, and to respond to the images presented in them. The articles present different facets and images of mothering. Through discussion we were able to assess how the participants in the study read the articles and whether they passively absorbed, critically considered, or even extrapolated beyond their messages. Participants worked in small focus groups, reading through each article and discussing the mothers and parenting practices represented in the stories. Participants included both younger and mature-aged students, as well as mothers, fathers, and some who were not parents.

The first article is "Toxic Mummy," an article about Britney Spears' custody case, a case in which she risked losing her two boys for behaving badly by partying, getting drunk, and acting as if she "had no idea what to do with [the boys]."[12] The next article discusses Angelina Jolie and the claims made by the mother of the girl she had adopted from Ethiopia, Zahara, who said she wanted her daughter back. The article focuses on Jolie's passion and love for her children, as well as her celebrity status.[13] The third article, "Jodie Foster Opens Up About Motherhood," discusses Jodie Foster's experiences and day-to-day activities as a mother.[14] Finally, the participants read an article discussing Nicole Richie's new role as a mother, how her life changed after having her baby, and whether or not she was coping well.[15]

How to be a Good Mother

The articles examined contained comments on the "good" or "bad" status of the mothers involved, offering evidence that these women were or were not doing a good job in their mothering roles. The articles set the bar high for these celebrity mothers. The value judgments made about the celebrities' mothering were reflected in participants' conversations, as they even commented on the extent to which these celebrities were worthy to mother their children.

Of the four articles, the one about Jodie Foster was generally considered by participants to be about a "good mother." This article received comments such as "with Jodie Foster, she's a good mom – she talks about the common tasks she has to do feeding fish, taking the cat to the vet, feeding her son, mending her son's clothes, so the common activities you think of when you think mom," and "Jodie Foster is the housewife staying home, mending clothes, doing the cooking and whatever, so she's constructed as that nurturing, down to earth practical stay at home mom that you can relate to." As such, Jodie Foster is seen as a "good mom" because she is portrayed as performing many of the tasks mothers "ought" to perform. The article rarely mentions her status as an actor, instead focusing on her role as a mother, quoting Foster as saying that occasionally,

> I'll have one of those days when I've fed the fish, cleaned 10 poops from the patio, taken the cat to the vet, sewn my son's stupid karate stars on until my fingers bleed . . . But there's absolutely no sort of acknowledgment or reward for this.[16]

Foster is portrayed as the all-sacrificing, loving mother who does everything for her children. This was conveyed to the participants, who frequently described Foster as a good mother due to the fact that she was depicted as performing "motherly" tasks. Interestingly, Jodie Foster was also described by many participants as a "normal" mom, often due to the fact that the article did not frequently draw on her status as a working, celebrity mother. For example, one student remarked that Foster was represented as "a really good mother" with another agreeing, remarking "yeah, all the hard work she does. And she knows it's still not enough." A third student summed this up succinctly by commenting that "Jodie Foster is portrayed as a good mom – a normal mom." So, although "good" mothers clearly have to devote extensive time to their children, they should also know it is "still not enough." Good mothers, as Hays writes, can never do enough for their children.[17] This is also the mark of a "normal" mother who focuses on her children rather than her career, or indeed, herself.

Interestingly, Foster's status as a lesbian mother was not commented upon in either the article or by the participants. Previous research has typically identified negative attitudes towards lesbian mothers,[18] but there was no negativity towards Foster in our focus groups on this account.

CLEMENCE DUE AND DAMIEN W. RIGGS

This is perhaps because participants judged the women in the articles purely on their mothering ability and rarely commented on the lack of discussion about the women's partners or absence thereof.

Angelina Jolie, however, did not garner the "normal" label, despite the fact that Jolie was also discussed as being "good," although to a much lesser extent. Instead, Jolie was most often referred to by participants as a "savior" because she has adopted so many children. This was seen in comments such as "she plans to adopt more kids, it says, along with her others already, has three other adopted kids, which makes her like a savior," and "Angelina is a celebrity interested in helping other people – using her money rescuing toddlers from near death – rescuing Africans and unwanted AIDS orphans." As such, the image attached to Jolie is not so much that of a good mother, but rather that of a savior. It's worth noting that the article doesn't discuss Jolie participating in traditional household tasks or everyday mothering activities like taking her children to the park. The article focuses on her adopting a child from Africa. Thus, while still about her "mother" role, it seems the fact that the article did not represent Jolie as participating in traditional female activities excluded her from being "good" in the same way as Foster.

The article about Nicole Richie largely positioned Richie as the "bad-girl-come-good-mom," a woman positively transformed upon becoming a mother. This was reflected in comments made by participants. For example, one participant remarked that the article says, " Nicole is loving motherhood and proving she can have it all," presenting an image of "her as having this whole package thing going on, kid, job, etc. . . . It also says she has come a long way from earlier, with Paris she was always trashy – partying and drinking." As can be seen, this participant placed her own value judgment on Richie, stating that before motherhood Richie was "trashy," but "had come a long way." She is now able to be a "good mother," as she no longer engages in these activities and is such a homebody she sometimes "doesn't leave the house for days."[19] This conforms to expectations placed on women to feel that motherhood is a transforming experience, which, of course, has to be for the better rather than the other way around!

Working Mothers

"Having it all" is another theme in the Richie article. The article states Richie is still working on her fashion label, and is therefore successfully combining work and motherhood. However, participants were quite clear they only considered her a good mother because her focus is now her baby, with her work coming second. This is reflected in comments such as, "she is a good mom as well and is managing to balance her career as well and only do minimal amounts of work." Thus it is to Richie's credit that she is able to "have it all," but this hinges on her prioritizing her child and "only doing minimal amounts of work" rather than working on a more full-time basis. This logic was not applied to her partner and baby's father, Joel Maddon, who was not drawn into the good/bad parent debate, despite the fact that he featured fairly prominently in the article and was away on tour, leaving Richie to care for the baby. Maddon wasn't "only doing minimal amounts of work," yet this was not picked up on or discussed by participants.

Similarly, it could be the case that participants did not apply the "good" mother label to Angelina Jolie because the article discussed her celebrity (and therefore, her working) status to a greater extent. Participants indicated they felt a tension between Jolie's ability to be a good mother while devoting significant time to career pursuits. For example, one participant stated, "she is the biggest celebrity for mothers, she's more of a celebrity because of how she is doing motherhood, going out and adopting children is what she is known for," while another commented, "Angelina, . . . she isn't a normal mother. She's still in the spotlight." It might be argued that "normal" here simply means not a celebrity, but this could also be read as suggesting that since Jolie has pursued her career throughout having children, she is unable to be called normal or good in the same way that Foster is. In fact, both women continued to work after they had children and the participants in this study were simply reacting to the messages they received in the articles they were reading.

How to be a Bad Mother

Keen to discuss how motherhood changes the lives of the party-women who now spend days on end without leaving the house, the media are also eager to demonize mothers who continue to act as they did in their pre-motherhood days. This was certainly the case with the Britney Spears "Toxic Mummy" article. This article explores the scrutiny Spears is under as a mother, citing as evidence her friends' concerns that she would overdose, her sexually suggestive behavior in public, and how she seems "unable to relate to her own children," supported by the observation that she was "picking them up and putting them down again."[20] In general, the negative depiction of Spears in this article was endorsed rather than criticized by participants, who were also frequently eager to add their own opinions about Spears' "bad" mother status. As one participant remarked, although "it says what she is doing is not abusive in the traditional sense, not abusive – she's not hitting her kids," nonetheless, because "she has no routine or anything," "she's still not a good mother." A conversation among participants ensued, one observing that "it actually says that she picks [the children] up and puts them down again – and doesn't know what to do with them," with another chiming in, "yeah so they're just like an accessory to her." A third goes further, remarking that "she obviously is going out partying and drinks, she is depressed all the time." Participants also seemed concerned about her maturity, stating that she is "so young . . . only like, barely 20."

These brief excerpts illustrate how participants frequently picked up on the negative "bad mom" images of Britney Spears, and expanded upon them with their own views; for example, it seemed to them the children were "just an accessory" and that "she is still not a good mother," even though the article stated that she was not abusive in the traditional sense. This is so despite the fact that some, perhaps most, of the behavior Spears is accused of exhibiting is not rare among mothers, even those we consider "good" mothers. Many mothers may have periods of time when they feel at a loss as to how to care for their children and many mothers may go through periods of depression. It's also true that many moms enjoy a glass of wine or two with friends occasionally, although the paparazzi are, thankfully, not recording every mom's every sip. These counter-arguments were not utilized by participants, who instead made comments extending the claims made in the article about Spears' "bad" mother status.

Conclusion: Mothering as Boring

Despite the mass media's fascination with celebrity mothers, the day-to-day effort involved in "mothering" and the commitment and serious work mothering requires are still undermined and devalued within our society. This was especially evident in our data in relation to the Jodie Foster article in which Foster, who received the most comments about being a good or normal mother, was also frequently dismissed as boring.

One participant explained that articles about bad mothers are more exciting than about good mothers, stating "they can't have an article that says that she likes being a mother because that's too boring." Another says outright that the article about Foster is boring, implying that motherhood is as well: "this article doesn't say bad things about Jodie or motherhood or anything, it is a very boring article actually, talks about general life and how things are . . . it is a pretty boring article."

Participants in this study frequently stated that they were unlikely to find it entertaining to read about the day-to-day workings of motherhood, despite the fact that they reinforced the model of intensive mothering as being "normal" or "good." This means that although mothers are expected to devote large amounts of time to caring for children, they remain unglorified and ignored for doing so and are generally considered boring. This dichotomy reflects the tensions Hays finds at the essence of intensive mothering: the requirement for mothers to intensively care for their children to the exclusion of all else at a time when the Western world values most the competition and individualism of the marketplace.

Douglas and Michaels state that the media reports they examined made it appear as though "celebrity mothers loved their kids unconditionally all the time; they loved being mothers all the time. . . . They had everything under control and their children were perfect because the celebrity moms always did everything right."[21] Participants were given an article, (the Spears article) in which this was not the case, but our study does support the claim that celebrity moms were required to behave in this selfless and perfect way to be considered good mothers.

The "good" or "bad" mother themes running through most of the articles were generally picked up on uncritically by participants; indeed, participants often went further to offer their own opinions on the celebrity moms. When asked later whether or how the articles were constructing arguments, the majority of the participants said the article did not argue for or against anything – just that it reported it. One participant stated that Britney Spears was "going through stuff which makes her a bad mom" and that this is what the article was about. The participants in the study frequently took on the messages contained in these articles uncritically, as can be seen in one participant's description of the article about Nicole Richie. She says the article "is not really an argument. It starts off saying she was this sort of person but now she is a mom she has changed and is getting better and taking her baby to toy shops."

In most cases the articles managed to impart a message about "good" or "bad" mothering to their audience, and in doing so they drew upon intensive mothering philosophies whereby children had to be the first priority of mothers. This was seen in the article about Jodie Foster, who was considered a good mom because of all the time she spent with her children and the fact that the article represented her as doing stereotypical "mom" work, for example, cooking, cleaning, and sewing. Ironically, this also made her and the article boring and the fact that the magazine reported such a story meant that the magazine must be "desperate" for material. While subscribing to intensive mothering philosophies which place children first and career and everything else second, a requirement is still placed on "good" mothers, namely, that they engage exclusively in "boring stuff."

The Angelina Jolie article, however, was not considered "boring." Jolie was primarily discussed as a savior in our focus groups, with some apparent hesitation to call her "good," perhaps because the article did not focus solely on her mothering role, but also her celebrity status. Interestingly, all of the articles were about women with careers, but the extent to which the articles focused on the women's preoccupation with mothering and their willingness to forsake their careers determined whether they were thought good or bad.

In contrast to Jolie and Foster, Britney Spears was considered "bad" because she has yet to give up her pre-motherhood party lifestyle and doesn't appear to have the innate mothering knowledge good mothers are presumed to naturally possess and effortlessly exercise. The "bad" mothering discourse was taken up by participants most enthusiastically, with conversations frequently straying from the article itself to more informal discussions of personal opinions and speculations concerning Spears' mothering ability.

The Nicole Richie article stated that Richie had given up her party lifestyle upon becoming a mother. Therefore, due to toy shopping trips and days without leaving the house, she was considered a "good mom." This was offset, however, by the fact that there were reports that she was "stressed" and "not coping," which frequently led participants to predict she was on the brink of behaving badly once again – that her transformation from "bad girl" to "good mom" may not be complete or permanent.

Mothers were largely only considered "good" where they were represented as giving up their lives for their children and performing household tasks which mothers stereotypically undertake. Moreover, participants seemed to believe no non-mother would willingly choose to undertake these tasks due to their boring monotony. This was not the same for fathers, who rarely entered the conversations. Clearly, the relative lack of celebrity dad articles in our magazine front pages reflects the lack of interest in the topic, and hence the relative lack of judgment, positive or negative, on fathers. Good mothers were required to be or become selfless devotees to their children. They were, in addition, also under constant threat of becoming bad when there were any signs they may not be dealing well with the many pressures mothering brings.

The fascination with celebrity mothers and whether they are "good" or "bad" reinforces many of the stereotypes surrounding how children should be parented. As Douglas and Michaels write, "Celebrity mom portraits resurrect so many of the stereotypes about women we hoped to deep-seat thirty years ago: that women are, by genetic composition, nurturing and maternal, love all children, and prefer motherhood to anything, especially work, so should be the main ones responsible for raising the kids."[22] Indeed, as we found, where celebrity mothers are *not* represented in this manner, they are not seen as "good" mothers.

Conversations about these articles indicate that women are still held up to high standards and the ideal of a "good" mother. No wonder many women feel they have to behave in a certain way to live up to the expectations society places on them to be "good" mothers. This is reinforced when confronted by images of celebrity moms, and is a pressure many parents feel, including us authors. As parents, we certainly find such normative images of motherhood and parenting to be exclusionary and divisive, but nonetheless we also feel compelled to engage with the norms they draw upon. Damien, for example, often feels disheartened when almost all references in magazines for parents are to heterosexual mothers. And the weight of the common expectations of what a "good parent" is supposed to look like (i.e., a mother) often hits him as he wrangles three children down a supermarket aisle and is met with bemused, bewildered or disapproving looks from other customers. Clemence similarly feels disheartened at the constant assumptions that she will stay at home to care for her children, or when family, friends, and colleagues stop asking about her paid work and solely ask about her children. Indeed, similar pressures are placed upon Clemence's partner Braden who, as he increasingly gives up time in his office to stay at home and share equally in the care of their children, constantly faces criticism and questioning about the fact that what he is doing is a woman's responsibility. As such, we would strongly argue that although it is undeniably a good thing when women are celebrated for their roles as mothers and for the care they provide to their children, the time is long overdue, *for the sake of all parents*, for mothers be given room to be "good" in a variety of ways and to pursue other commitments and interests while raising their children!

NOTES

1   Andrea Doucet, *Do Men Mother?* (Toronto: University of Toronto Press, 2006).

2   See, for example, Australian Bureau of Statistics, "Trends in Household Work," in *Australian Social Trends* (2009).

3   See Susan Maushart, *The Mask of Motherhood* (Sydney: Random House, 1997) for a discussion of the ways in which mothering splits heterosexual couples down traditional gender lines.

4   Sharon Hays, *The Cultural Contradictions of Motherhoood* (London: Yale University Press, 1996); Deidre Johnston and Debra Swanston, "Undermining Mothers: A Content Analysis of the Representation of Mothers in Magazines," *Mass Communications and Society* 6 (2003): 243–65.

5   Maushart, *The Mask of Motherhood*, pp. 236–7.

6   Susan J. Douglas and Meredith W. Michaels, *The Mommy Myth* (New York: Free Press, 2004).

7   Ibid., p. 13.

8   "How Hollywood Moms Get Thin So Fast," US Magazine.com, July 31, 2008, available online at www.usmagazine.com/cover-how-hollywood-moms-get-thin-so-fast.

9   "Celebrity Moms Love Mountain Buggy Strollers," *People*, May 7, 2007, available online at www.stylenews.peoplestylewatch.com/2007/05/07/celebrity-moms.

10 Graham Smith, "Regular Mom Katie Holmes takes Adorable Suri for Fun in the Park," *Mail Online*, August 12, 2008, available online at www.dailymail.co.uk/tvshowbiz/article-1042838/Regular-mom-Katie-Holmes-takes-adorable-Suri-fun-park.html.

11 For a discussion of this, see Douglas and Michaels, *The Mommy Myth*, p. 113.

12 "Toxic Mummy," *New Idea*, November 13, 2007.

13 "Ange's Tears – Don't Take Zahara," *New Idea*, November 28, 2007.

14 "Jodie Foster Opens Up About Motherhood," *Now*, August 16, 2007.

15 "Nicole Hits Back: 'I Love Being a Mum'," *Ok!* August 25, 2008.

16 "Jodie Foster Opens Up About Motherhood."

17 See Hays, *Cultural Contradictions*.

18 Victoria Clarke, "What about the Children? Arguments Against Lesbian and Gay Parenting," *Women's Studies International Fourm* 24 (2001): 555–70.

19 "Nicole Hits Back."

20 "Toxic Mummy."

21 Douglas and Michaels, *The Mommy Myth*, p. 116.

22 Ibid., p. 138.

CHAPTER 16

GOD, MOM!

The Blessings of Breasts and Womb

Once, when I was teaching my course on the Problem of Evil, I invited my friend and former teacher, Gerry Janzen, a leading scholar of the Hebrew Bible, to give a guest lecture on the Book of Job. The Book of Job is widely acknowledged as one of the most profound meditations on the problem of innocent suffering to be found anywhere in literature. In it Job, a pious man, suffers great loss and tragedy, including the deaths of his children. Suffering is the central theme of Job, but I didn't realize before Gerry's talk that it is also about motherhood.

"God is a woman"

For those who may be unfamiliar with this particular book of the Bible, let me give you a brief synopsis. It tells the story of Job, a righteous man who gets caught in the crossfire of a wager between God and Satan. God permits Satan to visit all manner of tragedy and affliction on poor Job as a test to see whether his piety is due to his good fortune. Job doesn't curse God as Satan predicted he would, but he doesn't exactly accept his misfortune with the serenity of a Stoic sage either. Instead, when his friends drop by to commiserate with him, he complains loudly and demands an explanation from God. His friends are horrified that he is questioning God and insist Job must have brought all these tribulations down upon himself through his sinful ways. Job declares his innocence, which prompts several lengthy exchanges between him and his friends. God finally shows up in a storm cloud to deliver a magnificent oration about divine creativity and the beauty and terrors of nature. Although God's speech is judged by many commentators to be more of an end run around Job's complaints than a satisfactory response to them, it does conclude with God taking Job's side in his debate with his friends – which is worth something! – and restoring most of what Job had lost in the calamities that befell him.

"And this relates to the theme of motherhood exactly how?" – or so I imagine you asking right now. That's a reasonable question, but stick with me here. Let's return to my classroom and to what Gerry had to say. As Gerry lectured, I listened with delight as he outlined what I found to be a highly original interpretation of the Book of Job that pivoted on what he believed was signaled by the divine name *Shadday*, commonly translated as "Almighty" and especially prominent in Job. According to Gerry, the name *Shadday* originated within a particular paradigm of divine-human relations that highlighted God's role as the guarantor of fertility, both cosmic and human. *Shadday* was the one who made wombs and land fertile, who led the ancestors to rich pastures, and whose most distinctive attributes were steadfast love and compassion. All these meanings are packed into the benediction that Jacob pronounces at Genesis 49:25, in which *Shadday* is evoked as the source of the "blessings of the breasts and the womb." The Hebrew word for womb has as its root the word for compassion, which suggests that *Shadday*'s, the Almighty's, compassion is literally womb-love, the deep feeling of a mother who cherishes the child that grew inside her. The word for breasts is resonant of the divine name *Shadday* itself. In light of these associations, Gerry urged us to reconsider the significance of God's speech about creation and wild nature at the end of the Book of Job, while thinking of the Almighty as issuing maternal blessings, of breast and womb. Once we do so, even the storm cloud from out of which God addresses Job – traditionally taken as merely an emblem of divine power and fury – becomes suggestive of fertility and nurturing care.[1]

Gerry's lecture forever altered my understanding of the Book of Job, but his interpretation depended so much on his prodigious philological erudition that I wondered how well my students were able to keep up.

At the start of the next class meeting, I asked them what they got out of Gerry's lecture. One young woman replied without hesitation, "God is a woman."

From Mother Goddesses to Classical Theism

Leaving aside the Book of Job, let's linger on this arresting and, for some, even scandalous notion that "God is a woman" – or, more precisely, a mother. On its face, this way of speaking may seem completely foreign to the Western monotheistic tradition that grows out of the Bible. However, it is at home within other religious traditions and reaches far back in human history. In fact, abundant archeological evidence from the Upper Paleolithic and Neolithic periods suggests that the earliest images of the divine were feminine *and* decidedly maternal. Stone Age figurines, generally thought to represent a fertility goddess, are notable for their huge breasts, swollen bellies, and round, plump buttocks, features that suggest a preoccupation with generation and nourishment, with "blessings of the breast and the womb." When humanity moves into the Bronze and Iron Ages and urban civilizations make their first appearance, female representations of the divine continue to abound, but are now often paired with male deities. Worship of the Mother Goddess persists to this day on the Indian subcontinent, where many regard her as the supreme deity. But, in the West, the rise and eventual dominance of biblical monotheism has led us to almost exclusively represent God as male – a way of speaking and thinking about God so deeply ingrained in us that we've lost sight of how peculiar it really is.

The language we use to speak about God is a longstanding subject of interest among theologians and philosophers of religion, who often stress how peculiar *all* of our God-talk is. To understand why that's the case, we need first to become familiar with what is frequently called "classical theism," the account of the nature and attributes of God developed over the centuries within Judaism, Christianity, and Islam. The Benedictine monk Anselm of Canterbury (1033–1109) sums up the basic premise of classical theism in his definition of God as "that than which nothing greater can be conceived." God represents the absolute maximum in power, understanding, goodness, and every other attribute we hold in high regard. God also lacks all those attributes ordinarily judged to be signs of weakness or imperfection, such as susceptibility to pain or doubt, the experience of involuntary passions or mood swings, and in general the capacity to be causally affected by anything God hasn't expressly willed. The technical term for this sort of invulnerability is *impassibility*, meaning that God acts on the world but is never involuntarily acted upon.

But if God is perfect, God is also *immutable* or unchanging, since any change in a perfect being could only be for the worse. Not being subject to the limitations of time and space, God is also *incorporeal*, meaning that God has no body. After all, having a body would restrict God to one location at a time and would limit God's power to what that single body could wield. An all-powerful being could suffer no such limitation. Moreover, bodies are made of parts and are as such prone to decomposition, unlike God, who cannot perish or even change. Finally, while certainly not a person in any ordinary sense of the word, as should be clear from all the preceding points, God is said to be capable of entering into something like a *personal* relationship with human beings and is said to care about their welfare.

That's classical theism in a nutshell: God is supremely powerful and perfect, with perfection interpreted to mean that God never suffers nor changes. Over the centuries there have been a few dissenting voices and plenty of quibbles over whether God's "maximal greatness" actually entails this or that attribute. But by and large there's consensus around this conception of God as transcending every limitation, as an impassible, immutable, and incorporeal being. Of course, philosophers and even some theologians have called attention to what they claim are numerous problems with this conception of God. For example, some wonder whether the notion of a maximally great being is even possible or coherent. A pertinent question was raised by none less than Homer Simpson when he wondered whether God could microwave a burrito so hot that he couldn't eat it. Others have asked how a God of supreme power and knowledge could exist without limiting human free will. If God knows everything we will do well before we do it, are we really exercising our freedom when we think we are choosing what to do? Still others have pointed out that the Bible includes stories portraying God as surprised (but doesn't God know everything?), regretful (but isn't everything in God's control?), and taking walks (but doesn't God lack a body?). To this last objection, at least, classical theologians have always had a pat answer. Biblical language is *anthropomorphic*, ascribing human qualities to God – not because these terms apply to God in any perfectly literal sense but because they are the best we can do in making sense of a reality that completely transcends anything else in our experience.

It's Like This

And now we've arrived at the problem of religious language which will bring us quickly to the question of whether a classical theist may speak of God as a Mother. Philosophers typically pose the problem of religious language this way: How can finite beings like us, using a language designed for talking about finite things, speak meaningfully about God, if God is an infinite being who lies beyond the range of our senses and imagination? Thomas Aquinas (1225–74), the great medieval theologian and proponent of classical theism, proposed one of the most enduring and influential solutions to this problem. Language about God can never be *literal*, he argued, since the literal meaning of words always refers to the ordinary objects of our experience, and God is neither ordinary nor an object of our experience. When we say that God is living, for instance, we don't mean that God is an organism sustained as we are by a biological process of metabolism. Or when we speak of the divine mind, we don't mean to compare our own relatively feeble minds to the mind of God or to imply that our mental life can supply any clues as to the manner in which God knows things. On the other hand, Aquinas does not think our talk about God is completely meaningless. Instead, he proposes that we treat religious language as *analogical*. That is, we talk about God on the basis of a series of analogies based on what we do know. Analogical language bridges the gap between the finite and the infinite by highlighting ways that God is similar to, although never quite the same as, the things in our experience. It's perfectly legitimate to speak of God as our Father, concludes Aquinas, even though God isn't our biological parent, because God cares for us and on occasion chastises us just as any good father does his children. Still, God is unlike even the best mortal fathers, surpassing ordinary fatherhood in ways that exceed our grasp. And that's the point of the analogy: God is *like* a father, a mental being and a living being, but immeasurably *better*, so much so that God can't really be identified with the sort of things we ordinarily denote with those terms.

But how about seeing God as the epitome of *maternal* care, as surpassing even the very best of mortal mothers in nurturance, receptive presence, and patient wisdom? Would Aquinas grant that it's equally legitimate to refer to God as our Mother? Within classical theism, God is incorporeal, a pure spirit, and consequently beyond gender. Having no body, no X or Y chromosomes, and none of the equipment standard to either male or female anatomy, God can't be male or female in any literal sense. The convention of using the male personal pronoun "he" when referring to

  GEORGE A. DUNN

God goes back at least to the time of the Bible, but perhaps we shouldn't get too attached to that usage, since we might end up over-literalizing what is just a metaphor. On the other hand, we probably want to avoid referring to God as "it," as that's far too impersonal and seems somewhat disrespectful. A solution adopted by many people who are sensitive to feminist concerns is to avoid using any pronouns whatsoever when speaking of God. That was the practice at the seminary I attended and, as you may have noticed, it's also been my practice here. The problem with this solution, though, is that it leads to weird and ungainly expressions – such as "God as God reveals Godself to God's people." If that grates your ears, try listening to phrases like that every day for two years.

So why not mix things up a bit by mingling references to God as Mother with the more traditional references to God as Father? After all, if my friend Gerry is right, the ancient Hebrews felt perfectly comfortable using the language of "womb" and "breast" to talk about God's blessings. Since the God of classical theism is represented as the source of our being – imparting life to all creatures, sustaining them in existence, and seeking their flourishing – motherhood offers a salient and apt metaphor for divine creativity. Moreover, within Christianity at least, the spiritual regeneration that believers claim to experience as God's preeminent gift to the faithful is routinely described as rebirth. Since only a mother can give birth, doesn't this analogy between spiritual regeneration and birth suggest the appropriateness of addressing God, the agent of that regeneration, as our Mother?

"Defective and misbegotten"

For Aquinas, however, terms associated with motherhood are completely unsuitable for God – not only because an exclusively male God was needed to legitimate the Church's exclusively male priesthood, nor solely because of what he (perhaps mistakenly) took to be biblical precedent. Rather, his denigration of motherhood has its roots in the chauvinistic biological theories of the ancient philosopher Aristotle (384–322 BCE), which the usually more cautious Aquinas regrettably swallowed hook, line, and sinker. According to Aristotle, the mother's contribution to conception was limited to the passive role of supplying the inert "matter." The active male "seed" infused that "matter" with "form" and disposed it to receive a rational soul. For Aristotle, in human reproduction, the father is the active and creative force, while the mother is merely passive and receptive. Remember our earlier discussion of the divine attribute of *impassibility*, the term used in classical theism to express the doctrine that a maximally great God is always the initiator of action in God's dealing with the world, never merely the passively acted-upon. Clearly, in Aristotle's account of human reproduction, the father's active role more closely resembles this idea of divine activity, while the passive and receptive role of the mother puts her at a greater distance from divine perfection. Accepting this account, Aquinas could never countenance motherhood as a legitimate metaphor for the creative power of God.

It gets worse. Aquinas not only endorses Aristotle's denigration of the mother's role in conception, but also agrees with Aristotle's belief that "woman is defective and misbegotten, for the active force in the male seed tends to the production of a perfect likeness in the masculine sex; while the production of woman comes from defect in the active force or from some material indisposition, or even from some external influence."[2] In other words, baby girls are produced when something goes wrong with the creative power of the male "seed," which naturally seeks to engender something just like itself. Aquinas hastens to add, however, that this "defect" occurs as part of God's provident design. Needless to say, there's something bizarre about God making the perpetuation of the species depend on a malfunction, some glitch in the system that causes masculine "seed" to deviate from its proper goal of becoming a male child to become a defective female instead. That alone is reason to suspect that the defect might be in the theory itself and not in half of the human race. And, of course, as we all know, modern genetics and embryology has conclusively vindicated this suspicion, removing at least one objection to speaking of God as our Mother.

But the root of the problem with Aquinas's rejection of Mother-language for speaking of God runs deeper than his faulty understanding of the birds and the bees. I would argue that it lies in his belief in divine *impassibility*, God's supposed inability to suffer, to be passive, to be emotional, or simply to be on the vulnerable end of any relationship. Aquinas was dead wrong when he described the mother's role in conception as entirely passive, but he may have been equally wrong in his failure to see how a certain sort of passivity and receptivity can also be a virtue, even perhaps a divine virtue. Consider in this connection philosopher Nel Noddings' description of how a mother responds to her child in distress:

> If she comforts the night-terrored child, her embrace shields from both terror and ridicule. She feels the excitement, pain, terror, or the embarrassment of the other and commits herself to act accordingly. She is present to the cared-for. Her attitude is one of receptivity.[3]

🐾 GEORGE A. DUNN

The good mother is anything *but* impassible in relation to her child. She doesn't simply act, but she *responds* from out of a deep receptivity to what the child is experiencing. And it's precisely that responsiveness, which Noddings calls "being present," quite apart from any particular words of comfort that the responsive mother may speak, that the terrified child seeks. What, besides a prejudice that requires God to be always active and virile – which, incidentally, happens to be one of the prejudices enshrined in classical theism – would prevent us from using the maternal response to her distressed child as one of our chief models for divine human relations?

"The true mother of life and all things"

Not every religious thinker in the West has shared Aquinas's conviction that the language of maternity was beneath the dignity of God. During Christianity's rise within ancient Rome, there were numerous groups on the fringes of Christian orthodoxy, known as Gnostics, whose writings frequently described God as both Mother and Father. But, according to religious scholar Elaine Pagels, these groups were eventually suppressed as heretical by the ecclesiastic authorities, for reasons she believes may have had a lot to do with male anxiety about the potential maternal language and symbolism might hold to empower women and threaten the Church's exclusively male hierarchy of priests and bishops.[4]

But there must be something appealing about the image of God as Mother because it has never entirely disappeared from devotional life. Research by medieval scholar Carolyn Walker Bynum has revealed just how common such language was in the writings of mystics and contemplative monks and nuns in the twelfth and thirteenth centuries, many of whom regularly turned to images of pregnancy and nursing – God's sheltering womb and bountiful breasts – to convey their sense of God's boundless love for all of creation. The High Middle Ages, the same era in which Thomas Aquinas promoted his offensive theory that women were "misbegotten" males, was also something of a heyday for expressions of piety that focused on the maternal aspects of God. God was said to exemplify to the highest possible degree the generative, sacrificial, loving, tender, and nurturing qualities that, according to Bynum, spiritual writers of this era associated with motherhood, qualities that are still required of mothers today.[5]

This renewed focus on the motherly qualities of God may have had something to do with another "heresy" that the Church was combating at the time. The Cathars were a sect branded as heretical for teaching that matter and spirit were irreconcilably opposed to each other. The goal of spiritual life for the Cathars was to liberate the soul from its imprisonment in this corrupt material world and hasten the soul's return to its true home in the spiritual realm. Language of divine maternity may have struck just the right note for those whose conception of spirituality did not require them to despise the body and scorn the gift of physical existence. As Bynum observes, maternal language for God is bound up with a celebration of flesh, matter, and physicality:

> For a theology that affirmed – over against Cathar dualism – the goodness of creation in all its physicality, a God who is mother and womb as well as father and animator could be a more convincing and sweeping image of creation than a father God alone.[6]

There is a profound physicality to a biological mother's love, for it's with her own body that she shelters and feeds the nascent life she brings into the world. To speak of God's love as maternal is therefore a powerful affirmation of material existence as God's gift, rather than something corrupt that stands between us and the divine.

Those who were drawn to maternal images tended to place their focus on God's gift of life, focusing on the divine activity of creation and nurture, rather than on divine wrath and judgment. A good mother will, of course, discipline her child when necessary, but only with the wellbeing of the child in mind. Discipline and correction are always expressions of love, never explosions of fury. Consequently, the conception of God as Mother tends to foster feelings of gratitude and to arouse a desire to help others, as it is natural for a child who has experienced good maternal care to find deep fulfillment in caring for others. The conception of God as Father, on the other hand, has often been associated with terror and fear of punishment or, worse, a perverse eagerness to be an instrument of divine retribution against the sins of others. Whereas fatherhood has often been associated with the role of the stern and demanding judge, motherhood is usually more closely associated with care and nurture.

Few, if any, medieval mystics have produced a more moving account of the experience of God as Mother than that of the Benedictine nun Julian of Norwich (1342–1416) in her classic work *Showings*, which is possibly the first book written by a woman in the English language. "This fair lovely word 'mother,'" she wrote, is so sweet and so kind in itself that it cannot be said of anyone or to anyone except of him and to him who is the true Mother of life and of all things. To the property of motherhood belongs nature, love, wisdom and knowledge, and this is God.[7]

Notice that Julian accepts Aquinas' doctrine of analogy. God is like a human mother, but at the same time God surpasses even the best human mothers inasmuch as God is the Mother of all things and fully identified with those properties that define motherhood in its most perfect expressions – "nature, love, wisdom and knowledge." Julian's use of the masculine pronoun when speaking of God the Mother is jarring, but this helps underscore the metaphorical quality of the language. God isn't literally a Mother; God isn't literally a "he." But if we are looking for something in our experience to serve as an analogy for God, the ultimate creator and nurturer of life, Julian believed there was no more powerful and appropriate image than that of a mother.

Mothers Made in the Image of God

We in the West have operated for two thousand years or so within a monotheistic tradition in which the dominant imagery for God has almost always been male, despite occasional exceptions found in the writings of visionaries like Julian of Norwich. But if my friend Gerry's interpretation of the Book of Job and other passages from the Hebrew Bible is right – and, for what it's worth, I think he's right on the money – the thought of God as Mother was never far from the minds (and presumably also the hearts) of many of the authors of the texts that most shaped our tradition. In the short space of this essay, we can only touch briefly on some of the ways that resurrecting that thought in contemporary times might make a difference in our lives.

We've already mentioned the affirmation of life, materiality, and the powers of fertility that resonate in the thought of divine Motherhood. Perhaps even more importantly, it allows us to imagine God as not simply an active power that zaps us into existence and then holds our feet to the fire waiting for us to transgress badly enough to deserve some additional but much less pleasant zap, but rather as one who bears us like a mother whose creative activity involves, among other things, providing a space in which we and God's other children can flourish. We come to think of God less as a severe judge who for this reason or that may choose to exercise his sovereign right to show mercy and more as a concerned mother who always cares for us even when we're at our worse, even when we're breaking her far-from-impassible heart. Feeling ourselves to be loved in the unconditional way a mother loves her child, buoyed in existence by the undeserved gift of that love, we might find it more difficult to sustain our own feelings of vindictive malice toward others, since those feelings are the very opposite of the maternal love on which our being depends.

For what's really at issue is what it means to have been created in the *imago dei*, the image of God. It's a central tenet of the Christian tradition that our moral, spiritual, and intellectual nature as human beings somehow mirrors the nature God, albeit in a finite and, regrettably, corrupted form. If we think of God primarily as a father, a lawgiver, a sovereign, or a judge, then it stands to reason that some of the luster associated with the divine nature will rub off on to the human beings who fill those roles. Not only will God be thought of as a father, but fathers will be seen as quasi-divine. When, however, we come to think of God less as the deliverer of laws and chastisements and more as the source of the blessings of breast and womb, then we might just have discovered new grounds for honoring those who have supplied those blessings in our own lives, our own dear mothers.

NOTES

1 Since that day when Gerry visited my class, he has published a book on Job that makes a rigorous case for this interpretation. See J. Gerald Janzen, *At the Scent of Water: The Ground of Hope in the Book of* Job (Grand Rapids: Erdmans, 2009).

2 *The Summa Theologica of St. Thomas Aquinas*, Vol. 1 (New York: Christian Classics, 1981), Q 92, Reply to Objection 1, p. 466.

3 Nel Noddings, *Caring: A Feminine Approach to Ethics and Moral Education* (Los Angeles: University of California Press, 1986), p. 59.

4 Elaine Pagels, *The Gnostic Gospels* (New York: Vintage, 1989), pp. 59–61.

5 Carolyn Walker Bynum, *Jesus as Mother: Studies in the Spirituality of the High Middle Ages* (Berkeley: University of California Press, 1984), pp. 131–2.

6 Ibid., p. 134.

7 *Julian of Norwich: Showings*, ed. Edmund Colledge and James Walsh (Mahwah: Paulist Press, 1977), p. 299.

A BRIEF AFTERWORD

Some Words from Contributors' Kids on Motherhood and Philosophy

What Does Your Mom Do?

"Does she work? Who pays her money?" (Jayden, 3, to his stay-at-home mother)

. . . [thinking] . . . "She writes stuff down." (Ben, 4)

"My mom is a doctor – a philosophy-doctor. She helps people – philosophy kids. She helps kids who don't know about philosophy." (Sonja, 4)

"That's easy. She makes the rules and changes diapers. She does laundry and plays with us and loves us." (Stephen, 5)

"She's a teacher." (Molly, 4)

"She makes up ideas for 5 dollars and then buys something for 6 dollars." (Tulah, 3)

"She teaches college students to read and write." (Wilkes, 6)

"She cares for us. She gives milk to the baby. She teaches philosophy." (Ella, 4)

What Do Philosophers Do?

"I don't know. I don't go to my mom's work! . . . [then she reconsidered] . . . 'Cept when I moved her books and drew our family on the board." (Ella, 4)

What Do You Think About Philosophy?

"I guess philosophy is cool because without it we wouldn't know what is real or fake. Philosophy asks all those questions, like are ghosts real, where do we go when we die, and what in science is true. But, I guess philosophy sucks, too, because Moms are always writing and don't get to spend more good time together with their kids." (Gavin, 11)

"Philosophers type papers, they teach, and they go to conferences on other continents and bring back special surprises for their kids." (Jayden, 6)

"Mamiiiiiiiuuuuuuuu." (Michelle, 10 months)

What Do You Want To Be When You Grow Up?

"A philosopher . . . or . . . . Um . . . maybe a neighbor." (Sonja, 4)

"I want to be a daddy." (Jayden, 6)

Some Other Deep Thoughts

"Daddy, why do you spend 50 percent of your life typing?" (Jayden, 6)

"We all got the same rules right?" (Zack, 8)

When asked where he was born: "GuateMaMa!" (Kevin, 2, born in Guatemala)

> *Ariadne*: "You can play in my house."
> *Boy*: "This isn't your house. It's *my* house."
> *Ariadne*: "You can pretend my house is your house."
> (Ariadne, 4, conversation in a playhouse in a public park)

"Mom, I love you, even when you're reading." (Sonja, 4)

READ ALL ABOUT IT

A Feminist Bibliography on Pregnancy and Mothering

Adams, Sarah LaChance. "Becoming with Child: Pregnancy as Provocation to Authenticity." In *New Perspectives on Sartre*. Eds Adrian Mirvish and Adrian van den Hoven, Cambridge Scholars Press, forthcoming.

Adams, Sarah LaChance. "Maternal Thinking (Ruddick)." In *Encyclopedia of Motherhood*. Ed Andrea O'Reilly, Sage, forthcoming.

Adams, Sarah LaChance. "Philosophy and Motherhood." In *Encyclopedia of Motherhood*. Ed. Andrea O'Reilly, Sage, forthcoming.

Adams, Sarah LaChance 2009. "The Pregnable Subject: Maternity and Levinas' Relevance to Feminism." In *Phenomenology 2008, Vol. 5: Selected Essays from North America*. Ed. Michael Barber, Lester Embree, and Thomas J. Nenon, Post scriptum OPO Series, Bucharet: Zeta Books.

Annas, J. 1986. "Pregnant Women as Fetal Containers." *Hastings Center Report* 16 (6):13–14.

Bailey, Alison 1997. "Mothers, Birthgivers and Peacemakers: A Critical Reflection on Maternal Peace Politics." In *Perspectives on Power and Domination*. Ed. Lawrence Bove and Laura Duhan Kaplan, New York: Rodopi.

Bailey, Alison 1996. "Mothering, Diversity and Peace: Comments on Sara Ruddick's Feminist Maternal Peace Politics." In *Bringing Peace Home: Feminism, Violence and Nature*. Ed. Karen J. Warren and Duane L. Cady. Bloomington: Indiana University Press.

Bailey, Alison 1994. "Mothering, Diversity and Peace Politics: A Critical Analysis of Sara Ruddick's *Maternal Thinking: Toward a Politics of Peace*," *Hypatia* 9 (2): 188–98.

Bailey, Alison and Jacqueline Zita 2007. "The Reproduction of Whiteness: Race and the Regulation of the Gendered Body." *Hypatia* Special Issue, ed. Alison Bailey and Jacqueline N. Zita, 22 (2): vii–xv.

Betterton, Rosemary 2002. "Prima Gravida: Reconfiguring the Maternal Body in Visual Representation." *Feminist Theory* 3 (3): 255–70.

Bigwood, Carol 1991. "Renaturalizing the Body (With the Help of Merleau-Ponty)." *Hypatia* 6 (3): 54–73.

Blum, Linda 1999. *At the Breast: Ideologies of Breastfeeding and Motherhood in the Contemporary United States*. Boston: Beacon Press.

Brody, Donna 2001. "Levinas's Maternal Method from 'Time and the Other' Through *Otherwise Than Being*: No Woman's Land?" In *Feminist Interpretations of Emmanuel Levinas*. Ed. Tina Chanter. University Park: Pennsylvania State University Press, 53–77.

Cahill, Heather 1999. "An Orwellian Scenario: Court Ordered Caesarean Section and Women's Autonomy." *Nursing Ethics* 6 (6): 494–505.

Card, Claudia 1996. "Against Marriage and Motherhood." *Hypatia* 11 (3): 1–23.

Chodorow, Nancy 1999. *The Reproduction of Mothering*, 2nd edn. Berkeley: University of California Press.

Collins, Patricia Hill 1994. "Shifting the Center: Race, Class, and Feminist Theorizing about Motherhood." In *Representations of Motherhood*. Ed. Donna Bassin, Margaret Honey, and Meryle Mahrer Kaplan. New Haven: Yale University Press.

Corea, Gina 1988. *The Mother-Machine: Reproductive Technologies from Artificial Insemination to Artificial Wombs*. Boston: Beacon Press.

Cudd, Ann E. 1990. "Enforced Pregnancy, Rape, and the Image of Women." *Philosophical Studies* 60 (1): 47–59.

Davis-Floyd, Robbie 1992. *Birth as an American Rite of Passage*. Berkeley: University of California Press.

De Beauvoir, Simone 1953. *The Second Sex*, trans. H. Parshely. New York: Bantam.

DiQuinzio, Patricia 1999. *The Impossibility of Motherhood: Feminism, Individualism and the Problem of Mothering*. New York: Routledge.

Downe, Pamela 2001. "Stepping on Maternal Ground: Reflections of Becoming an 'Other-Mother'." *Journal of Association for Research on Mothering* 3 (1): 27–40.

Fentiman, Linda 2009. "New Markets in Mothers' Milk: How Breastfeeding and Human Milk Have Become Commodities," *Nevada Law Journal* 10 (1).

Glenn, Evelyn Nakano, Grace Chang, and Linda Rennie Forcey (eds.) 1994. *Mothering: Ideology, Experience, Agency*. New York: Routledge.

Guenther, L. 2008. "Being-from-Others: Reading Heidegger after Cavarero." *Hypatia* 23 (4): 99–118.

Guenther, L. 2006. *The Gift of the Other: Levinas and the Politics of Reproduction*. Albany: State University of New York Press.

Guenther, L. 2006. "'Like a Maternal Body': Levinas and the Motherhood of Moses." *Hypatia* 21 (1): 119–36.

Guenther, L. 2005. "Lucky Burden: Beauvoir and the Ethical Temporality of Birth." *Symposium: Canadian Journal of Continental Philosophy* 9 (2): 177–94.

Guenther, L. 2005. "Unborn Mothers: The Old Rhetoric of New Reproductive Technologies." *Radical Philosophy* 130: 2–6.

Haslanger, Sally and Charlotte Witt (eds.) 2005. *Adoption Matters: Philosophical and Feminist Essays*. Ithaca: Cornell University Press.

Held, Virginia 1993. *Feminist Morality: Transforming Culture, Society and Politics*. Chicago: University of Chicago Press.

Hillyer, Barbara 1993. *Feminism and Disability*. Oklahoma City: University of Oklahoma Press.

Huntley, Rebecca 200. "Sexing the Belly: An Exploration of Sex and the Pregnant Body." *Sexualitie*s 3 (3): 347–62.

Katz, Claire Elise 2002. "The Significance of Childhood." *International Studies in Philosophy* 34 (4): 77–101.

Keller, Jean. "Rethinking Ruddick on 'Adoptive' Mothering." In *Sara Ruddick's Maternal Thinking: Philosophy, Practice, Politics*. Ed. Andrea O'Reilly. Toronto: Demeter Press, forthcoming.

Kittay, Eva Feder 1999. *Love's labor: Essays on Women, Equality, and Dependency*. New York: Routledge.

Kittay, Eva Feder 1999. "'Not *My* Way Sesha, *Your* Way, Slowly': 'Maternal Thinking' in the Raising of a Child with Profound Intellectual Disabilities." In *Mother Troubles*. Ed. Julia Hanigsberg and Sara Ruddick. Boston: Beacon Press, 3–27.

Klassen, Pamela 2001. *Blessed Events: Religion and Home Birth in America*. Princeton: Princeton University Press.

Kristeva, Julia 2002. "Stabat Mater." In *The Portable Kristeva*. Ed. Kelly Oliver. New York: Columbia University Press.

Kukla, Rebecca 2008. "Measuring Mothering." *International Journal of Feminist Approaches to Bioethics* 1 (1): 67–90.

Kukla, Rebecca 2006. "Ethics and Ideology in Breastfeeding Advocacy Campaigns." *Hypatia* 21 (1): 157–80.

Kukla, Rebecca 2005. *Mass Hysteria: Medicine, Culture and Mothers' Bodies*. Lanham: Rowman and Littlefield.

Lauritzen, Paul 1989. "A Feminist Ethic and the New Romanticism – Mothering as a Model of Moral Relations." *Hypatia* 4 (3): 29–44.

Layne, Linda 2003. *Motherhood Lost: A Feminist Account of Pregnancy Loss in America*. New York: Routledge.

Leonard, Victoria Wynn 1996. "Mothering as Practice." In *Caregiving: Readings in Knowledge, Practice, Ethics, and Politics*. Ed. Suzanne Gordon, Patricia Benner, and Nel Noddings. Philadelphia: University of Pennsylvania Press, 124–40.

Lewin, Ellen 1994. "Negotiating Lesbian Motherhood: The Dialectics of Resistance and Accommodation." In *Mothering: Ideology, Experience, Agency*. Ed. Evelyn Nakano Glenn, Grace Chang, and Linda Rennie Forcey. New York: Routledge.

Lim, Hilary 1999. "Caesareans and Cyborgs." *Feminist Legal Studies* 7: 133–73.

Longhurst, Robyn 1998. "(Re)presenting Shopping Centres and Bodies: Questions of Pregnancy." In *New Frontiers of Space, Bodies, Gender*. Ed. Rosa Ainley. London: Routledge.

Lundquist, Caroline 2008. "Being Torn: Toward a Phenomenology of Unwanted Pregnancy." *Hypatia* 23 (3): 136–55.

McLeod C. 2002. *Self-Trust and Reproductive Autonomy*. Cambridge, MA: MIT Press.

Martin, Emily 1987. *The Woman in the Body*. Boston: Beacon Press.

Meyers, Diana 2001. "The Rush to Motherhood: Pronatalist Discourse and Women's Autonomy." *Signs* 26 (3): 735–73.

Meyers, Diana Tietjens, Kenneth Kipnis, and Cornelius F. Murphy, Jr. (eds.) 1999. *Kindred Matters: Rethinking the Philosophy of Family*. Ithaca: Cornell University Press.

Minaker, Joanne C. "Law Mothering." In *Encyclopedia of Motherhood*. Ed. Andrea O'Reilly, Sage, forthcoming.

Minaker, Joanne C. "Public Policy and Mothers." In *Encyclopedia of Motherhood*. Ed. Andrea O'Reilly, Sage, forthcoming.

Moloney, Sharon. "Birth as a Spiritual Initiation: Australian Women's Experiences of Transformation." *Australian Religion Studies Review*, Special Supplement, 22 (2). Forthcoming.

Moloney, Sharon 2008. "Mothers and Daughters at Menarche: An Indigenous Inspired Quiet Revolution." *Journal of the Association for Research on Mothering* 10 (2).

Moloney, Sharon 2007. "Dancing with the Wind: A Methodological Approach to Researching Women's Spirituality around Menstruation and Birth." *International Journal of Qualitative Methods* 6 (1).

Moloney, Sharon 2006. "Dismantling the Fear of Birth." *Natural Parenting* 16.

Moloney, Sharon 2006. "The Spirituality of Childbirth." *Birth Issues* 15 (2): 41–6.

Moloney, Sharon 1998. "Breastfeeding as Fertility Suppressant: How Reliable Is It?" *MIDIRS Midwifery Digest* 8 (3).

Morgan, Lynn R. and Meredith W. Michaels (eds.) 1999. *Fetal Subjects, Feminist Positions*. Philadelphia: University of Pennsylvania Press.

Mullin, Amy. "Filial Responsibilities of Dependent Children." *Hypatia* 25 (1) forthcoming.

Mullin, Amy. "Paid Childcare, Responsibility and Trust." In *Sara Ruddick's Maternal Thinking: Philosophy, Practice, Politics*. Ed. Andrea O'Reilly. Toronto: Demeter Press, forthcoming.

Mullin, Amy 2007. "Children, Autonomy and Care." *Journal of Social Philosophy* 38 (4): 536–53.

Mullin, Amy 2007. "Children, Caregivers, and Friends: Models of Care." In *Taking Responsibility for Children*. Ed. Samantha Brennan and Robert Noggle. Waterloo: Wilfrid Laurier University Press, 47–71.

Mullin, Amy 2007. "Giving as well as Receiving: Love, Children and Parents." *Symposium: Canadian Journal of Continental Philosophy* 12 (2).

Mullin, Amy 2006. "Parents and Children: An Alternative to Unconditional and Selfless Love." *Hypatia* 21 (1): 181–200.

Mullin, Amy 2005. "'Like a Mother': Paid Mother-work Performed in Private Spaces." In *Motherhood and Space*. Ed. Caroline Wiedemer and Sarah Hardy. New York: Palgrave Macmillan, 203–20.

Mullin, Amy 2005. *Reconceiving Pregnancy and Childcare: Ethics, Experience and Reproductive Labor*. Cambridge: Cambridge University Press.

Mullin, Amy 2005. "Trust, Social Norms and Motherhood." *Journal of Social Philosophy* 36 (3): 316–30.

Mullin, Amy 2004. "Pregnancy." In *Sexuality: The Essential Glossary*. Ed. Jo Eadie. London: Arnold, 170.

Mullin, Amy 2002. "Pregnant Bodies, Pregnant Minds." *Feminist Theory* 3 (1): 27–46.

Narayan, Uma and Julia J. Bartowiak (eds.) 1999. *Having and Raising Children: Unconventional Families, Hard Choices, and the Social Good*. University Park: Pennsylvania State University Press.

Nelson, Hilde Lindemann (ed.) 1997. *Feminism and Families*. New York: Routledge.

Nelson, Hilde Lindemann and James Lindemann Nelson 1989. "Cutting Motherhood in Two: Some Suspicions Concerning Surrogacy." *Hypatia* 4 (3): 85–94.

Noddings, Nel 1984. *Caring: A Feminine Approach to Ethics and Moral Education*, 2nd edn. Berkeley: University of California Press.

Oakley, Ann 1980. *Woman Confined: Towards a Sociology of Childbirth*. Oxford: Martin Robinson.

Oksala, Johanna 2006. "What is Feminist Phenomenology? Thinking Birth Philosophically." *Radical Philosophy* 26 (July/August): 16–22.

O'Leary, J. 2009. "Never a Simple Journey: Pregnancy Following Loss." *Bereavement Care* 28 (2): 12–17.

O'Leary, J. 2005. "The Baby Who Follows the Loss of a Sibling: Special Considerations in the Postpartum Period." *International Journal of Childbirth Education* 20 (4): 28–30.

O'Leary, J. 2005. "The Trauma of Ultrasound during a Pregnancy Following Perinatal Loss." *Journal of Loss and Trauma* 10: 183–204.

O'Leary, J. 2004. "Grief and Its Impact on Prenatal Attachment in the Subsequent Pregnancy." *Archives of Women's Mental Health* 7 (1): 1–15.

O'Leary, J. 1992. "The Parenting Process in the Prenatal Period: A Developmental Theory." *Pre and Perinatal Psychology Journal* 7 (2): 7–9.

O'Leary, J. and C. Gaziano 1999. "The Role of Childhood Memory Scores in Parenting in Pregnancy and Early Postpartum." *Journal of Prenatal and Perinatal Psychology and Health* 13: 3–4.

O'Leary, J. and Thorwick, C. 2008. "Maternal-Paternal Representation of Pregnancy and Attachment to the Unborn Child during Pregnancy Following Loss." *Attachment* 2 (3): 292–320.

O'Leary, J. and C. Thorwick 2006. "Fathering Perspective during Pregnancy Post Perinatal Loss." *Journal of Obstetric, Gynecologic, and Neonatal Nursing* 35 (1): 78–86.

O'Leary, J., C. Gazanio, and C. Thorwick 2006. "Born after Loss: The Invisible Child in Adulthood." *Journal of Pre and Perinatal Psychology and Health* 21 (1): 3–23.

Oliver, Kelly 1997. *Family Values: Subjects Between Nature and Culture*. New York: Routledge.

Olkowski, Dorothea 2006. "Only Nature is Mother to the Child." In *Feminist Interpretations of Maurice Merleau-Ponty*. Ed. Dorothea Olkowski and Gail Weiss. University Park: Pennsylvania State University Press, 49–70.

O'Neill, Onora and William Ruddick (eds.) 1979. *Having Children: Philosophical and Legal Reflections on Parenthood*. New York: Oxford University Press.

O'Reilly, Andrea (ed.) 2008. *Feminist Mothering*. Albany: State University of New York Press.

O'Reilly, Andrea (ed.) 2007. *Maternal Theory: Essential Readings*. Toronto: Demeter Press.

O'Reilly, Andrea 2006. *Rocking the Cradle: Thoughts on Feminism, Motherhood and the Possibility of Empowered Mothering*. Toronto: Demeter Press.

Overall, Christine 1993. *Human Reproduction: Principles, Practices, Policies*. Toronto: Oxford University Press.

Petchesky, R. 1987. "Fetal Images: The Power of Visual Culture in the Politics of Reproduction." *Feminist Studies* 12 (2): 263–92.

Reinelt, Claire and Mindy Fried 1992. "'I am this child's mother': A Feminist Perspective on Mothering with a Disability." In *Perspectives on Disability*, 2nd edn. Palo Alto: Health Market Research.

Reynolds, Tracy 2001. "Black Mothering, Paid Work and Identity." *Ethnic and Racial Studies* 24 (6): 1046–64.

Rich, Adrienne 1986. *Of Woman Born*. New York: Norton.

Rodemeyer, Lanei 1998. "Dasein Gets Pregnant." *Philosophy Today* 42 (Supplement): 76–84.

Rowland, R. 1992. *Living Laboratories: Women and Reproductive Technologies*. Bloomington: Indiana University Press.

Ruddick, Sara 1995. *Maternal Thinking: Toward a Politics of Peace*. Boston: Beacon Press.

Sandford, Stella 2001. "Masculine Mothers? Maternity in Levinas and Plato." In *Feminist Interpretations of Emmanuel Levinas*. Ed. Tina Chanter. University Park: Pennsylvania State University Press, 180–202.

Seavilleklein, V. 2009. "Challenging the Rhetoric of Choice in Prenatal Screening." *Bioethics* 23 (1): 68–77.

Sherwin, S. 1991. "Abortion Through A Feminist Ethics Lens." *Dialogue* 30: 327–42.

Simms, Eva-Maria 2001. "Milk and Flesh: A Phenomenological Reflection on Infancy and Coexistence." *Journal of Phenomenological Psychology* 32 (1): 22–40.

Soliday, E. 2009. "Medical Patients' Rights Reflected in Women's Reported Childbirth Experiences." Paper presented at the Philosophy of Pregnancy, Childbirth, and Motherhood Conference, Eugene, Oregon.

Thomas, Carol 1997. "The Baby and the Bath Water: Disabled Women and Motherhood in Social Context." *Sociology of Health and Illness* 19 (5): 622–43.

Thompson, Judith Jarvis 1971. "A Defense of Abortion." *Philosophy and Public Affairs* 1 (1): 47–66.

Trebilcot, Joyce (ed.) 1983. *Mothering: Essays in Feminist Theory*. Totowa: Rowman and Allanheld.

Tronto, Joan C. 2002. "The 'Nanny' Question in Feminism." *Hypatia* 17 (7): 34–51.

Villarmea, Stella 2009. "Rethinking the Origin: Birth and Human Value." In *Creating a Global Dialogue on Value Inquiry*. Ed. Jinfen Yan and David Schrader. Lewiston: Edwin Mellen Press.

Villarmea, Stella 2005. "Good, Freedom, and Happiness: A Kantian Approach to Autonomy and Cooperation." In *New Women of Spain: Social Political Studies of Feminist Thought*. Ed. Elisabeth de Sotelo. Münster: Lit, 244–56.

Villarmea, Stella 1999. "The Provocation of E. Levinas for Feminism." *European Journal of Women's Studies* 6 (3): 291–304.

Welsh, Talia 2008. "The Developing Body: A Reading of Merleau-Ponty's Conception of Women in the Sorbonne Lectures." In *Intertwinings: Interdisciplinary Encounters with Merleau-Ponty*. Ed. Gail Weiss. Albany: State University of New York Press, 45–59.

Whitbeck, Caroline 1975. "The Maternal Instinct." *Philosophical Forum* 6 (2–3): 321–32.

Willett, Cynthia 1995. *Maternal Ethics and Other Slave Moralities*. New York: Routledge.

Wynn, Francine 2002. "The Early Relationship of Mother and Pre-Infant: Merleau-Ponty and Pregnancy." *Nursing Philosophy* 3: 4–14.

Young, Iris Marion 1990. "Pregnant Embodiment: Subjectivity and Alienation." In *Throwing Like a Girl and Other Essays in Feminist Philosophy and Social Theory*. Bloomington: Indiana University Press, 160–74.

NOTES ON CONTRIBUTORS

KIM ANNO, MFA, is a professor and chair of the painting department at the California College of the Arts in San Francisco. She is both a painter whose work resides in museum collections nationally such as SFMOMA, the Honolulu Academy of Art, Brooklyn Museum, Columbia University, and the Getty Institute, as well as a writer on philosophic ideas about art. She is working on a project about abstraction outside the canon of Modernism. Currently, she is running for site governance council at her son's public school.

JENNIFER BAKER earned a PhD in philosophy at the University of Arizona and is an Assistant Professor at the College of Charleston. She has three children, one delivered through the most torturous scheme nature has ever devised, the others through lovely c-sections. She writes on virtue.

ELIZABETH BUTTERFIELD, PhD, is Assistant Professor of Philosophy at Georgia Southern University, where she regularly teaches a course on existentialism. Her primary research interests include the later philosophy of Jean-Paul Sartre, feminism, and ethics. These days she spends a great deal of time singing "Wheels on the Bus" and spinning in circles with her wonderfully giggly 2-year-old.

CLEMENCE DUE is a doctoral candidate at the University of Adelaide. Her PhD research involves media representations of race and belonging, but as a "working mom" with a young family she is also interested in representations of parenting and traditional gender roles.

GEORGE A. DUNN is a lecturer in the philosophy and religion department of the University of Indianapolis and a regular visiting lecturer at the Ningbo Institute of Technology in Zhejiang Province, China. Most importantly, he is the father of Ariadne Blayde, a sophomore studying playwriting at Fordham University. Despite being named after the mortal bride of Dionysus, the Greek god of drinking and debauchery, Ariadne is remarkably serious, studious, and sober for a young woman her age. Go figure.

JANET ELLIOTT has a degree in elementary education, with a concentration in English literature. She taught junior high social studies and language arts for six years in Indiana and Michigan before deciding to become a full-time stay-at-home mom.

KEVIN ELLIOTT received his PhD from the University of Notre Dame and is presently an Assistant Professor of Philosophy at the University of South Carolina. Janet and Kevin have been quite invested in figuring out the best strategies for helping their children (Jayden, age 6, and Leah, age 3) to get a good night's sleep.

SARA GOERING is Assistant Professor of Philosophy at the University of Washington, Seattle. She works primarily in feminist bioethics, with particular interests in disability rights and justice for marginalized populations. Her two children, Ella and Graham, not only inspire fantasies about off buttons, but also share highly entertaining philosophical reflections about the world.

SUE ELLEN HENRY is an Associate Professor of Education at Bucknell University, where she teaches social foundations of education, multiculturalism and education, and a course on democracy and education. Her research interests focus on issues of social class in classrooms and the role of emotion in teaching and learning. Together with her husband Abe, she works at creating a life that combines good care for her three children (Jacob, age 9, Ruby, age 7, and Benjamin, age 4) with good care for herself and her relationships. So far, it's going okay.

AMY KIND is Associate Professor of Philosophy at Claremont McKenna College. She works primarily in the philosophy of mind, and her published articles concern topics such as consciousness, the imagination, and introspection. Raising two young boys means that she now knows as much about construction vehicles, superheroes, and Transformers as she does about Descartes and the mind-body problem.

NIN KIRKHAM is a lecturer in philosophy at the University of Western Australia and her special fields of interest are ethics (virtue ethics, bioethics, and environmental ethics), continental philosophy, and the philosophy of mind. She combines research and teaching in philosophy with the care of her two young children, Eleanor and Sam.

SHEILA LINTOTT is an Assistant Professor of Philosophy at Bucknell University. Her main area of research is in aesthetics and she is particularly interested in the intersections between aesthetics and feminist theory and aesthetics and environmental philosophy. She is co-editor (with Allen Carlson) of *Nature, Aesthetics, and Environmentalism: From Beauty to Duty* (2008) and has published articles on aesthetics and feminist thought in a number of academic journals. She lives in Pennsylvania with her husband Eric and their children, Sonja and Jack. To her great relief, Sheila is confident that motherhood has made her a better philosopher and that philosophy makes her a better mother.

BERTHA ALVAREZ MANNINEN received her PhD from Purdue University in 2006. Her dissertation, and most of her subsequent research, has been in medical ethics, including the ethics of abortion. In addition, she has published articles on the ethics of euthanasia, stem cell research, and the intersection of metaphysics and bioethics. She is currently an Assistant Professor of Philosophy at Arizona State University at the West campus. Her "free time" is mostly spent changing t-shirts and onesies, mostly after every meal she tries to feed her 9-month-old daughter Michelle. On a good day, she ends her nights with a round of Dr. Seuss books, lullabies, and night-time cuddling.

CHRIS MULFORD was an aimless liberal arts BA when she first gave birth in 1968. Starting out from her rocking chair, she began a lifelong study of breastfeeding. In order to go where the mothers were, she trained as a nurse in 1974 and completed a BS in nursing in her mid-forties. In 1985 she was in the first cohort of International Board Certified Lactation Consultants (IBCLCs). Chris has worked clinically in hospitals, in homes, and at WIC clinics. She has taught parents, physicians, nurses, and nutritionists and is active in ILCA, her professional organization.

Breastfeeding has taken her around the globe, to do advocacy in Geneva at the International Labor Organization, to teach in Swaziland on an assignment from UNICEF, and to work with the World Alliance for Breastfeeding Action headquarters in Malaysia. She currently is a member of the US Breastfeeding Committee and two state breastfeeding coalitions. She and George Mulford, her life partner of 46 years, have two children, Zoe (41) and Toby (31).

AMY MULLIN is Professor of Philosophy at the University of Toronto. She is interested in the moral responsibilities of caregivers (including mothers) and recipients of care (including children). She publishes work on feminist theory, topics in the history of philosophy, and aesthetics. She has three school-aged children.

LAURA NEWHART is an Associate Professor of Philosophy at Eastern Kentucky University. Her areas of research include feminist theory and biomedical ethics. She lives in Richmond, Kentucky with her 2-year-old son Kevin.

GLENN PARSONS teaches philosophy at Ryerson University in Toronto. His main research interest is the concept of beauty; he is the author of *Aesthetics and Nature* (2007) and, with Allen Carlson, *Functional Beauty* (2008). Glenn and his wife Lindsay have two children, Alice and William.

DAMIEN W. RIGGS is a lecturer in social work at Flinders University. His research areas include critical race and whiteness studies, LGBTQ psychology, and family and parenting studies. He is the author of *Becoming Parent: Lesbians, Gay Men, and Family* (2007) and *Masculinities, Sexualities and Family* (2010).

SHERYL TUTTLE ROSS, PhD, is an associate professor of philosophy at the University of Wisconsin-La Crosse. She has been practicing Vipassana meditation for nine years and has been a mother for twelve years (not including the pre-kid Barkley years) Her children Joie and Aiden keep her humble and busy. Her research interests in the field of aesthetics include propaganda art, political humor, and guilty pleasures.

MAUREEN SANDER-STAUDT is an assistant professor at Arizona State University where she lives with her partner, three children, and animal companions. She specializes in feminist care ethics, and has published on the topics of care giving and virtue ethics, artificial womb technology, and the comparative moral status of embryos in abortion, *in vitro* fertilization, and crimes against pregnant women. Her current interests are in the areas of reproductive technology, political practice, and family ethics. She is currently working on projects that explore care as a corporate virtue, and a care ethical assessment of polygamous practices in the US.

JUDITH WARNER'S book *Perfect Madness: Motherhood in the Age of Anxiety* was an instant *New York Times* bestseller when it was published in February 2005. She currently writes the "Domestic Disturbances" column for the *New York Times*. She is also the author of a range of nonfiction books, among them *You Have the Power: How to Take Back Our Country and Restore Democracy to America* (with Howard Dean) and the bestselling biography *Hillary Clinton: The Inside Story*. A former special correspondent for *Newsweek* in Paris, she reviews books for the *New York Times* and has written about politics and women's issues for magazines including *The New Republic* and *Elle*. She lives in Washington, DC with her husband and their children.